Global Lies?

Also by Mark D. Alleyne

INTERNATIONAL POWER AND INTERNATIONAL COMMUNICATION
NEWS REVOLUTION: Political and Economic Decisions about Global Information

Global Lies?

Propaganda, the UN and World Order

Mark D. Alleyne

First published 2003 by
PALGRAVE MACMILLAN
Houndmills, Basingstoke, Hampshire RG21 6XS and
175 Fifth Avenue, New York, N.Y. 10010
Companies and representatives throughout the world

PALGRAVE MACMILLAN is the global academic imprint of the Palgrave Macmillan division of St. Martin's Press, LLC and of Palgrave Macmillan Ltd. Macmillan® is a registered trademark in the United States, United Kingdom and other countries. Palgrave is a registered trademark in the European Union and other countries.

ISBN 0–333–92004–X hardback
ISBN 1–4039–2100–8 paperback

This book is printed on paper suitable for recycling and made from fully managed and sustained forest sources.

A catalogue record for this book is available from the British Library.

Library of Congress Cataloging-in-Publication Data
Alleyne, Mark D., 1961–
    Global lies? : propaganda, the UN and world order / Mark D. Alleyne.
        p. cm.
    Includes bibliographical references and index.
    ISBN 0–333–92004–X – ISBN 1–4039–2100–8 (pbk.)
        1. United Nations–Public relations–History. 2. Propaganda–History.
    I. Title.

    JZ4984.5.A46 2003
    659.2′934123–dc21   2003040539

10 9 8 7 6 5 4 3 2 1
12 11 10 09 08 07 06 05 04 03

Printed and bound in Great Britain by
Antony Rowe Ltd, Chippenham and Eastbourne

Dedicated to my mother Cynthia Yvonne Alleyne

Las bocas están cerradas y selladas con candado de terror!

Joe Arroyo
La Guerra de los Callados

Contents

List of Tables and Charts

List of Illustrations

grounds that "the highest interests of the corporation are involved in the health of the earth's society". (Photo courtesy Xerox Corporation)

Preface

When I started work on this book in 1998 I only knew that a chapter in my *News Revolution* was very underdeveloped and that the topic deserved a book of its own. In *News Revolution* I had barely scraped the surface of how the UN had systematically tried to become an international intellectual force. But over the course of four years this book evolved into more than I could have reasonably expected.

It is a book that can be read a number of different ways. The most straight-forward way is to see it as a bureaucratic history of an important yet obscure part of the United Nations. Another way is to see it as a way of more comprehensively understanding the UN's first 50 years because all the histories of that period have not given substantial attention to the organization's public information program. Yet a third way is to see it as a different way of understanding international relations. I devote some time to discussing this point in the final chapter because the field of international relations (IR) has not traditionally been accommodating to studies of this sort.

The satisfaction I gleaned from writing the book is based on my fascination with the intersection of mass communication and political power. When I started graduate work at Oxford in this specific area I was virtually alone and had to chart out on my own a program of study and readings. However, I am pleased to see that almost 20 years later those of us who try to blend what is sometimes called communication research with international relations have not only grown in number but that much of this work is now being relied upon to solve some of the key problems that dog international life.

From the very start of my career in academe I have maintained that my research should be relevant to improve what I consider to be the gravest maladies of the human condition, such as ignorance, bigotry, violence and injustice. So throughout the four years of work on this book I sought to view the work from the perspective of the common reader seeking to understand and deal with these problems, while trying to balance my commitment to the scholarly integrity of the work.

The world events that occurred while I was at work on this book sadly reinforced the urgency of the need to come to terms with many of the issues spanned by this investigation. In defiance of the IR maxim that "a punitive peace is an unstable peace", the various penalties imposed on Iraq after the Gulf War continued. The violence between Palestinians and Israelis escalated. The civil war in Colombia showed no sign of ending despite its 40-year history. War crimes tribunals on Rwanda and the former Yugoslavia continued. Suicide terrorists attacked the United States World Trade Center and the Pentagon. And an International Criminal Court was created in 2002.

In all the cases listed above, the UN was a player in some way. This was a striking departure from the organization's essential marginalization during the Cold War. For a scholar of the UN, the four years of writing this book were heady times to be around the organization. Although polls showed the UN ranking slightly higher than governments in the estimation of world public opinion, the world had no competing organization to be to the world all the things the UN tried to be. In addition to being a voice for abused children, AIDS victims, oppressed minorities and women, the UN was called upon to implement a peacekeeping operation in the wake of almost every major war. This was all done under the unforgiving glare of "real-time" international media scrutiny.

The title of this book suggests that it might be a tale of the UN as convener of a duplicitous discursive formation. However, nothing could be further from what I intend this book to be. While I am not a foe of the UN, I also did not intend to write a book that would be unconstructively critical. The final judges on how good a job I have done will be the readers.

I owe a debt of gratitude not only to you, the reader, who has taken the time to select this book to read, but also to the many people who have for a long time pointed to the relevance of this area of research in international relations and whose various intellectual contributions helped me refine my understanding of my chosen topic. In Chapter 7 I make the point that even though a number of North American and European writers turned their focus to the so-called "soft" dimensions of international relations in the 1990s (such as culture, communication, ideology and race), these concerns were put on the agenda of world politics and intellectual discourse about international problems a long time before. Caribbean, Latin American, African and Asian intellectuals, activists and politicians provided the intellectual weight that made "national self-determination" a "human right" and sparked such initiatives as the New World Information and Communication Order (NWICO). The task was whether others would hear and heed them. And even though by the turn of the century it was common in North American academic circles to hear that the NWICO was a dead concept, the then popular constructivist and postmodern approaches to IR actually owe a debt to that tradition of inquiry. I make this point because one might be tempted to classify this book as solely part of the emerging constructivist approach to IR, however I would prefer that it be considered part of a long, rich tradition of critical inquiry by those who have gone before me and have been rich fonts of inspiration. The incomplete list includes such intellectuals as Walter Rodney, Nelson Mandela, Eric Williams, Stuart Hall, Michael Manley, Ali Mazrui, Susan Strange, Conor Cruise O'Brien, and Herbert Schiller.

In tune with what I say is the "new" international relations – where ethnocentrism and intellectual snobbery should not confine either the definition of credible subjects or intellectuals in the field – this book begins with a quote from a work by the famous Colombian artist Joe Arroyo.

From Bob Marley's performance at Zimbabwe's Independence festivities to the revolutionary lyrics of Peter Tosh, and to Live-Aid, music has been as much a part of international relations as conventional diplomacy. It is my hope that young scholars will be bold enough to devote themselves to the task of making these seemingly strange connections in order to understand better how our world works. In the context of the book, Arroyo's lyrics about war and murder might refer not only to the timidity of the UN to confront the thorny issue of propaganda but could also describe the fear that might overcome some writers who want to take international relations in this direction.

MARK DACOSTA ALLEYNE
Chicago
Spring 2003
markalleyne@prodigy.net

Acknowledgements

First in line to receive my thanks must be the very loyal, hard-working UN Secretariat staff in New York, without whose help and co-operation this project would not have been realized. The list includes Shashi Tharoor, his predecessor at the helm of the Department of Public Information (DPI) Kensaku Hogen, Gillian Sorensen, Oleg Astapkov and Paula Refolo.

Of course, any scholarly work I produce is a reflection on all the good that has come from interactions with so many dedicated librarians. The Government Documents librarian at the University of Illinois, David Griffiths, was especially helpful. There is also a long list of librarians and staff at the UN's Dag Hammarskjöld Library who were invaluable. They included the now-retired Phyllis Dickstein and Rima Bordcosh, Maureen Ratynski, Yenjit Mapairoj, Samia Karoum, Alan Aalto and Kikuko Maeyama. At the UN Photo Library my work benefited from the kind assistance of Veena Nanchanda and Reynaldo Reyes. At the Schomburg Center of the New York Public Library I must thank Lela Sewell-Williams (who later relocated to Howard University's Moorland-Spingarn Center). In Los Angeles, Guille Pulido of UCLA was also especially helpful. My research also enjoyed a considerable boost from the assistance of the staff at UCLA's Film and Television Archive, especially reference librarian Lisa Kernan. I am also indebted to the Main Library, Northwestern University, Evanston, Illinois, where the competent cataloging of, and easy access to UN documents made my work faster and more enjoyable during the summer of 2001. Valuable research assistance was also rendered by the Xerox Corporation, especially Donna S. Liapari in Rochester, New York.

I also received loyal, competent help from a list of research assistants: Laura Fernandez, Bertin Kouadio, Dorcas Gakure, Kimberly Owens, Rhona Dass and Janice Yung.

The former Director of the Institute of Communications Research – Clifford Christians – had faith in me, sometimes when he had only my word to take. I am very grateful for his support. I have also benefited from the professional support of my colleagues Paul Zeleza, Leon Dash, James Miller, and Dr Karin Dovring, and greatly from the support of Professor Toy Caldwell-Colbert, Provost of Howard University.

There is also a considerable list of people from my social world in Chicago, New York, Colombia and Barbados, who lived with continued tales about this book for four years or as long as they have known me. I am sure many of them will be surprised and relieved to see that a book did eventually result from such complaints. The list includes Nerlys Canabal, Carmenza Muñoz,

Reudon Eversley, Greg Moore, Judy Mason, Pamela Davis, Sarita Villarreal, Dr Patrick Michel and Andy Mack.

The anonymous scholarly reader for Palgrave took this book very seriously, read it carefully and provided extremely constructive comments that helped to improve the work. To him or her I express sincerest thanks.

At Palgrave Macmillan I must thank numerous persons whose professionalism brought this book from a dream to reality. The now retired Tim Farmiloe acquired the work, and I would like to think that he made a very smart decision. I benefited immensely from Kerry Coutts' and Alison Howson's important input all along the way. And in the latter stages the talent of Caroline Ellerby (one of the best copy-editors I have ever worked with) and Guy Edwards helped to improve the final product. At Palgrave in New York, Michael Flamini continued to be an expert in the publishing world, and a source of tremendous support in my career as an author.

Nelsonito and Ana Lucía have been my faithful companions.

Nobody who has been of help in any way during the writing of this book is responsible for any of its shortcomings.

1
Propaganda for Peace?

The setting

When the United Nations (UN) civil service was established in 1946, the first UN Secretary-General, Trygve Lie, appointed eight Assistant Secretaries-General. An Assistant Secretary-General in charge of the Department of Public Information (DPI) was one of them. This meant that the new organization gave "public information" a status on a par with some of the other functional areas of its business that were also given their own Assistant Secretaries-General. The seven other Assistant Secretaries-General were for: "Trusteeship and Information from Non-Self-Governing Territories"; "Economic Affairs"; "Conference and General Services"; "Security Council Affairs"; "Administrative and Financial Services"; "Legal Affairs"; and "Social Affairs".[1]

The first Assistant Secretary-General of Public Information was the Chilean Benjamin Cohen, who came from the post of Chief of the Information Planning Section in the secretariat of the first General Assembly in London. Cohen was a graduate of the University of Chile and Georgetown University. His impressive resumé included stints as Chile's Ambassador to Bolivia and Venezuela. He had also been a journalist and newspaper editor.[2] The *United Nations World* magazine of March 1947 described Cohen as a man who had no hobbies other than reading. He was also described as a linguist who "thinks with equal ease in Spanish, English and French, knows Italian and Portuguese and dabbles in German and Russian".[3]

It was to this urbane diplomat and newspaperman that the task of being the UN's first official propagandist was handed. Cohen's new job was created in large part to respond to the possibility that the evil work of Joseph Goebbels might be replicated in the post-Second World War world. Goebbels' Nazi propaganda program had been so successful that the founders of the UN needed to make sure that there would be an entity ready to counteract such mobilization for hate should it ever happen again. However, at the time there was a deliberate attempt by the new organization to suppress

1

Figure 1.1 Benjamin Cohen of Chile served eight years (1946–54) as Assistant Secretary-General for Public Information, the longest term of any head of the DPI in the twentieth century. Cohen is shown here (center) in this 1952 scene from the first UN television program produced for Latin America, "Mesa Redonda de Las Naciones Unidas". He is flanked by Dr. Miguel Albornoz, Alternate Representative of Ecuador to the UN, and Gustavo Martinez-Cabañas, Deputy Director-General of the UN Technical Assistance Administration.

even the hint of similarity between what Goebbels had done and what Cohen would do. For one thing, while hatred was the stock-in-trade of Nazi propaganda, peace and international understanding would be the goal of the UN program. There was even denial that what the UN was doing was setting up a propaganda project. And no two people could be as dissimilar as the blue-blooded Chilean and the Nazi of working-class origins who had died with his wife in a suicide pact a year earlier after they had poisoned their six children.

The outfit that Cohen headed was made up of four Divisions and two Services. The Divisions were press, radio, films and other visual information, and publications and reference. One of the Services ran a network of the DPI's overseas information centers, and the other was a liaison to educational institutions and non-governmental organizations. The DPI served the news media by such means as a teletype service and providing advance copies of speeches, but it also generated the UN's own publications, including posters, articles and magazines.[4] By 2000 the DPI consisted of three Divisions – News and Media Services, Public Affairs, and Library and Publications – and two Services – Information Centres, and Communications and Coordination. But the tasks being accomplished could not even have been imagined in 1946; they included maintaining a World Wide Web site that gave public access to UN documents since 1993, as well as all UN resolutions in history, and audio of UN press briefings and radio programs. In addition, the DPI was running a training program for journalists from poor countries and hosting thousands of high-school and university students each year for "Model United Nations", simulations of meetings of various parts of the UN Secretariat in which young people play the roles of delegates in order to better understand UN politics. The expected tasks of servicing the news media were still a key part of the DPI's role, but new technology and changed attitudes towards cultivation of public opinion had altered and expanded the range of activities now called "public information".[5]

Ingrid A. Lehmann, a UN official with more than 20 years' experience in peacekeeping and public information work for the organization, has described "public information" as

> the policy and practices of the United Nations and other international organizations to disseminate their information materials (print, audio, visual) worldwide, through media contacts, direct mailing and a system of information centers in key capitals, as well as the field headquarters of peacekeeping missions. The information products are usually couched in neutral, objective language, which meet the strict UN criteria of impartiality. The term *public affairs* has also been employed by some recent missions, as well as *education*, in particular reference to voter education and human rights education.[6]

Although it is very tempting to think of what the UN calls "public information" as merely the organization's public relations or propaganda, the way Lehmann writes about the topic suggests that she believes public information is a very different practice from public relations. Indeed, when she defines public relations she says it is something that is carried out by governments and corporations. Public relations is

> the efforts of governments, companies and individuals to communicate their point of view with the intention of persuading and influencing attitudes and behavior. Particularly useful is the concept of "corporate image-making", which has been successfully used by some governmental agencies, including, for a brief period, by the United Nations. It often

employs opinion surveys, target audience analysis, campaign plans and other professional public relations strategies.[7]

Lehmann's attempt to draw a distinction between public information on the one hand, and public relations or propaganda on the other, is but another example of the discomfort felt at the UN about what its public information work is. The uneasiness was apparent from the very start when the basic principles of UN public information policy were set out in a Technical Advisory Committee's recommendations, which were adopted by General Assembly resolution 13(I), of 13 February 1946 (see Appendix II). The committee's advice was contained in 16 recommendations, the second of which stated explicitly that the proposed "Department of Public Information" should not disseminate "propaganda", however what exactly constituted the "propaganda" that the committee thought fit to name within quotation marks was not defined. The full recommendation was as follows:

> The activities of the Department of Public Information should be so orga-nized and directed to promote to the greatest possible extent an informed understanding of the work and purposes of the United Nations among the peoples of the world. To this end the Department should primarily assist and rely upon the co-operation of the established governmental agencies of information to provide the public with information about the United Nations. The Department of Public Information should not engage in "propaganda". It should on its own initiative engage in positive infor-mational activities that will supplement the services of existing agencies of information to the extent that these are insufficient to realize the purpose set forth above.[8]

Recommendation 3 noted that the general policy of the United Nations should be to give "the press and other existing agencies of information ... the fullest possible direct access to the activities and official documentation" of the UN.

Responsibility for the formulation and execution of the UN's "information policy" was to be in the hands of the UN Secretary-General and the Assistant Secretary-General in charge of the DPI (recommendation 4), subject to the authority of the UN's principal organs.

Recommendation 5 urged that there be a "common information policy" between the UN and its specialized agencies, and that this should be taken into account when the Economic and Social Council negotiated agreements with the specialized agencies.

A further eight recommendations outlined the possible form and nature of the DPI's work.

It was proposed that the DPI should have branch offices "to ensure that peoples in all parts of the world would receive as full information as possible about the United Nations". The work of the new department would fall into six categories of functions: "press, publications, radio, films, graphics and exhibitions, public liaison and reference". With regard to the first category, the DPI would "provide all the services for the daily, weekly and periodical press, both at the headquarters of the United Nations and through its branch offices, that may be required to ensure that the press is supplied with full information about the activities of the United Nations".

The prohibition of "propaganda" and duplication of the work of other bodies mentioned in recommendation 2 were re-emphasized in recommendation 9, which stated that all the DPI's publications should be within those limits.

The Technical Advisory Committee proposed that the DPI should promote the use of radio, and suggested that work in this area be based on consultation with national radio broadcasters. This recommendation said in part that:

> The United Nations should also have its own radio broadcasting station or stations with the necessary wavelengths, both for communication with Members and with branch offices, and for the origination of United Nations programs. The station might also be used as a center for national broadcasting systems that desire to co-operate in the international field.

This was a fascinating suggestion because the idea of the UN having its own broadcasting station would be proposed and discussed for the next 50 years without ever becoming a reality. Also, with the benefit of hindsight, it was conspicuous that none of the committee's suggestions mentioned television, which would become the most powerful mass medium (at least in the most influential UN member countries) in the second half of the twentieth century.[9] In addition to radio, the other media named by the committee to promote the UN's work were "documentary films, film strips, posters and other graphic exhibits".

The DPI and its branch offices were to "actively assist and encourage national information services, educational institutions and other government and non-governmental organizations of all kinds interested in spreading information about the United Nations". To do that the committee recommended that the DPI "operate a fully equipped reference service, brief or supply lecturers, and make available its publications, documentary films, film strips, posters and other exhibits for use by these agencies and organizations".

These founding visions of what the DPI should be were not limited to the idea that it would be a conduit for a one-way flow of information about the UN, however. It was also suggested that the department and its branch offices "analyze trends of opinion throughout the world about the activities of the United Nations and the extent to which an informed understanding of the work of the United Nations is being secured". In other words, the DPI was to be the eyes and ears of the UN.

This idea of the department functioning in an interactive fashion was buttressed by the suggestion that an Advisory Committee, to be selected based on expertise and geography, might be established to advise on UN information policy. The Secretary-General might consult the press and governments on how the Advisory Committee might be created. The recommendations speculated that national and regional Advisory Committees be set up once the central Advisory Committee had been created.

Chapter 2 looks critically at the ecology of the DPI during the 50 years after the Technical Advisory Committee's recommendations. This was a long road of debate in UN committees and at the General Assembly, and resulted in a number of reports on the status and future of the DPI. The department has been as remarkable for its lack of change as it has been for its reforms.

But a question has to be asked here about the very idea of "public information" and its place within the evolution of international relations.

Cultural relations, public information or propaganda?

"Public information" is one of the least known and understood areas of United Nations work. That public information activities are so obscure is fascinating because it appears to be one of the most significant aspects of UN operations in terms of the large percentage of the UN Secretariat budget allocated to it and the fact that public information was, in 1946, one of the first departments of the organization to be created.

At the beginning of its life, the UN spent as much as 10.6 per cent of its regular budget on public information,[10] and even though that percentage declined and rose over the following decades it was always a significant part of UN spending. The DPI's budget for the 1998–99 biennium was $135.5 million, 5.37 per cent of the total UN budget of $2.526 billion for that two-year period.[11]

The history of the United Nations' public information program is directly linked to the evolution of war as a means by which state and non-state actors conduct their international relations. It is also historically tied to the evolution of mass-media technology and the science of psychology.

The twentieth century saw international relations become a much more democratic arena than ever before, and these changes provoked the need for actors in international politics to pay more attention to cultivating what has now become known as "public opinion". The conduct of war was more "democratic" because it gradually ceased to be an activity between armies and mercenaries, and became one involving nation-states and their populations.[12] Diplomacy became more democratic with the arrival of what is now called the "open diplomacy" proposed in President Woodrow Wilson's "Fourteen Points" of 1918. The first of the points called for an end to the secret diplomacy (the custom of conducting interstate relations to that point) in favor of "[o]pen covenants of peace, openly arrived at".[13] The last of Wilson's points urged the creation of "a general association of nations for the purpose of affording mutual guarantees of political independence and territorial integrity to great and small states alike",[14] which led to the creation of the League of Nations that lasted from 1920 to 1946 when it was succeeded by the United Nations.

Democratic war

To illustrate how the nature of war had changed, Finch provides a useful quote from an Australian magazine in 1939, in the wake of Japan's "rape" of Nanking and on the eve of the Second World War:

> The days of professional armies are over. No longer do trained combatants take to the field against trained combatants purely because that is what they are paid to do. For wars, like everything else, have been modernised. They are bigger, and brighter, and better, and bloodier than ever before. In a 1939 war everyone would be included ... everyone, including our women and children.[15]

More recently, Millen-Penn has declared that:

> In the twentieth century we are all combatants. Millions who died in World War II, the hundreds of thousands in Vietnam, the millions who have died in local or limited wars in Latin America, Africa, and now in Europe – in Bosnia today – were not and are not soldiers.[16]

Because war now involved civilians almost on equal terms as it did professional soldiers, governments going to war needed to make sure that their civilian populations were psychologically prepared for the sacrifices that war entailed. Such sacrifices included being prepared to die or have family members die, enduring property loss, and suffering rationing and shortages of basic necessities. "To convince one's own civilian population that they must identify with the aims of the war to the point of martyrdom is a necessity of modern warfare," Finch explains. "To convince the population of the combatants, and of neutral nations, that they should disown the war is also highly desirable, for the negative impact it has, in the first place, upon potential recruitment, and later, upon desertion and surrender rates".[17]

By 1939 the historian E. H. Carr was already theorizing that "power over opinion" was one of the three main forms of power in international relations, along with economic and military power. In his realist critique of idealist views of world politics, Carr argued that international relations were essentially about power. States with power are the most able to pursue their objectives. Propaganda was the specific means by which a state gained power over opinion. Carr noted that power over opinion became a more important factor as the number of people involved in the political process increased:

> The radio, the film and the press share to the fullest extent the characteristic attitude of modern industry, i.e. that mass-production, quasi monopoly and standardization are a condition of economical and efficient working. Their management has, in the natural course of development, become concentrated in fewer and fewer hands; and this concentration facilitates and makes inevitable the centralized control of opinion. The mass production of opinion is the corollary of the mass-production of goods.[18]

By 1948, with the experiences of Nazi propaganda still very recent, Speier was even making the distinction between the different types of propaganda used in war strategy. There was "tactical" propaganda, designed to break the will of enemy troops, and "strategic" propaganda directed at sapping the morale of enemy civilians.[19]

The increased use of propaganda to conduct war and regular diplomatic relations has been described by some writers as one of the defining features of international relations in the twentieth century. According to Finch: "While the key features of psychological warfare were employed before the twentieth century, the scale of its use and the central place it came to occupy in national strategy, first during World War One and then, at a greatly increased level, in the Second World War, locate psy-war as one of the defining features of the century".[20]

Because of these new imperatives of war, many attempts to define propaganda have done so by associating it with military practice. A popular American textbook on the subject, in use at the end of the twentieth century, defined propaganda as "the deliberate, systematic attempt to shape perceptions, manipulate cognitions, and direct behavior to achieve a response that furthers the desired intent of the propagandist".[21] The authors then go on to distinguish between different types of propaganda, using cases of interstate war throughout the text to explain their understanding of propaganda: "white propaganda" ("from a source that is identified correctly, and the information in the message tends to be accurate");[22] "black propaganda" (that which is "credited to false source and spreads lies, fabrications, and depictions");[23] and "gray propaganda" ("somewhere between black and white propaganda").[24]

However, the position of this book is that propaganda should not be defined in such narrow terms. Advances in social thought by the end of the twentieth century provided a more sophisticated means of understanding the psychological and social dynamics of conflict. In order to understand what propaganda is, we must understand how and why people organize themselves into groups, how they demarcate difference between their groups and others, and how these differences are maintained through communicative practice over time. By doing that we take ourselves out of the limited box of thinking of propaganda's place in international relations as just something states do at times of war. For example, before governments run mass-media campaigns to boost their war efforts, they often engage in communicative practices that are just as important or even more important in molding national resolve. These methods include indoctrinating citizens with nationalist ideology from infancy through pledges of allegiance and biased textbooks, and instilling reverence for national symbols, such as flags and monarchs. Therefore, the approach of this book to propaganda is that there cannot be one normative definition of the concept.

Propaganda should be seen as a phenomenon of all domestic and international societies in which a variety of communicative practices are employed (wittingly or not) to produce consequences that become obvious either in the short term or after a much longer period of time. This perspective means that the intellectual discourse on propaganda should draw on research and theory as varied as anthropologist Benedict Anderson's "imagined community",[25] the work of critical historians on the political uses of distorted school textbooks,[26] and the large body of related ideas and debates in postmodern, poststructural and postcolonial theories by such writers as Homi Bhabha, Jean Baudrillard and Roland Barthes. This perspective is critical to gaining a greater appreciation of the intellectual project of this book because many of the cases discussed throughout are about racial and nationalist conflicts that incubated over long periods of time. To reduce the consideration of such problems as South African apartheid and the genocides in Rwanda and the Balkans to merely the mechanics of propaganda campaigns during a slice of the century would be to miss the point entirely.

Democratic diplomacy

Point one of Wilson's "Fourteen Points" that called for an end to secret diplomacy was expressed in Article 18 of the League of Nations Covenant. It required that "all international engagements (treaties and agreements) entered into by any Member of the League must be registered with, and published by, the Secretariat".[27] The "old diplomacy" was characterized by foreign policy being conducted by a very small, closed elite that entered and left arrangements in secret, paying little attention to what the general public thought. The argument for the "new diplomacy" was that it would produce a safer world since mutual suspicion would be minimized because covenants would be open and subject to "democratic control" by "an activist public opinion".[28]

After being skeptical of the "new diplomacy" in the early editions (dating back to the 1940s) of his widely used text on international relations, Hans Morgenthau was declaring by the 1970s that the strategic use of information and communication had created the new age of "nationalistic universal-ism".[29] Morgenthau believed that modern means of mass communication (such as radio and satellites) were significant in two major ways: (a) as means by which states tried to achieve their ends in the era of "nationalistic uni-versalism" that characterized the post-Second World War era; and (b) as a factor in the decline of diplomacy. "While nationalism wants one nation in one state and nothing else, the nationalistic universalism of our age claims for one nation and one state the right to impose its own valuations and stan-dards of action upon all the other nations," Morgenthau explained.[30] He said propaganda, although not clearly understood in theory and practice, had become a major way in which states conducted relations with other states:

> Psychological warfare or propaganda joins diplomacy and military force as the third instrument by which foreign policy tries to achieve its aims. Regardless of the instrument employed, the ultimate aim of foreign policy is always the same: to promote one's interests by changing the mind of the opponent.[31]

Morgenthau also identified the efficient nature of modern international communication as one of a few factors – such as the end of secret diplomacy and the rise of "parliamentary diplomacy" (diplomacy via international con-ferences) – that account for the disintegration of traditional diplomacy.[32] Of course, the traditional secret diplomacy did not suddenly end in the twen-tieth century, but diplomacy was certainly much more open than it had been in previous generations.

Psychology

Planners of both war and diplomacy benefited from the findings of a new science that came into its own in the early years of the 1900s. Psychology is "the study of how human beings and animals sense, think, learn, and know".[33] It is an interdisciplinary field with many branches, such as clini-cal psychology and cognitive science, but the branch of psychology that has been most useful to the conduct of war and diplomacy is social psychology, the field of research that explores "the problem ... of how and why people change their attitudes".[34] Significant texts were Harold Lasswell's study of the use of propaganda during the First World War, *Propaganda Technique in the World War* (1927), and Walter Lippmann's theory of public opinion con-tained in his *Public Opinion* (1922). Lasswell defined "propaganda" as "the management of opinions and attitudes by the direct manipulation of social suggestion rather than by altering other conditions in the environment or in the organism".[35] In other words, Lasswell conceived of propaganda as not an activity that necessarily introduced new ideas but one that worked on existing views and prejudices.

Over the years not every writer on the subject has been careful to include this key distinction in defining propaganda. For example, Karin Dovring, one of Lasswell's collaborators, has given a slightly different spin to this definition by saying that propaganda is the manipulation of symbols to control attitudes on controversial matters.[36] Similarly, a former British Council functionary, J. M. Mitchell, has defined it as "[t]he diffusion of information and ideas, which may be true or false, in order to gain an advantage in a contest".[37] Still another connotation of the word "propaganda" is "lack of objectivity in the presentation of information, tendentious distortion of truth, even outright deception".[38] But, as we shall see in Chapter 4, propaganda shares with pornography the problem that it is difficult to define.

The deeper research into how human beings think, carried out in the early twentieth century, helped to make military strategists and diplomats more sophisticated in manipulating the factor that became a more important variable in politics – public opinion. The phenomenon has been given various definitions, ranging from "opinions held by any population"[39] to "attitudes, perspectives, and preferences of a population toward events, circumstances, and issues of mutual interest".[40] One of the authors of the League of Nations Covenant, Robert Cecil, is quoted as saying that everything depended on public opinion and that "the public must have an opinion on international affairs, and that its opinion must be right".[41] However, the durability of tendencies towards the old diplomacy revealed that there was a fear and distrust of public opinion. Indeed, it might be correct to say that decision-makers do not fear public opinion per se but the opinions of specific publics because public opinion is actually the sum of opinions culled from the various groups that comprise any society. These social groups are based on class, ethnicity, occupation, gender and other characteristics. So when supporters of Article 18 of the League Covenant spoke of public opinion they were thinking of themselves, namely "the middle class, or the educated working class".[42]

Theories of public opinion have provided ideas about how opinions are acquired by various social groups, especially the notion that in any attempt to influence a particular nation attention should be focused on converting the so-called "opinion leaders". Theories such as these have given the UN's public information strategy an elitist nature – more resources are focused on cultivating support from the small percentage of society viewed as opinion leaders (such as journalists and university teachers) than on more popular groups (such as labor unions and churches).[43] The Nazi war machine learnt from psychological and public opinion research a number of techniques that were used to cultivate a supportive (or at least passive) public in Germany and territories under German control, as well as to attack the will of enemy troops and civilians. Among these was the idea that successful propaganda did not have to be based on truth but on perceptions of the truth, myths, and "stereotypes" – a term used by Lippmann to describe people's perceptions of reality that form the "pseudo-environment" in which we live.[44] So existing myths and stereotypes of various ethnic groups could be manipulated and exploited. Also, propagandistic messages could be very effective if they were packaged in entertainment programs, such as movies, that did not overtly appear propagandistic. Hence the Nazis invested heavily in a film industry that produced movies with subtle anti-Semitic content that exploited existing stereotypes and myths.

Cultural internationalism

Just as the UN's public information program emerges from a history of research into how people think, it is also the beneficiary of what the historian Akira Iriye has called "cultural internationalism". It was a development in international relations that was well under way by the time the UN was founded. The League of Nations had played a critical role in sustaining it, and when the UN's founders decided to create a Department of Public Information from the start of the organization they were simply trying to sustain this phenomenon.

Iriye defines "internationalism" as "an idea, a movement, or an institution that seeks to reformulate the nature of relations among nations through cross-national cooperation and interchange". The specific form of internationalism called "cultural internationalism" Iriye defines as "a variety of activities undertaken to link countries and peoples through the exchange of ideas and persons, through scholarly cooperation, or through efforts at facilitating cross-national understanding".[45] Cultural internationalists believe that such activities maintain international peace. Iriye says the phenomenon originated in the late 1800s, in North America and Europe, to counteract "the seemingly endless preoccupation of the great powers with military strengthening and colonial domination".[46]

However, the history of cultural internationalism is contradictory because in its early days in the late 1800s and early 1900s its proponents embraced only the so-called "civilized" races of the world. Membership and control of organizations that were established with a cultural internationalist ethic – such as the Universal Postal Union (UPU), the International Council of Women, and the International Olympic Committee (IOC) – was largely confined to North America and Europe. "One of the remarkable coincidences of history is the fact that internationalist movements were making rapid gains in the West at the very moment when prejudices against non-Western people were also becoming widespread," Iriye has concluded. "It is hard to escape the conclusion that before the First World War few in Europe or North America developed a conception of global internationalism, embracing different races and peoples".[47] Another irony of the times is that Woodrow Wilson, whose "Fourteen Points" gave birth to the League of Nations and were a good example of internationalism, also has a record of being one of the most racist presidents in American history.

Although this contradiction still persisted in many of the examples of internationalism present at the end of the twentieth century – as the discussion of "universality" in Chapter 4 of this book will show – the 1900s were characterized by an expansion of internationalism. In the first half of the century the prime example was the League of Nations that maintained both a Committee on Intellectual Cooperation and an Information Section, which was part of its Secretariat. One project of the committee was a campaign to get countries to revise textbooks to be less narrow and nationalistic in perspective. Other highlights of internationalism during the years after the 1919 Paris Peace Conference and the start of the Second World War were the effort to create a world language – Esperanto; growing popularity of international student exchange; international collaborative efforts at art preservation; and the 1928 Kellogg-Briand Pact that outlawed war as a means of settling disputes.

The Atlantic Charter that set the foundation for the United Nations is also part of this trend. Its signatories agreed that the provision of economic and social welfare were the basis of international peace. Similarly, the United Nations Educational, Scientific and Cultural Organization (UNESCO) was created by the Allied Education Ministers with the aim of eradicating war by promoting ideas that would foster peace. Perhaps there is no better example of how far internationalism had come during the century than the election of two Africans – Boutros Boutros-Ghali (1992) and Kofi Annan (1997) – to the post of UN Secretary-General. Having a person of non-European descent lead a world institution would have been unthinkable by many European and North American internationalists of the early twentieth century and interwar years.

In the late 1960s, Council of Europe official Gerard Herberichs noted that there was a link between the increased recognition of something called public opinion and the rise of internationalism. He argued that much internationalist doctrine worshipped public opinion by assuming that public opinion was peace-loving, and as such could be cultivated to promote the creation of international organizations. The 1907 Hague Convention, Article 12 of the League of Nations Covenant, the Universal Declaration of Human Rights, and the preamble to UNESCO's Constitution are just some of the international treaties cited by Herberichs to illustrate this belief in "the somewhat simplistic doctrine that public opinion wants peace and international organization".[48] This view, he argued, was irrational because there was no evidence that international public opinion was of such character. However, in the spring of 2003 the mass demonstrations on all continents against Anglo-American war on Iraq were perhaps evidence that this assumption is correct.

International cultural relations

The growth in importance of public opinion, the systematic study of how mass persuasion works and this wider awareness of the strategic value of culture in international relations were among the factors that stimulated many of the world powers to increasingly invest in international "cultural relations" programs as the century progressed.

J. M. Mitchell, who spent a career working in the field for the British government, defined cultural relations as the "fostering of co-operative relationships between cultural and educational institutions and individuals so that nations can interrelate intellectually, artistically and socially".[49] It is a blanket term that refers to various forms of international exchange among people. These exchanges can occur via mass media, through educational exchanges, language training or tourism. The term refers to forms of contact intended to construct international understanding, empathy, and foster a world society, as well as strategic communication that aims to give one actor in international politics an advantage over another. The reason why strategic international communication is considered by this author and others as a form of international cultural relations is that many of the practices intended, or perceived, to create a pacific global system actually originated in the strategic activities of states. So the practice of "cultural diplomacy" – which is the "involvement of culture in international agreements; the application of culture to the direct support of a country's political and economic diplomacy"[50] – is a form of cultural relations. But the key distinction is that cultural diplomacy is conducted only by government agencies, while cultural relations are undertaken by both government agencies and private individuals and organizations.

Cultural diplomacy is only one part of cultural relations. The US government uses the term "public diplomacy" instead of cultural diplomacy. Institutions that actually have the benign image of running programs to develop international understanding, actually are also means by which nation-states conduct their public relations and try to win public opinion and markets in foreign countries. Such bodies include the Alliance Française of France (established in 1883), British Council (1935) and BBC World Service (1932) of the UK, the Japan Foundation (1972), the US Information Agency (1953), the Goethe Institute of Germany (1951) and the Cervantes Institute of Spain (1991). These countries can afford to maintain international shortwave broadcasting services, educational exchange schemes and language training programs to maintain their good images. Because institutionalized international cultural relations of this sort are financially and technologically intensive, it means that only a small proportion of actors in international affairs have this capability.

When the Germans and Italians established schools and institutes in various parts of the globe in the 1930s, to maintain the allegiance of nationals and influence foreigners, they were employing techniques in cultural relations set in vogue by the French from as far back as the nineteenth century. After France was defeated by Prussia in 1871, the Alliance Française was started in 1883 so that France could invoke "her cultural patrimony as a means of rehabilitation".[51] The Alliance Française was to teach French in the colonies and elsewhere. It was followed 31 years later, in 1902, by the Lay Mission for non-religious teaching overseas. Third and fourth French institutions of international cultural relations followed in 1910: the national office for school and university exchanges, and the Bureau for Schools and French Foundations Abroad (*Bureau des écoles et des oeuvres françaises a l'étranger*).[52] Because the French pioneered institutionalized cultural relations, their model – which involved language teaching, "education", exchanges and even religion – was copied by the countries that adopted cultural relations in the twentieth century.

There was a marked difference between the crude forms of propaganda used during the First World War and before, and the techniques employed later in the century. In the interwar years and during the Second World War the powers perfected their techniques by using the French model to make their strategies subtle and more pervasive. The methods used during the First World War were largely written propaganda messages, such as the pamphlets and books used by the British to get support in the US after two-thirds of American newspaper owners were found to be neutral,[53] and the leaflets that were dropped from balloons over enemy territory.[54] Radio was in fact used in war as far back as the Russo-Japanese War (1904–05) when it was employed in naval communication, and was confined to the military sphere in the First World War. But it was only with Nazi propaganda of the 1930s that the institution of radio, which was previously regarded as a benign invention for domestic entertainment, became a weapon in struggles to influence public opinion.[55]

In the late 1930s France was the only state with a "cultural service" up to the task of combating Italian and German propaganda.[56] It was about that time that the British started institutionalized cultural relations. The British had disbanded their propaganda organization of the First World War but were persuaded to re-examine their position in the face of Nazi propaganda. UK propaganda during the First World War was handled by the News Department of the Foreign Office. The budget for such activities in 1918 was £2 million. That figure was scaled down immediately on completion of the war to £80 000, and Foreign Secretary Lord Curzon declared in 1919 that: "British propaganda in Foreign Countries shall, in future, be regarded as part of the regular work of His Majesty's Missions Abroad".[57] In 1930 the Treasury began annual grants for "books, lectures, films and miscellaneous minor services".[58] Four years later a Committee of International Understanding and Co-operation was set up to co-ordinate the work of the General Post Office Film Unit, the Travel Association, the Department of Overseas Trade and the News Department of the Foreign Office. This short-lived committee became the British Council, the first budget of which, in 1935, was £5000. The increased importance the British government attached to cultural relations, especially in the wake of war, can be gleaned from the rapid expansion of this budget; in 1937/38 it was £60 000, in 1938/39 £130 000, and in 1944/45 it was £2.1 million. By 1947 the British Council had 53 institutes worldwide, with seven in Egypt alone.[59]

The other form of British international cultural relations that would remain an institution in the UK's foreign relations from the 1930s onwards was the British Broadcasting Corporation (BBC). The BBC's Empire Service was started in 1932, becoming the first regularly scheduled shortwave service in the world, broadcasting 10 hours a day. The history of international shortwave broadcasting in the years between that milestone and the outbreak of the Second World War is fascinating because it reveals that international broadcasting expanded as conflict heightened.

Between 1932 and 1937 the BBC added further transmitters but broadcast only in English and never exceeded 17 hours a day on air.[60] However, during those same years Russia, France and Germany experimented with external broadcasting in foreign languages, and Japan and Italy got their own international shortwave services in 1935. During this period the Abyssinian War and the Spanish Civil War provided the first occasions for the use of shortwave broadcasting as a weapon of political warfare. Largely in response to this occurrence, the BBC finally assumed broadcasts in foreign languages in 1937, adding Arabic, Spanish and Portuguese. Two years later the number of foreign languages broadcast by the BBC increased to nine. In the meantime, Hitler employed broadcasting in the campaign against Czechoslovakia. The BBC reached its peak of wartime operations in 1944 when it was broadcasting in almost 50 languages, amounting to a total of about 130 hours daily from 43 transmitters.[61]

States also followed the lead of the Church by investing in a strategic cultural relations technique that controlled people's minds subtly over a period of time – education. A 1937 UK Foreign Office memorandum noted that:

> Education is the basis of all organised cultural propaganda, and a special feature of its modern development is its determination to secure a hold on the education of foreign children at as early an age as the government of the foreign country concerned will allow. In this respect it may be said that the totalitarian State, abroad as well as at home, is following the example of the Church, though with a very different set of principles in view. In its full development, the organisation of German or Italian cultural propaganda in a foreign country begins with the schools. Very often pupils will be attracted to a German or Italian elementary school by the offer of education at a nominal fee or even gratis; thereafter they will proceed to a State School, in the curriculum of which every effort has been made to secure a privileged position for the teaching of German or Italian. There follows a course either at a local university (at which there will always be a professor of German or Italian language and civilisation), accompanied by generous facilities (scholarships, free journeys, etc.) for travel or study in Germany or Italy, or else at a German or Italian university. Finally, for

the former student or for others who may be interested, there is usually a club or institute with every social and intellectual amenity through which contact can be maintained with what should, by now, have become the student's spiritual home. To this may be added such further influence as may be exerted by the visits of prominent statesmen, artists or men of learning, the visits of theatrical companies, the showing of German and Italian films and the energetic advertisement and sale of German or Italian products of all kinds.[62]

After the war the British government decided to continue "national propaganda overseas" with the aims of: (a) supporting British foreign policy; (b) preserving and strengthening the Commonwealth and Empire; and (c) increasing British trade and protecting British investments overseas.[63] The Ministry of Information that had been set up for the war was abolished and replaced by a decentralized system in which British propaganda was conducted from the Foreign Office, the Commonwealth Relations Office, the Colonial Office and the Board of Trade, which all set policy, and from the "operational" agencies of the British Council, the BBC and the Central Office of Information. Although the Cold War, decolonization and international economic difficulties were a challenge to British propaganda activities in the immediate post-Second World War period, by 1952 the "Overseas Information Services" had been "steadily whittled down", being effectively cut in half during the years since 1947 due to annual budget cuts and inflation. In 1952 these services accounted for 0.25 per cent (£10 million) of UK government expenditure.[64]

Despite its history of stops and starts, the UK's international cultural relations never again had the temporary and somewhat disorganized character of the interwar and war years. The Drogheda Committee enquired into British international cultural relations at the beginning of the 1950s and recommended a significant expansion. The advice was heeded, and by the 1980s the BBC was broadcasting in English and 36 other languages for almost 735 hours a week, and the British Council had 116 libraries around the world and was assisting annually about 56 000 students overseas in learning English.[65]

Similar to the UK, the US institutionalized its international cultural relations, after France and the Axis powers, in a late, reactive fashion, but unlike that of the British, American international cultural relations enjoyed a steady expansion from the 1930s onwards and of an entirely different type. Preston asserts that US international cultural relations were less subtle, aimed at converting others to an American way of thinking rather than to listen to foreign concerns.[66] The US government opened a Division of Cultural Relations in 1938, followed two years later by the office of the Coordinator of Inter-American Affairs. Months after the attack on Pearl Harbor of December 1941, the Voice of America (VOA) began broadcasting.

The Office of War Information was also established in 1942, along with its overseas component, the US Information Service.

Whereas in Western Europe it was fascism that provided the spur for Britain to enter the propaganda war and institutionalize its cultural relations, the Cold War was the spark for the expansion of this new area of US foreign policy. In 1945, the year of the UNESCO constitution, the US had 48 cultural relations officers and 70 libraries in 30 countries.[67] About the same time there were 21 cultural centers abroad and 300 American schools in "other American Republics".[68] In 1946, while Stalin was according top priority to political indoctrination at home, Senator J. William Fulbright introduced Public Law 584 that started the famous international academic and cultural exchanges.

The major milestone in the history of US public diplomacy was the passage of the Smith-Mundt Act in 1948, the basic legislation authorizing US informational and educational exchanges. In 1952 the US government spent over $162.8 million on these exchanges and other forms of international cultural relations, including $7.3 million in the Fulbright Scholarships. In addition, that year the Mutual Security Agency spent $21.7 million on "overseas Information Work".[69] Such activities got an even greater institutional character in 1953 with the setting up of the United States Information Agency (USIA), the jurisdiction of which covered the Voice of America. But while the VOA was overtly "telling America's story abroad" (in the words of the USIA's motto), the Central Intelligence Agency (CIA) was covertly financing Radio Free Europe and Radio Liberty to pursue the Cold War over the airwaves. Radio Free Europe was started in 1950 for broadcasts to eastern Europe. Radio Liberty started transmissions in 1953 to the various linguistic groups within the USSR. Both stations were based in Munich and claimed they were funded by non-governmental sources until their backing from the CIA was revealed many years later.[70]

The history of this battle of the airwaves during the Cold War seems as intriguing as a spy novel. The Eastern bloc jammed the VOA, Radio Free Europe and Radio Liberty. During the Cold War the entire Eastern bloc jammed broadcasts from the West. The Soviet Union alone is said to have used 2000 transmitters for the purpose of jamming, and Poland allegedly spent £500000 per annum on jamming before it stopped in 1956.[71] Floating transmitters in the Mediterranean were used to outfox the jammers, as was a "balloon campaign" that repeated the practice employed in the First World War of using balloons to drop propaganda leaflets in enemy territory. The balloon campaign started in 1951 and by 1956 was carrying 250 million copies of the leaflets.[72]

Cultural relations as a means of pursuing international policy is extremely capital intensive, and for this reason only a handful of states are actually able to pursue government-sponsored cultural relations worldwide. These tend to be the states with extensive commercial and military interests: Japan,

Germany, Russia, France, Canada, Britain and the US. However, this does not mean that other states do not underwrite certain types of cultural relations. By the end of the century more than 80 states were sponsoring some form of shortwave broadcasting and the reach of these stations was enhanced by the technical capability of the World Wide Web to relay audio and video, allowing listeners to acquire programs "on demand" and obviate the need to fiddle with broadcast schedules and reception problems. Some of the most prominent small states that maintain shortwave services are those that need to manage specific crises in their foreign relations, such as Cuba, Taiwan and Israel.

Each member of this elite club of states organizes its cultural relations according to one of three possible models that have been identified by Mitchell: "direct government control", where a department of government is set up for handling all the cultural relations of the country, the best example being the USIA, which was subsumed again within the State Department at the end of the twentieth century; "indirectly through non-governmental, autonomous agencies", such as the British Council that has some autonomy even though it is mainly funded by the government; and a "mixed system", such as that of Germany, in which the "government retains overall control but funds and contracts non-official agencies to operate independently within their competences".[73]

This book will show that one of the successes of UN public information work is its contribution to making some concepts (such as "human rights") part of the "common sense" of international values and norms. Similarly, cultural relations has become part of the wallpaper of international politics to the extent that in many cases the fact that it is a strategic practice has become invisible.

One way this invisibility occurs is through the tendency for some state-sponsored international broadcasting to become "surrogate" domestic services for foreign publics. The lesson from the conduct of cultural diplomacy via international broadcasting in the years since the Second World War is that institutions created to manage "crises" often take on a purpose of their own that is quite separate from the original objectives. In various parts of the world the broadcasts of the BBC, VOA, Radio Liberty and Radio Free Europe became essential sources of information for audiences without comparable domestic radio stations or with unreliable, state-controlled media. The international radio of foreign governments is described as providing "home service" or surrogate broadcasting in such situations. Rampal and Adams have noted that even during the Falklands War many Argentineans listened to the BBC (the broadcaster of the enemy) for reports on the war; Iranians and Iraqis got their reliable information during their eight-year war from the BBC and VOA; and the VOA was also a key source of news about events in China for millions in the People's Republic of China during the democracy movement of May 1989.[74]

So high are the reputations of these international broadcasters that friendly governments also retransmit their programs on their domestic services and this was especially the case with the BBC World (radio) Service in the former colonies of the British Empire after decolonization.[75] The BBC benefited from such good will when it created its World Service TV in the early 1990s.[76] President of the Czech Republic, Vaclav Havel, in the wake of President Clinton's plan to abolish Radio Free Europe, wrote personal letters to leading members of congress to whip up opposition to the president's plans.[77] A similar plea came from the former Soviet dissenter, Elena Bonner.[78]

Another way in which international cultural relations has become an almost invisible feature of contemporary international politics is through the way that global inequalities have facilitated the dependence of poor states on international cultural relations for information and education, almost as though information disseminated in this way is not part of the propaganda instruments of other states. This is succinctly and poignantly expressed by Hachten, who says:

> Generally, Third World nations are on the receiving end of public diplomacy because most lack the communication capability to compete globally. A partial exception has been the extensive radio broadcasting by a few developing nations – the Voice of the Arabs station under Egypt's Gamal Nasser, for example. On the other hand, many Third World nations have benefited from the cultural exchanges and educational assistance from developed nations – all aspects of public diplomacy.[79]

Without the resources to engage in international promotion on the scale of elite states and without large cultural industries of their own, many small countries, as Hachten observes, accept "gifts" of books, scholarships and other tools of influence as forms of aid. Similarly, some governments actually rely on the foreign broadcasts of the elite players as means of communication to their people. Kunczik provides a quote from L. F. Kaemba, the information attaché at the Zambian embassy in Washington DC, who admitted: "I have to work at times with the Voice of America. I may find it necessary to broadcast to Zambia and explain something that has taken place at the United Nations, perhaps in reference to the Zambia economic mission or within the Security Council. I pick up a phone and call someone with whom I have previously made contact at VOA and say, 'At such and such a time can you let me broadcast to Zambia?'"[80]

It is very questionable whether this state of dependence is as beneficial as Hachten suggests, because it means that many states are kept in the passive state of being receivers of the worldviews of others. They cannot manage their public relations on a continuing basis as the richer countries can. What image maintenance they do carry out is often through North American and European public relations and lobbying firms whom they usually hire for specific tasks. Kunczik gives a number of examples. In 1989, in the wake of allegations by Amnesty International of human rights violations in Turkey, the Turkish government hired Saatchi and Saatchi. The company was given a budget of £1 million for promotion in the UK alone. When the socialists came to power in Greece in 1981, Prime Minister Papandreou hired the New York PR company Fenton Communications Inc., for $6000 a month, to help allay American fear about a socialist government. In 1982, in order to get Congress to agree, over Israeli opposition, to the sale of AWACS reconnaissance planes to Saudi Arabia, the kingdom paid $400000 to Cook, Ruef & Associates Inc. In 1985, the UNITA rebels in Angola reportedly spent $600000 on cultivating their image abroad; the Angolan government countered by hiring the PR company of Gray & Co., which also represented Japan, South Korea, Saudi Arabia, Canada, Turkey, Morocco and the Cayman Islands.[81]

Of course, cultural relations continues to be a means by which states manage crises, the original purpose for which it was invented. As we have seen above, war has most often been the impetus for starting or reviving international cultural relations, especially cultural diplomacy. Military conflict is a rather straightforward example of what could be defined as a crisis, but the definition is also a subjective one to be made by the state opting to use international cultural relations as a means of conducting its international relations. It is the *potential* for crisis to arise that explains the maintenance of standing institutions conducting international cultural relations even more so than specific, identifiable crises.

This relationship with actual, prospective, perceived or created crises is the basic configuration of how international cultural relations is a resource for power in international relations. The cases from the World Wars and the Cold War discussed above were examples of the use of cultural diplomacy and propaganda in actual crises. The 1980s and early 1990s provided several examples of governments using public diplomacy and the careful management of journalistic coverage for strategic ends in "crisis" situations. Reporters were not allowed to be present, or were present under very controlled circumstances during Israel's operations in Lebanon and Britain's war in the Falklands in 1982, the US in Grenada in 1983, the French in Chad in 1988, the US in Panama in 1989, and the Persian Gulf War in 1991/92.

The UN public information project

International cultural relations and cultural internationalism use the same techniques that have been perfected by experience and research on psychology, public opinion and propaganda. But although international cultural relations and cultural internationalism are related norms in international relations, the key distinction is that the former is usually motivated by the foreign policy priorities of nation-states while the declared brief of the latter is a complete transformation of the nature of international relations to produce a peaceful world system. It could be argued that the cumulative effect of some types of international cultural relations could transform the whole international system. For example, programs such as student exchanges, transnational broadcasting and language training could enhance international understanding. However, if they do this would be a byproduct of the primary goals of the states that sponsor them because states use international cultural relations, especially cultural diplomacy, to gain them strategic advantage. So only the League of Nations and its successor, the United Nations, have been the actors in international politics with a mission of this size to use these techniques to completely reform the international system and construct a peaceful world order.

Benjamin Cohen's contribution to a 1949 book on world peace reflects the kind of thinking in the early days about how the UN functionaries conceived of the role of public information and the mass media within the overall project of the UN. Cohen said there were three dimensions to the DPI's work: disseminating factual information on the UN; surveying "public opinion"; and education. He pointed out that the UN reframed from "propaganda" (his quotation marks), and when he described the education work of the DPI he clearly assumed that such work was value-neutral and not propagandistic. He noted:

> Teaching about the United Nations, recommended to governments by the General Assembly, has developed into a major activity for the Department of Public Information. It is done through the distribution of sample materials and publications; the furnishing of speakers to institutions; forums and debates of all kinds; the production and circulation of documentary motion pictures and film strips; the establishment of reference collections and centers in particularly all countries which are members of the United Nations, in some non-member states, in trustee and non-self-governing territories. Thousands of voluntary workers, in almost every land, have been mobilized in this campaign to develop an intelligent participation of peoples in the activities of the United Nations.[82]

The emphasis on public information was the policy outcome of a syllogism popular among the founders of the UN: the more informed an individual is, the more equipped he or she will be to understand his or her responsibilities in the new world order the UN established. And, as the previous reference to Gerard Herberichs shows, already seductive by 1946 was the optimistic faith in an international public opinion that was assumed to be peace-loving. According to Cohen:

> We believe that well-informed individuals will be able to pass intelligent judgment on matters of public concern; we believe also – and the General Assembly has endorsed such a view – that enlightened peoples will understand fully their responsibility in the shaping and conduct of international affairs.[83]

The problem

Some of the reasons why the UN's public information program should be the subject of an intriguing book should already be quite obvious. It is fascinating that an organization that has the promotion of international peace as its primary goal uses techniques that have most often been used in world politics to support conflict. It is even more fascinating that this organization should feel obligated to constantly deny throughout its history that it is not in the business of spreading propaganda. But, despite the UN's defensiveness, the public information program has been one of the most durable and visible parts of the UN's bureaucracy. This fact makes it very surprising that very little has been written about it by writers outside of the UN.

The project of this book is to explain how United Nations public information policies and practice have collectively been a problem for the UN and to put in one place an investigation of its role in international politics. The book presents a set of ideas about how the public information program relates to existing theories of international relations and how we might theorize its role. This problem has four dimensions, each of which can be summed up by four separate questions that will be examined in separate chapters.

I have given careful thought to the sequence in which I examine these questions because I must consider some of them before I move on to others. For example, I could not consider public information in relation to other tools used to conduct international relations (the last of the questions) without dealing with all the issues raised by the preceding questions that set the context for tackling this question. Similarly, I felt I had to tackle the question about the relationship between the public information program and the UN's public relations problems first because it is the most basic question any individual would ask about this subject based on even the most cursory knowledge of the UN. These questions are explained in turn below.

(1) **Why does the public image of the United Nations remain distorted despite the fact that it has had an international public information program throughout its history – a program that often absorbs more than 5 per cent of its budget?** This question is handled in Chapter 3. It was one of the most fascinating and enjoyable parts of the book to investigate because it required looking at the UN's representation in popular culture, especially by the world's most powerful media. As is the case with many large international organizations, the UN has been haunted by the problem that the public often remembers its problems and failures more than its achievements. Compounding the problem is the fact that the news values of the world's most powerful media are often based on the exceptional and the negative than the routine and positive. So the UN constantly has to manage its public image and respond to controversies. Some of its image problems have been provoked by its own officials (such as revelations that former UN Secretary-General Kurt Waldheim

was a Nazi), and others have been caused by specific policies and programs (such as the failure of UN peacekeeping in Somalia). In addition, public opinion can be influenced by the representation of the UN in popular culture, especially through the most popular media such as fictional movies. One of the interesting findings of this book is that representation of the UN in popular American movies gradually changed either in response to, or related to, changes in the place of the UN in the ideological superstructure of international politics. A subsidiary question tackled by this chapter is whether the UN can realistically do more than it has done, or is doing, to renovate and manage its image.

(2) **How do we resolve the contradiction between the UN's prohibition of propaganda as a threat to world peace and its own "public information" activities that seem in many cases to be examples of propaganda?** Chapter 4 provides an explanation of the DPI's work within the context of the international discourse on propaganda. In the 1900s, especially after the Nazi campaigns, propaganda became a pejorative concept in international relations and there have been various instruments of international law against it. However, resolutions by the UN General Assembly have recognized that there is a role for positive propaganda in international politics. This chapter looks at the position of the DPI amidst this dichotomy of "good" and "bad" propaganda. This is actually a return to a topic I first explored in my 1997 book *News Revolution: Political and Economic Decisions About Global Information.* However, in Chapter 4 of this book I give the question much more extensive treatment. I try to answer the question by using two case studies – the UN's campaign to promote the universality of human rights, and the UN's campaign against apartheid in South Africa.

(3) **How can UN public information policy and strategy be refined to keep pace with the evolution of the international system and communication technology?** This section, Chapter 5, is called "Lubricating the Wheels" because it considers the number of factors that must be taken into consideration in dealing with this question, which has plagued the UN's public information program from its inception. This chapter argues that the very model of the UN's public information strategy – based on the "two-step" theory of development communication – must be scrutinized carefully and even revised. Just as the communication technology and practice of the twentieth century allowed the flourishing of internationalism and international cultural relations, the twenty-first century began with all the promises presented by the Internet. In addition, the UN has to respond to and be a player in a political environment where UN peacekeeping has radically expanded and the number of global actors competing to mold international public opinion is much more numerous than in 1946, ranging from the Cable News Network (CNN) to public relations firms acting on behalf of states and other actors.

(4) **Does the track record of over 50 years prove the utility, and even "success", of the United Nations public information program?** Chapter 6 begins the process of placing the UN's public information program within the wider context of the study of international relations. One of the chapter's basic functions is to remind the reader that public information is but one of a number of tools that actors in international politics use to pursue their objectives. Other tools include sanctions (of various kinds, including economic and sporting), military force, conventional diplomacy, espionage, cultural diplomacy and even marriage (a tool that was very common during times when monarchical rule was more widespread than it is today). However, what makes public information a unique tool is that it is used as part of a larger project of "multilateral governance" by an international intergovernmental organization (IGO).

This book was written after I had spent several years researching and writing on the politics of UNESCO, and that expertise will be gleaned throughout the following chapters as I compare and contrast the roles of the DPI and UNESCO in world politics. UNESCO was conceived as the functional international organization that would promote and perpetuate the universality of values beneficial to international peace, especially through programs of international collaboration in education, science, culture and communication. Therefore, the values UNESCO promotes are the same as, or similar to, those of the DPI. However, UNESCO came upon hard times in the 1980s when two of its founding members (the US and UK) withdrew in disagreement with UNESCO's communication program. One of the findings of this book is that UNESCO's problems had a direct and profound impact on the DPI as the UN General Assembly sought to keep alive aspects of UNESCO's communication program via different means.

Chapter 2 provides the basic background information about the UN's Department of Public Information necessary to understand clearly the succeeding chapters. Chapter 7 concludes the work by gathering together the key findings of the previous chapters and considering them within the wider context of knowledge and theory.

The book concludes with an argument for a more interdisciplinary approach to the study of international relations, especially in the consideration of a topic such as the one treated here. This argument is implicitly supported by the work of others who have written on related dimensions of the UN's role in global politics. Although this is the first book-length study of the UN's public information program by a scholar not working full-time or under contract for the UN, I am not the first to pay scholarly attention to what I will call the UN's "virtuality". In his 1968 book *The United Nations Sacred Drama*, Conor Cruise O'Brien, an ex-UN official, argued that a "factual" description of the UN was impossible because its "existence is diffused so largely in the realm of fantasy".[84] The key to understanding the UN's place in international politics, he argued, was in discerning the roles of myth, ritual and drama in human life. The UN's rituals are a means of channeling aggression in a harmless way, a substitute for action. Cruise O'Brien argued that, in considering the UN:

> style and gesture, and even décor, may be more significant than the analysis of voting patterns, and the impact of a scene or a personage more significant than the letter of the Charter. Since the United Nations makes its impression on the imagination of mankind through a spectacle presented in an auditorium with confrontations of opposing personages, it may be said to belong to the category of *drama*. Since the personages, individually or collectively, symbolize mighty forces, since the audience is mankind and the theme the destiny of man, the drama may rightly be called *sacred*. I use the word as implying association, not with supernatural order, but with those human needs which address themselves to such an order: the needs which create prayer, ritual and holy symbols. The origin of the United Nations drama is essentially the same as that of all sacred drama, in fear and in prayer. In the ancient drama the fear was of the gods, and prayer was addressed to the gods. In this modern drama, man's fear is of man, and his prayer addressed to man.[85]

The timing of journalist Cruise O'Brien's analysis is fascinating because he offered a perspective on the UN that would not be "discovered" by scholarly work in international relations for another 30 years! It is then that we find François Debrix, building on postmodern social theory and constructivist international relations paradigms, arguing that the UN originated from the need to discursively construct international relations in a different way after the Second World War, and hence the UN performs a "signifying mission".[86] "The UN does not have to approximate a (collective) reality that may never be," declares Debrix. "Simply, it is the sign of something else: the will of sovereign states to find a common resolve and cooperate only on certain issues".[87]

Cruise O'Brien pointed out in 1968 that writers on the UN sometimes unwittingly proclaim the UN's symbolic/dramatic function in world politics with the language they use. For example, a former head of the DPI, Hernane Tavares de Sá, published a critical book about the UN in 1966 using theatric metaphor in both the book's title and the sub-divisions inside. Tavares de Sá's *The Play Within The Play: The Inside Story of the UN* has parts with such names as "The Plot", "The Players", "The Stage" and "The Rehearsals".[88]

These approaches to the UN by Cruise O'Brien and Debrix are great departures from traditional studies of the organization in both substance and form. Both books may even appear rather strange, eccentric and inaccessible to those used to more conventional writing on the body. For example, Debrix's work begins with a review of a photo exhibit on the UN, and

Cruise O'Brien's book features a number of doodles about scenes at the Secretariat in the late 1960s.

It is in the spirit of a similar desire to take the study of international relations in bold, new, interdisciplinary directions that this book is written. Neo-realist theory has given greater weight to factors such as mass media in the process of international relations, and views war as having less utility than it had previously. However, neo-realism is still reluctant to abandon the notion that the state is the primary actor in international politics. By considering this case, which investigates not only a dimension of international communication but also the politics of an international organization under global conditions that seem more chaotic than orderly, this book is a critical engagement with the assumptions of the rationalist orthodoxy of international relations.[89]

2
Global Information Machine

The UN in the world: the DPI in the UN

The United Nations appears to be a very puzzling organization indeed. Although the Cold War was the single most important feature of international relations in the 40 years after the Second World War, a scholar could conclude in 1995 that the UN "played no major role".[1] Similarly, at the end of the century commentators were lamenting the famous failures of the UN to keep the peace and avoid genocide in Rwanda and Bosnia.[2] However, during the first 50 years of the UN's life, the representation of the body in Hollywood films had gradually changed from that of a benign institution in need of public support to that of a power-hungry predator, capable of invading the US or of blackmailing Chinese officials to force them to the negotiating table (see Chapter 3). Small, vulnerable states allege that the UN is controlled by the powerful countries that have permanent seats on the UN Security Council, the UN's most powerful organ. The North American and European states counter that the UN is in the hands of African, Asian and Latin American states that gained a majority in the General Assembly in the wake of decolonization in the 1960s and 1970s. At the end of the century the UN's largest contributor, the US, stopped paying dues to the organization claiming the UN was mismanaged and inefficient.

The UN's founders perhaps anticipated that the organization would engender such schizophrenic reactions when they created a Department of Public Information (DPI) as one of the first parts of the UN Secretariat in 1946. The basic function of the DPI is to inform the world of what the UN is and what it does. So we cannot fully appreciate its reason to be without a basic understanding of the role the UN plays in world politics.

When the UN was born on 24 October 1945, it was the completion of another important stage in the modern evolution of world politics. The first stage was the creation of the League of Nations after the First World War. The league was the brainchild of President Woodrow Wilson who, in his "Fourteen Points", envisaged an international system based on the principle of national self-determination, open diplomacy and an international body that would settle disputes. However, the league could not prevent the outbreak of world war again, and even before the Second World War was over President Franklin D. Roosevelt and Prime Minister Winston Churchill met to draft plans for a new world order. That proposal – the Atlantic Charter of 1941 – expressed the essence of Roosevelt's belief in the connection between his notion of "four freedoms" and world peace. Roosevelt believed that in a world where these freedoms were guaranteed there would be less recourse to conflict. The four freedoms were: freedom of speech and expression, freedom of worship, freedom from want, and freedom from fear. The Atlantic Charter also reaffirmed the belief in the principle of national self-determination.

In 1942, 26 countries pledged to observe the Charter. Two years later, in 1944, China, the USSR, the UK and the US drafted plans for the world organization that was to become the United Nations. The British, Soviets and Americans later agreed on a voting procedure for the organization that gave them veto power in what was to become the UN Security Council. The United Nations Conference on International Organization opened in San Francisco in 1945, and two months later the UN Charter was completed and signed. The UN officially came into existence on 24 October 1945 when the required number of states ratified the Charter.

The Charter and various UN conventions and resolutions seek to establish codes of conduct in international relations that are designed to maintain world peace. Some of these principles include: the idea that there are basic "human rights" to which all people are entitled; respect for self-determination of peoples and the sovereignty of states; respect for the rule of law; peaceful resolution of disputes; and the norm of collective security. The other way the UN endeavors to maintain world peace is through the norm of functionalism. The UN Secretariat in New York City is the center of a functional system of international organizations (often called the "United Nations system") that was theorized as a means of maintaining international peace. Functionalism is a theory of the organization of international relations which hypothesizes that international peace and welfare will be maintained by a system of functional international organizations, each responsible for a specific area of transnational interaction and concern (e.g. meteorology, civil aviation, health, etc.). It is based on four assumptions:[3]

- All states have a harmony of interest that allows them to cooperate for mutual benefit.
- Political and technical matters (such as health provision, civil aviation and the mails) can and should be separated in international relations.
- There would be no recourse to war if economic and social welfare were achieved throughout international society.
- Functional organizations would have a positive spillover influence on areas of international relations not yet covered by functional agencies.

Functionalism assumes that order in international relations is a higher goal than justice and equality. The man considered the father of functionalist thought, David Mitrany, promoted the "principle of functional representation" that said that parties who are deemed insignificant in the broader scheme of international relations or whose stakes in an issue area are relatively small could be excluded from decision-making. Small states would get "working democracy" in lieu of "voting democracy", and they would be consoled by "an assurance of peace and a growing measure of social equality through the working of international service". Mitrany justified this by asserting that the "formal principle of equality...at best has never been more than a political fiction".[4]

The housekeeping affairs of the world are handled by a vast network of international organizations that adhere in varying degrees to Mitrany's outlook on international affairs. All of these organizations are called UN "Specialized Agencies". They have their own memberships, organizational structures, finances and internal politics. Some are actually older than the UN but became part of the UN system after the UN was created. By taking care of economic and social welfare it is assumed that at least one critical factor in the descent to war will be taken away. Chapters IX and X (Articles 55–72) of the UN Charter defined this network of agencies and the relationship they should have with the United Nations. They were described as bodies "established by intergovernmental agreement and having wide international responsibilities, as defined in their basic instruments, in economic, social, cultural, educational, health and related fields", whose relationship to the UN would be through the Economic and Social Council (ECOSOC). Article 63 gave the ECOSOC the power to define the type of relationship Specialized Agencies would have with the UN and the responsibility for co-ordinating their activities through collaboration with the agencies themselves, the General Assembly and member states.

It is important that the Specialized Agencies were introduced in the UN Charter in Chapter IX, which dealt with the UN's role in terms of international social and economic co-operation. Article 55 noted that "the creation of conditions of stability and well-being" were "necessary for peaceful and friendly relations among nations". Based on this assumption, according to Article 55, the UN aimed to promote human rights, solutions to economic and social problems, cultural and educational co-operation and "higher standards of living, full employment, and conditions of economic and social progress and development". Article 56 obligated UN members to pursue these goals. The definition of the Specialized Agencies and their relationship to the UN in Article 57 was presented, therefore, as a nexus to these assumptions about what should be the role of the UN in the new world order created after the Second World War.

This recognition of the link between economic and social welfare and peace is one key difference between the post-Second World War peace system and the peace system that succeeded the First World War. So, for example, the World Meteorological Organization (WMO) co-ordinates matters related to predicting weather and climate change, the International Civil Aviation Organization (ICAO) regulates air safety, and the International Labor Organization (ILO) deals with labor standards. Although the United Nations Educational, Scientific and Cultural Organization (UNESCO) became one of the bodies most associated with debates about international communication, it was really a forum body for discussing and studying problems in the areas of education, science, culture and communication. It could not set international communication policy the way the International Telecommunication Union (ITU) and Universal Postal Union (UPU) were able to in their respective areas of telecommunications and the mail.

One of the reasons why world peace remained elusive despite the creation of the League of Nations and the UN was the contradictory behavior of the powers that established these organizations. For example, during the era of the League of Nations, European colonialism in Africa and Asia progressed. Also, despite the high-minded proclamations of the Atlantic and UN charters, many people still had to engage in armed conflict to free themselves from imperialism after these documents were proclaimed; these conflicts included Algeria, Kenya and Vietnam. For several years after the US signed on to the UN Charter its citizens of color still had to wage a civil rights struggle to win the outlawing of discrimination in such areas as housing, public accommodation and employment. And although South Africa was one of the earliest members of the UN it maintained a system of racial apartheid for most of the succeeding 50 years. The African National Congress and its leader, Nelson Mandela – who became an international hero because his commitment to armed struggle cost him a quarter of a century in a South African prison – waged the anti-apartheid struggle. Similarly, the UN merely created a forum in which the competing claims of Jews and Palestinians for a state in the Middle East would be played out during the next 50 years.

So in many ways the project of the UN remains very much a work in progress. However, one would be hard pressed to find an argument for the view that there has been regression in the character of both international and domestic politics and that the UN has not been a key player in bringing about the progressive changes that have occurred. Some of the most prominent of these changes include the fact that the vast majority of the territories that were under the yoke of formal colonialism in 1946 are no longer in that situation; apartheid was ended in South Africa at the beginning of the 1990s; and since the founding of the UN humanity has not seen international conflict of the magnitude witnessed in the two World Wars.

During its first 50 years, the United Nations was composed of six principal organs: the International Court of Justice (the World Court), the Security Council, the General Assembly, the Economic and Social Council, the Trusteeship Council and the Secretariat.

The General Assembly was the most popular body because it consisted of all the member states of the UN, each of which had one vote, and was the world's best-known forum for the discussion of international affairs. A two-thirds majority of UN members present and voting was required for General Assembly decisions on the important issues specified in Article 18 of the UN Charter. On other matters, a simple majority made decisions. The General Assembly performed a key role in the execution of decisions needed to keep the UN functioning. For example, it decided the level of assessment for each member to share the organization's expenses, considered and approved the UN budget, and shared with the Security Council the responsibility for electing members of the International Court of Justice and for appointing the UN Secretary-General. It also elected the members of the Economic and Social Council and some members of the Trusteeship Council, as well as the 10 non-permanent members of the Security Council.

It is in the composition of the Security Council that the power differentials in world politics were most evident. Article 24 of the UN Charter gave this UN organ "primary responsibility for the maintenance of international peace and security". It had five permanent members – the UK, the US, the People's Republic of China, France and the Russian Federation – who had to concur with at least four other members of the council for any vote on an issue other than a procedural matter to be approved.

The range of activities supervised by the Economic and Social Council seemed almost limitless because it was the UN organ charged with promoting world economic and social welfare. The *United Nations Handbook* – an influential reference source on the UN published annually by the government of New Zealand – has summarized the work of the ECOSOC as follows:

> ECOSOC makes or initiates studies and reports with respect to international economic, social, cultural, educational, health and related matters. It makes recommendations on such matters to the General Assembly, to the members of the UN, and to the specialized agencies concerned. It also makes recommendations for the purpose of promoting respect for, and observance of, human rights. It prepares draft conventions for submission to the General Assembly on matters within its competence and calls international conferences on such matters. It enters into agreements with specialized agencies and makes arrangements for consultation with non-governmental organisations.[5]

The International Court of Justice made decisions on cases submitted to it by states, and it provided legal advice to the UN organs and the Specialized Agencies. The Trusteeship Council was established to provide oversight on the administration of the various trust territories in existence during the early years of the UN, however by the end of the century all of these areas had ceased to be trust territories.

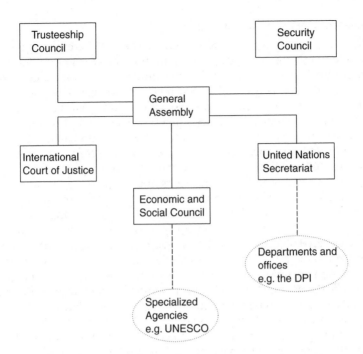

Chart 2.1   The DPI and UNESCO in the UN structure.

Chart 2.1 illustrates where the focus of this book, the DPI, fell within this structure. The DPI is a department within the UN Secretariat in New York. Because UNESCO had a mandate directly related to the work of the DPI, the chart also indicates the position of that organization within the structure of the UN system. UNESCO was a UN Specialized Agency that was affiliated to the UN through the Economic and Social Council, as all Specialized Agencies were.

In looking at any graphic description of the UN or the "UN system", it is tempting to think of the various departments and agencies as being autonomous entities. However, it should be quickly explained that member states constantly try to micro-manage these bureaucratic parts and the programs they run. This feature of UN politics is perhaps best known in the case of the Security Council where much has been written about the use or misuse of the veto privilege of permanent members. But less well-known are the coalition politics, horse trading and rhetorical sparring that occur in the General Assembly and various committees over such programs as the DPI. As far back as 1960, the dynamics of policy-making in the area of public information attracted scholarly attention in two separate articles from Richard N. Swift and Leon Gordenker, two professors at prestigious American universities.[6]

A public information bureaucracy

Very few actors in international relations rival the information output of the United Nations system. Other very powerful information-producers in world politics include states – especially influential nation-states such as France, the UK, Germany and the US, which not only generate information through their embassies and other diplomatic offices around the world but also use "cultural (public) diplomacy" organs such as the British Council and the Alliance Française to disseminate their views on world affairs, trying to win friends and influence people. And transnational corporations such as Coca-Cola, IBM and Sony are also powerful information players, in this case using paid advertising and public relations in their quests to find and maintain markets in every corner of the globe. But while the information campaigns of corporations are to expand their markets and serve their shareholders, and states use their campaigns to pursue their national interests, the declared objective of the UN is to serve all members of international society. The functions of the various bodies in the UN system cover every aspect of human life, from World Health Organization (WHO) programs to eradicate diseases such as polio and smallpox, to the safeguarding of the rights and welfare of refugees by the UN High Commissioner for Refugees (UNHCR), to the protection of workers' rights by the International Labor Organization (ILO). Many of these projects simply cannot work without information campaigns of some kind, ranging from making people aware of the availability of helpful resources to communicating with donor states and foundations to ensure the continued flow of resources.

A snapshot into this vast information bureaucracy was provided in 1995 when the DPI published a guide to help those searching for information about the various activities of the UN.[7] The primary subject categories listed in the book alone numbered more than 250. The total number of UN offices, programs and Specialized Agencies was 53, the vast majority of which – 38 – had officers, divisions or departments devoted to "public affairs", "external relations", "information" or "press". For example, the International Monetary Fund (IMF) had a "Public Affairs Division", the United Nations Development Fund for Women (UNIFEM) had an "Information Officer", and the United Nations Development Program (UNDP) had a "Division of Public Affairs". So the DPI is actually only one public information program among many, and in addition to its general mandate of promoting the work of the UN, at that time it was handling the specific public information needs of two departments at the Secretariat: the Department of Peace-Keeping Operations and the Department of Political Affairs. The 1995 guide made no reference to the then dawning significance of the Internet. Just five years later, every single significant actor in international relations, especially the UN offices, programs and agencies, would be expected to have a presence on the World Wide Web and did so. This development added further information media and workers to the equation.

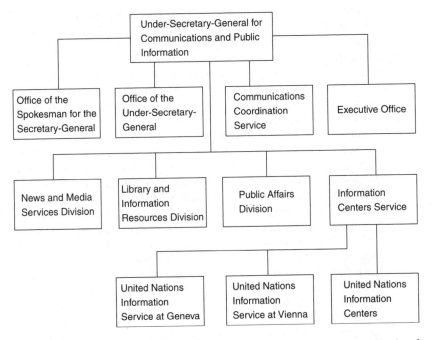

Chart 2.2 United Nations Department of Public Information – organizational structure 2001.

The United Nations' budget cycle covers two years, and the total UN budget for the 1998–99 biennium was US$2.526 billion.[8] The DPI accounted for 5.37 per cent of that figure ($135 million), more than the UN spent on Human Rights and Humanitarian Affairs (4.96 per cent) and International Justice and Law (2.10 per cent).

During the 1998–99 period there were 730 permanent posts in the DPI.[9] The department's hierarchy consisted of the Office of Under-Secretary-General for Communications and Public Information at the top, three divisions and one service on the level below, and at the bottom level the UN Information Service at Vienna and Geneva and the network of UN Information Centers around the world (see Chart 2.2).

The organizational configuration of the DPI at the end of the century was set out in a 1999 "bulletin" – the equivalent of an executive order – by UN Secretary-General Kofi Annan. This outlined the five dimensions of the DPI's work. The Department

(a) Assists the Secretary-General in the discharge of his or her responsibilities under the Charter of the United Nations and the mandates of the General Assembly, the Security Council and other United Nations legislative bodies in raising public awareness of the issues and aims of the United Nations and promoting an informed understanding of its work among all peoples of the world;

(b) Provides a full range of public information services to the global news media, non-governmental organizations, academic institutions, parliamentarians, business and professional organizations and other key redisseminators and directly to the general public, both at Headquarters and through its network of information centers abroad;

(c) Promotes the integration of the United Nations information outreach and support for an internal "culture of communication" through the in-house network of United Nations informational focal points and the system-wide Joint United Nations Information Committee; and keeps the Secretary-General and other senior officials informed of major news developments of direct relevance to the United Nations;

(d) Establishes and monitors, through the Publications Board, Secretariat-wide policies for the preparation, production, distribution and sale of print and electronic publications; coordinates the implementation of the biennial publications programme of the United Nations; manages the Dag Hammarskjöld Library; and provides comprehensive library services to delegations, members of the Secretariat and independent researchers;

(e) Coordinates and manages the United Nations home page and Web site; chairs the Interdepartmental Working Group on the Internet; and builds and maintains a multilingual, media-friendly United Nations presence on the Internet.[10]

The Under-Secretary-General for Communications and Public Information – a top-level UN civil servant who was appointed by the UN Secretary-General based on background and the need to have diverse geographical representation of UN officials and staff – ran the shop and was accountable to the Secretary-General. Answering to the Under-Secretary-General were Directors of the Office of the Spokesman for the Secretary-General, the Public Affairs Division, a News and Media Division and a Library and Information Resources Division. Also reporting to the Under-Secretary-General were Chiefs of the Information Centers Service and the Communications Coordination Service. In other words, the DPI included a myriad of diverse activities that represented the public face of the UN, including the guided tours of the UN headquarters in New York, the UN bookshop, the UN's library and the accreditation of journalists covering the UN, its activities and special conferences.

The bureaucratic organization of the DPI underwent a number of reconfigurations over the years, including changing its name to the Office of Public Information (OPI) from 1958 to 1978,[11] but the basic functions of most of its components remained the same. The Technical Advisory Committee that recommended the UN have a public information program suggested the creation of a global network of information centers that would be conduits for the two-way flow of information between the UN and its public. By 2000 there were over 60 such centers, covering all regions of the world.[12] The network came under the supervision of the Chief of the Information Centers Service. Similarly, the News and Media Division was made up of three units – a Press Service, a Radio and Television Service, and a Media Monitoring and Analysis Section – that conducted basic activities of the DPI throughout the years of its existence. The Press Service generated press releases and a number of publications for the media and general public. It also accredited journalists covering the UN. The Radio and Television Service produced a number of news and documentary audio-visual programs and also maintained the UN's audio-visual and photo libraries, and the Media Monitoring and Analysis Section reported on how the UN was covered by the world's media.

Although the Public Affairs Division had the most elaborate and varied brief of the DPI's divisions, ironically it had the smallest staff. Of the 730 permanent positions at the DPI during the 1998–99 period, only 47 were in Public Affairs, compared to 275 at the information centers (the largest allotment of permanent staff) and 133 in the News and Media Division (the second largest).[13] The Public Affairs Division's Promotion and Planning Service promoted the thematic focus of the UN's work in such areas as "sustainable development" and "human rights" by helping to develop and propagate the initiatives used by the UN to gain awareness, such as special

Figure 2.1   United Nations Radio commentators report on a meeting of the Security Council, 18 April 1973. At the time the DPI's Radio Services disseminated productions in 40 languages for rebroadcasting in 145 states and territories.

decades, international years and conferences. Its Public Liaison Service ran the guided tours, produced exhibits, maintained the Non-Governmental Organization (NGO) Resource Center at UN Headquarters, ran the annual DPI/NGO conference, and co-ordinated the annual Training Programme for Broadcasters and Journalists from Developing Countries.

The Library and Information Resources Division included the UN's library, the Publications Service, which published a number of UN periodicals, and the Sales and Marketing Section, which "establishes and exploits a market for United Nations publications and related items, and supervises the United Nations Bookshops in New York and Geneva".[14]

Operating out of the Under-Secretary-General's Office was the Communications Coordination Service, a focal point for the strategic planning and management of the UN's public information policy. It was also the part of the DPI charged with "managing and enhancing the United Nations presence on the Internet, including the United Nations Web site in all official languages".[15]

The Communications Coordination Service was established in 1999 and was one of two strategies devised by the Kofi Annan administration to tackle the long-standing problem of co-ordinating the various parts of the public information work of the UN and the UN system. The second strategy was the creation of the post of Director of Communications in the Office of the Secretary-General to co-ordinate a Communications Group that consisted of representatives from the Specialized Agencies and all departments in the Secretariat. The Group, which included the Under-Secretary-General for Communications and Public Information, met frequently to devise a common public information strategy for the United Nations.[16] Early in the UN's life, in July 1946, the new DPI and the Specialized Agencies met to see how they could co-ordinate their work, and this led to the creation of the Consultative Committee for Public Information (CCPI), which comprised representatives from the Specialized Agencies and the DPI. The DPI served as its secretariat and met once a year.[17] In 1974 the CCPI was merged with the Programme Committee of the Centre for Economic and Social Information to form the Joint United Nations Information Committee (JUNIC). JUNIC became the forum in which public information professionals in the UN system met to discuss and co-ordinate their activities as well as plan campaigns. It reported to the UN's Administrative Committee on Coordination (ACC), a body chaired by the UN Secretary-General, which met twice a year. The ACC was created in 1946 at the request of the ECOSOC to supervise the implementation of the agreements between the United Nations and the Specialized Agencies. Its mandate expanded over the years to include the promotion of co-operation within the UN system of organizations, and its name was eventually changed to the United Nations System Chief Executives Board for Coordination (CEB).

The DPI was supposed to be at the center of the public information practice that JUNIC co-ordinated. However, this fact could sometimes be lost because the public information programs of the UN system were so numerous and extensive. The rapid increase in public information activities during the 1970s prompted a 1983 report from the Secretary-General's office as a reminder of the intended role of the DPI in these matters:

> In the medium-term plan and programme budget documents, the impression is conveyed that the Department of Public Information is the only point of information activity within the United Nations. From 1971 on, however, there has been an ever-growing dispersion of information functions and resources to other departments and offices. It is estimated that for the 1982–1983 biennium there are at least 72 posts outside the budget for the Department which are being utilized for information programmes. While there are some advantages to be gained from such an approach, it would be prudent to ensure that the Department, which was designated by the General Assembly as the focal point for co-ordination and implementation of the information activities of the United Nations, is able to exercise that role.[18]

Each year JUNIC also presented a report to the United Nations Information Committee, the body of the General Assembly that oversaw the United Nations public information program. The General Assembly set up the Information Committee in 1978 during the heady days of the proposed "New International Economic Order" (NIEO) and the "New World Information and Communication Order" (NWICO). Its predecessor was the Consultative Panel on Public Information that was created by the General Assembly in Resolution 1405 (XIV) of 1 December 1959 "to advise the Secretary-General on information policies and programmes in order to ensure maximum effectiveness at minimum cost". The new committee met once a year and provided the Secretary-General with a "general framework for action in the information field".[19] Although by 2000 both the NIEO and the NWICO movements were more part of UN history than contemporary policy, the Information Committee's brief – from a 1979 General Assembly resolution – had remained the same. It existed:

(a) To continue to examine United Nations public information policies and activities, in light of the evolution of international relations, particularly during the past two decades, and of the imperatives of the establishment of the new international economic order and of a new world information and communication order;

(b) To evaluate and follow-up the efforts made and the progress achieved by the United Nations system in the field of information and communications;

(c) To promote the establishment of a new, more just and more effective world information and communication order intended to strengthen peace and international understanding and based on the

free circulation and wider and better balanced dissemination of information and to make recommendations thereon to the General
Assembly...[20]

Membership of the Information Committee grew steadily from 66 in 1979
to 95 by 2000. Its annual sessions in the spring ran for as long as two weeks,
and its annual reports were several pages long. Its debates and reports were
the most insightful windows into divisions among UN member states concerning international communication and trends in UN public information
policy-making. Indeed, it can be argued that the Information Committee
became, over time, much more than a forum for debate and the overseeing
of UN public information policy; it was an arena in which states and political groupings of states sparred on their propaganda wars and from which
they sought UN propaganda support during conflicts. For example, the
committee's 2001 report stated that:

One delegation denounced the aggression against it in the form of radio
and television broadcasts from another country as flagrant violations of
international law. Those were illegal acts that were being committed
using increasingly sophisticated technology, he said, and he demanded a
cessation of that aggression. Exercising its right of reply, another delegation noted that this was not a constructive interjection, to which the former delegation responded that the money used on the media aggression
could be put to good use by the Organization and reiterated his condemnation of this aggression against his country.[21]

Similarly, later in the report it was noted that:

Several speakers called for increased dissemination of information on the
question of Palestine, and called for an enhanced role for the Committee
in uncovering the facts related to the suffering of the Palestinian people
and the acts of aggression perpetrated against them. One speaker mentioned that the archives of the United Nations were filled with information, reports, resolutions and recommendations related to the question
of Palestine and the internationally accepted rights of the Palestinian
people, and stressed the need for the Department to utilize those documents through all means to expose the oppressive policies to which the
Palestinian people were being subjected.[22]

Each year, the Information Committee tried to accommodate all of these
contentious exchanges within draft resolutions that eventually went to the
full General Assembly for passage. In 2001 the committee's Draft Resolution
A on "Information in the Service of Humanity" recommended that the
member states of the General Assembly uphold the principles of the NWICO.

Draft Resolution B on "United Nations Public Information Policies and Activities" was specifically directed to the UN's public information program, committing the DPI to such imperatives as multilingualism in its output, helping to bridge the "digital divide" and promoting special UN conferences.

Although these General Assembly resolutions shared the posturing and rhetoric of resolutions passed on other topics, the creation of the Information Committee had serious consequences for the workload and ideological role of the DPI. The new committee was more than a "talk shop"; it was where actual projects to rectify global communication problems were proposed for the DPI to complete. For example, in its 2000 report the committee said the DPI "should maintain and improve its activities in the areas of special interest to developing countries ... and that such reorientation should contribute to bridging the existing gap between the developing and developed countries in the crucial field of public information and communications". It also urged the DPI to "enhance its role" in the "efforts of the Secretary-General in closing the digital divide as a means of spurring economic growth and as a response to the continuing gulf between developed and developing countries".[23]

In pointing attention to the inequalities in international communication, the Information Committee was being loyal to the brief given to it by the UN General Assembly in 1979 in Resolution 34/182. However, although the committee was sticking to the letter of its purpose, the substance of its recommendations with respect to the DPI were contradictory. While it reaffirmed General Assembly Resolution 13 (I), the brief for the work of the DPI, it drifted from that very same brief by suggesting that the DPI undertake work well outside its remit. This was what occurred in 1981 when the DPI began running a Training Program for Broadcasters and Journalists from Developing Countries. Between 1981 and 2000 the DPI trained in New York 303 media professionals from 100 countries.[24]

The role of the DPI was also expected to expand in another way. In addition to the expectation that it would play an active role in rectifying information and communication inequalities, the General Assembly began specifically identifying the DPI as the UN counter-propaganda organ in national and regional struggles in which the UN was a key player. On this matter, the motivating factor was the increased role of propaganda as a tool for conducting international relations – one of the key trends of international politics in the twentieth century (see Chapter 6).

The UN was at the forefront of the propaganda war during the apartheid regime of South Africa over the two key issues of the country's occupation of what was to become the new state of Namibia and white minority rule in South Africa.[25] General Assembly resolutions singled out the DPI as the UN department that would lead the charge against South Africa's well-known efficient propaganda machine. For example, General Assembly Resolution number 31/150, of 20 December 1976, stated that the Secretary-General should direct the DPI to

> ... aquire and distribute appropiate films on Namibia ...
> (b) To prepare, in consultation with the South West Africa People's Orga-
> nization, a film on the contemporary situation inside Namibia and the
> struggle of the Namibian people for genuine national independence;
> (c) To continue publicity through television, radio and other media;
> (d) To continue to give publicity to the United Nations Council for
> Namibia and the South West Africa People's Organization on televi-
> sion in the United States of America and other major Western coun-
> tries, in order to mobilize support in those countries for the genuine
> national independence of Namibia ...

The resolution also went on to say that the DPI should: "continue to make every effort to generate publicity and disseminate information with a view to mobilizing public support for the independence of Namibia". DPI-run projects, especially the production of over a thousand radio programs annually, were among the factors that eventually led to Namibian independence in 1990 and non-racial elections in South Africa four years later.[26] This "good propaganda" campaign of the UN is discussed in more detail in Chapter 4.

The DPI was singled out in a similar fashion with regard to the question of Palestine. General Assembly Resolution 50/84(C) of 15 December 1995 requested the DPI to

> ... disseminate information on all the activities of the United Nations sys-
> tem relating to the question of Palestine, including reports on the work
> carried out by the relevant United Nations organizations;
> (b) To continue to issue and update publications on the various aspects
> of the question of Palestine in all fields, including materials concern-
> ing the recent developments in that regard and, in particular, the
> achievements of the peace process;
> (c) To expand its audiovisual material on the question of Palestine,
> including the production of such material;
> (d) To organize and promote fact-finding news missions for journalists to
> the area, including the territories under the jurisdiction of the
> Palestinian Authority and the occupied territories;
> (e) To organize international, regional and national encounters for
> journalists;
> (f) To provide, in cooperation with specialized agencies of the United
> Nations system, particularly the United Nations Educational,
> Scientific and Cultural Organization, assistance to the Palestinian
> people in the field of media development.

In 1995, the DPI launched an annual training program for Palestinian journalists and broadcasters. The program was part of the DPI's "Special

Information Program on the Question of Palestine" and was designed to assist the Palestinian people in strengthening their media capability. Eight Palestinian journalists participated in the first training program, held from 6 October to 22 November, attending briefings by officials of the UN and UN Specialized Agencies, participating in a one-week skills training workshop with CNN in Atlanta, two weeks of classes at Columbia University's School of International and Public Affairs, and one week of briefings at US government branches. For the rest of the 1990s the DPI ran a similar program each year for more or less the same number of Palestinian journalists.

The fact that the Information Committee originated with the rancor at the UN over the NIEO and NWICO is very significant because it provides a lens through which not only the nature of the Information Committee's debates and decisions but also the type of tasks the DPI was called upon to perform in the successive years can be assessed. The increased involvement of the DPI in "service" projects to redress the world's communication "imbalances" of the type described above began at the same time that UNESCO – the Specialized Agency mandated to do such work – was stymied by the US and UK. These two most powerful members of UNESCO actually quit the body in the early 1980s on the grounds that its championing of the NWICO was unwanted "politicization". UNESCO lost a quarter of its budget from the withdrawal of the US, UK and Singapore, and was therefore forced to tone down its radical program of international communication reform. As a result the new Information Committee was to be the vehicle that transferred this ideological project to the UN Secretariat and, more specifically, to the DPI.

In addition to continuing the NWICO discourse, the Information Committee was also essentially a means by which the member states attempted to maintain their control over the DPI, making it clear that the power of DPI bureaucrats over UN Secretariat public information policy would always be subject to careful scrutiny and control.

Perpetual re-evaluation

Over the first 50 years of the UN, three themes recurred in relation to its public information program. The first was controversy over waste and mismanagement, the second was a desperate search for more clearly defined "target audiences" for the UN's public information campaigns, and the third was uncertainty over the role of UN public information policy and practice within international politics.

Expenditure and management

Because the DPI had been plagued with questions about its worth and competence, it had been subject to what seemed like perpetual re-evaluation throughout its existence. Evaluation and re-evaluation of programs that use public funds are the norm in order to avoid waste and corruption. But just a few years into the life of the UN questions were being raised as to whether the money spent on public information was not a waste in itself. So began a history that involved the DPI frequently under attack and subject to a number of periodic reviews to define its mission, refine its techniques and ensure that it did not waste UN funds. Two matters were constant features of the first 50 years of the DPI – calls from the General Assembly for spending on the DPI to be cut, and calls from the General Assembly for the DPI to carry out more tasks.

In the early days, the DPI was the focus of UN spending on public information, but by the mid-1970s the UN system as a whole had a public information bureaucracy that included the DPI and several Specialized Agencies devoted to spreading the word about the UN and its interconnected parts. The growth in UN public information work was a result of the expansion of the UN system, and also of the evolution of international politics. Decolonization created scores of new states and expanded the realm of international public opinion to be cultivated, the number and importance of NGOs increased, and there was a greater need for collective action through the UN on such transnational issues as the environment, refugees and health. In 1948 the UN's total budget was $38 388 000 and the first public information budget accounted for about 10 per cent of this ($4 080 000). But in 1971 the UN budget was $192 149 300 and the proportion of money allocated to public information had declined to 4.15 per cent ($9 245 563).[27] In 1979 the UN system as a whole spent $52 114 000 on public information work, a figure that included money from the regular budgets and extra-budgetary sources; the resources spent on public information were increasing rapidly as the comparative figure for 1977 had been $13.5 million less.[28] In 1977–78 the entire UN system had information offices in 74 cities, amounting to "148 information points".[29]

It was just six years into the life of the United Nations that the Assistant Secretary-General for Public Information was claiming that "[t]he demands for public information services from the United Nations far exceed the budgetary resources placed at the disposal of the Department by the General Assembly".[30] This comment was quoted in a review of the DPI's "Basic Principles" by an 11-member Sub-Committee of the General Assembly's Fifth Committee with the aim of helping the General Assembly formulate an appropriate 1953 budget for the DPI. According to the sub-committee: "the basic policy of the United Nations, in the field of public information, is ... to promote to the greatest possible extent, within budgetary limitations, an informed understanding of the work and purposes of the Organization among the peoples of the world" (see Appendix V). To keep within these "budgetary limitations", the sub-committee suggested the DPI should make its clients pay for more of the materials that were then distributed free. Number 10 of the principles said that although free distribution of materials was needed to carry out public information work, the DPI should "actively encourage the sale of its materials" whenever possible, and that in some cases "it should seek to finance production by means of revenue-producing and self-liquidating projects". However, the sub-committee's attitude to spending by the DPI was contradictory. While the Basic Principles were that the DPI's work should occur "within budgetary limitations", the sub-committee recommended in its report consideration of establishing a United Nations Press, similar to a university press, and noted in number five of the Basic Principles that the UN should have its own broadcasting facilities. These two proposals certainly would have added considerably to the cost of the UN's public information program had they been implemented.

The 1953 Basic Principles were a distinct renovation of those of 1946 because of their stipulation that the DPI devote special attention to the needs of "under-developed areas". In successive years the DPI would undertake a number of projects to serve the perceived needs of disadvantaged groups and regions, a mission that, though noble, provided further strain on the department's budgetary and human resources. The sub-committee's justification for this significant policy innovation was that:

> In view of the high importance which aid to under-developed areas has come to assume in relation to many of the Organization's activities, it was felt that a specific directive to pay particular attention to the special problems and needs of such areas might appropriately be included in any basic policy statement relating to information services. It was considered, moreover, that since the tasks that might usefully be undertaken in the field of public information are practically limitless, special consideration should be given to the needs of those areas where, in relation to other areas, information media are less fully developed.[31]

However, the UN was so preoccupied with the cost of its public information program that within a few years it appointed an "Expert Committee" to recommend "possible modifications to ensure a maximum of effectiveness at the lowest possible cost".[32] Experts found that because the term "budgetary limitations" in the 1953 Basic Principles was never defined, the net effect was a "series of ad hoc cuts in information expenditure".[33] In 1956 the General Assembly's Fifth Committee had recommended that spending on public information (excluding the Visitor's Service and the Sales and Circulation Service) should be limited to $4.5 million annually within three years. However, the Secretary-General drew attention to this problem of the General Assembly specifying tasks for the UN's public information operations while at the same time calling for thrift. "The Assembly itself, while emphasizing the need for economy, has not specified any activity which should be cut out or cut down," a memo from the Secretary-General's office declared.[34]

During the next 20 years the problem of an expanding public information program with diminishing resources would get worse and would be

compounded by the fact that the players in the UN system's public information bureaucracy became more numerous. The expanding UN bureaucracy motivated the UN to explore ways in which there could be greater
co-ordination throughout the system. From 1968 the Joint Inspection Unit
(JIU) began a series of investigations on co-ordination and co-operation
among the members of the UN system. Its particularly critical report on
co-ordination in public information was released in 1981 and castigated the
UN system for essentially wasting scarce resources by simply not co-ordinating
public information policy and practice. "One dares not, at present, even speak
of integrated actions or joint programmes in the field of public information,"
the document concluded.[35]

This assessment by an internal unit of the UN is very significant in light
of the historical context. The UN, particularly UNESCO, was at the time
embroiled in the debate over the NWICO. NWICO advocates had placed the
need to end world communication imbalances on the agenda of UN public
information policy-making by asking the DPI and other UN public information organs to carry out media training and to publicize the NWICO concept. By the mid-1980s both the US and the UK had quit membership of
UNESCO, claiming that the organization was not only threatening freedom
of the press by promoting the NWICO but that it was also mismanaged. The
JIU report is some evidence that a number of the criticisms of the UN made
by NWICO detractors at the time were not far from the mark. While the
NWICO sought government policy and action to end global communication disparities, the UN itself was a poor example of what more government
activity in the field of information and communication might mean.

At the time, public information bureaucrats, the ACC and the Committee
for Programme and Co-ordination (CPC) had all recognized the need to
avoid duplication, and therefore a number of ad hoc working groups had
been established under JUNIC. JUNIC had started a process where public
information work would be co-ordinated according to yearly plans of
action.[36] In keeping with the tenor of the times, the common theme chosen by JUNIC for 1980–81 was the New International Development Strategy
and the promotion of the NWICO. Sub-themes were the International
Drinking Water Supply and Sanitation Decade and the International Year for
Disabled Persons. However, out of the $52 million spent by UN agencies on
public information work in 1979, $387019 was devoted to joint projects, the
bulk of which went to two initiatives: the monthly newspaper *Development
Forum* and a "World Newspaper Supplement".[37] It is indeed interesting that
UNESCO – the agency spearheading the NWICO – was singled out by the
JIU as one of the least enthusiastic about co-operation and co-ordination.
The agency told the JIU that each UN organ had specific objectives and programs that did not make co-ordination and co-operation among agencies in
public information easy.[38] The report concluded: "So long as the Member

States of the United Nations system continue to permit publicity on individual organizations or their heads – building up empires – instead of making them co-ordinate their efforts towards the global aims of development as envisaged by the New Economic Order, the role of JUNIC and the contribution of the members of JUNIC will remain a formality".[39]

Doubts regarding the worth and efficiency of the public information program continued into the 1980s. At one point the CPC recommended that the DPI's budget be suppressed to "well below average" growth and the money saved be redeployed to the transport programs of the Economic Commission for Africa (ECA), the Economic Commission for Latin America and the Caribbean (ECLAC), the Economic and Social Commission for Western Asia (ESCWA) and the Economic and Social Commission for Asia and the Pacific (ESCAP).[40] No doubt one reason why public information was seen as expendable was the inefficient way in which some very public areas of it was conducted. For example, subscribers to the *UN Chronicle* received only six issues in 1984 even though it was supposed to be a monthly, and there were gaps between the publication dates of the English, French and Spanish versions.[41]

By the late 1990s there had been a number of cuts in the DPI's funding and manpower, reductions so severe that a Task Force appointed by the Secretary-General to look at the DPI emphatically said in 1997 that the cuts had gone far enough. However, in 1999 the CPC still expressed concern that "the inadequacy of resources was the cause of a number of difficulties faced by the Department in implementing its activities", and that "because of the reduction in resources, many United Nations information centers could not play a meaningful role".[42] Despite the "culture of communications" that was heralded for the UN by the Task Force and by the DPI leadership afterwards, in 1999 the CPC reported that the DPI was still having problems identifying its audiences, getting policies through the slow bureaucracy and decentralizing the distribution of information.[43] The CPC lamented the lack of an efficient, speedy means to respond to press queries and noted that there were "no guidelines on media relations issued to the Secretariat as a whole, and senior officials do not feel encouraged to speak to the press".[44]

Target audiences

Are the DPI's clients individual members of the public, or media and government organs that redisseminate information to individuals? In other words, should the DPI be viewed as a mass-media outlet to the general public or more as a wire service the audience of which is actually news media? The fact that the UN has had difficulty answering such a basic question helps explain why the DPI suffered from an identity crisis throughout the first 50 years of the organization.

The ambiguities began with the founding principles of 1946, which said the DPI should "promote to the greatest possible extent an informed understanding of the work and purposes of the United Nations among the peoples of the world", and in order to do so "should primarily assist and rely upon the co-operation of the established governmental and non-governmental agencies of information to provide the public with information about the United Nations". The DPI was charged with ensuring "that peoples in all parts of the world receive as full information as possible about the United Nations". The department was also to open "branch offices" as soon as practically possible (see Appendix II). Such wording implies that the DPI's clients would be both news organizations and the general public. However, the matter becomes complicated when one considers that the UN has been shy about reaching over governments and propagandizing foreign publics, a de facto violation of the principle of national sovereignty. More intriguing is the fact that public information work that is not focused on a particular opinion class is likely to be ineffective or inefficient. Similarly, the target audience can vary according to the issues concerned.

The Expert Committee that had reviewed public information policy and practice in 1958 found that the DPI (or OPI as it was then called) could not answer the basic question of to whom UN public information programs should be directed. It suggested that the audience be made up of four categories:

(a) Those governmental agencies and public institutions that are concerned with influencing public opinion, for example, Ministries of Information and Institutions for political, social and economic research.

(b) Those persons and organizations concerned with the media of mass communication and professionally engaged in providing information, instruction and entertainment to the peoples of the world – editors, journalists, writers in the press and other publications, as well as those responsible for the planning of radio, television, graphics and cinema production.

(c) Those persons and organizations that show real interest in the aims and activities of the United Nations and are ready to commit themselves in service to it – including international and national United Nations associations and other non-governmental organizations with general and special interests in political, social, economic and educational questions.

(d) Persons and institutions concerned with education. This would include Ministries and Departments of Education, schools, colleges and universities, teachers, professors and other eminent educationalists.[45]

According to the committee: "The existing pattern of information activity [was] too diversified to be effective".[46] The reorientation it recommended would entail "a shift of emphasis in the method of dissemination of information from 'mass approach through media of mass communication' to the selective approach of public relations, and working through existing organizations, governmental and non-governmental, and through individuals who are disseminators of information and exercise influence, or, occupy positions involving exercise of influence in the formation of public opinion".[47] In effect the recommendation was that the DPI should adopt a "two-step" model of communication for the diffusion of its ideas. The model (then popular with American communication consultants) suggests that the appropriate means of fostering social change is to first reach opinion elites, who will then provide direction for the rest of society below[48] (see Chapter 5).

Although the DPI used the famous means of social communication that had been subject to much scholarly investigation over the years, in the following years there would not be any serious study of the UN's target audiences or the impact of its messages for fear of the UN actually becoming too powerful a player in international politics. The idea that the DPI existed to communicate indirectly with the public provided a buffer against criticism that the UN might be trying to undermine the power of governments, an issue raised in 1972 in a study by the United Nations Institute for Training and Research (UNITAR). The study originated from doubts over international public awareness of the UN expressed by Secretary-General U Thant at the Twenty-First Session of the UN General Assembly. It was concerned with "the role of the news media in spreading information on the world organization, and with the coverage of United Nations policies and activities by the world press, radio, and television", and it was intended to provide "some bases for practical thinking about possibilities of widening and improving public information on the United Nations, of making the world organization better known and better understood".[49] The UNITAR investigation questioned why the Basic Principles of UN public information policy were not being revamped to keep in step with the times. For example, the 1946 principles stated that the UN "cannot achieve the purposes for which it has been created unless the peoples of the world are fully informed of its aims and activities". But the UNITAR report pointed out that it was not possible for the world to be ever *fully* informed; *adequately* informed might be more reasonable, but then this still begs the question of *how much* and *what kind* of information is adequate. Also, *all* people of the world do not have to be informed of all aspects of the UN's activities. In particular cases, only *some* constituencies (e.g. governments and special interest groups) need to be informed of specific UN initiatives. Another example is that the existing principles suggested the DPI should "primarily" assist and rely upon the co-operation of established governmental and non-governmental information agencies, and "supplement" the work of these organizations. However, the UNITAR study saw the UN as not having the means to directly reach the world's publics because: (a) governments deliberately did not want it to do so and did not want to lose control over their domestic information environments; and (b) the DPI did not have the resources. The report added that:

> As a matter of fact, the amount spent yearly by the United Nations on *all* information activities would not suffice to cover even 15% of the budget of one of the major international news agencies. The total yearly

operating costs of the "big five" (AP, UPI, Reuters, Agence France Press [sic], TASS) probably amount to more than the whole regular budget of the United Nations.[50]

Fourteen years later a CPC investigation concluded that within the DPI there were no common understandings of what "impact" meant, or even who the "target audiences", "end-users" or "redisseminators" were. The reviewers blamed this lack of agreement on two factors:

First, individual divisions have traditionally interpreted these terms in the light of their own role and responsibilities regarding, for example, press, films or radio audiences, and this tradition persists...Secondly, many of the outputs are designed to reach very specific audiences, which tends to discourage the use of common definitions.[51]

There was also the additional problem that the DPI did not even do routine evaluations, and this seemed to be a deliberate policy. The CPC reviewers offered three explanations for this:

First, it has been pointed out that there is no consensus among Member States on how the opinions or attitudes of target audiences should be changed. For example, certain issues that are regarded as politically sensitive, such as human rights and disarmament questions, are frequently cited by the Department as a reason for not measuring impact. The second factor that impedes the conduct of impact studies is that target audiences are often not usually clearly defined, therefore making the change of awareness or perception even more difficult to measure. The third factor is that while staff members within the Department generally review qualitative feedback on end-user reaction, it is rarely systematically analysed.[52]

The international role of UN public information

If there is reluctance to clearly define a target audience then it is obvious that there must also be ambiguity about what is the exact role of UN public information policy in international relations. Indeed, the reluctance to have a clearly defined target audience is due to the UN's shyness from making the DPI a stronger player in world politics.

In 1946 the role of the DPI was made very clear by historical circumstances. The UN had taken the place of the failed League of Nations, and needed to get its message out and win over public opinion. In addition, racist war propaganda had played a key role in the war just ended, and the international system needed a communication actor that would counter tendencies to incite war via mass media in the future. However, 20 years later the international system had grown much more complex. The basic problem was now whether the DPI should be a passive provider of information or actually try to move international opinion and action. Related to this basic problem was the issue of how the UN could determine that the public information program was in fact meeting its objectives.

At the beginning of the 1970s, Secretary-General U Thant described the DPI as an "international information service"[53] and the Secretariat was claiming that the UN could not afford to be antagonistic through its public information activities since its primary goal was to resolve conflict:

> In terms of policy, these limitations derive from the fact that, essentially, the United Nations is a political organization, charged with the task of containing and comprehending – in the hope and with the object of harmonizing – conflicting interests, in the common cause of promoting peace, fundamental human rights and respect for international law, so as to attain social progress and better standards of life in larger freedom. These ends are pursued by the Organization through its various principal organs and through the functional institutions and bodies established by it – whether in the political field or in those of economic and social development. Given this central political reality, it would seem to follow that any and all information activity conducted on behalf of and under the collective authority of the total United Nations membership could not deviate from the basic political postulates of "objectivity" and "universality". It must necessarily confine itself, particularly when dealing with matters of controversy, to its mandate merely to "make available" to "all the peoples of the world through any appropriate media", information which is strictly "objective and factual". <u>Thus, United Nations information programmes, no matter to what field they relate or how actively or purposely they are conducted, must continue to be fashioned and articulated essentially as programmes aimed at explanation and clarification and not exhortation.</u>[54] [Underlining in original document]

The same 1971 document suggested that the DPI's job must be "to tell the peoples of the world, not <u>what</u> to think, but what to think <u>about</u>". However, the next paragraph contradicted this in its explanation of cases where there should be exceptions to this rule.

> At the same time, in certain fields, where the Organization itself has, as a whole, taken a definitive and action-oriented stand – as, for example, economic and social development, promotion of human rights, decolonization, elimination of racial discrimination and, more recently, protection of the human environment – the United Nations Office of Public Information cannot any longer restrict itself to merely neutral stances or statements. It must go beyond this and actively identify itself with these

universally approved causes and movements. Not to do so would not only be falling short of historic responsibility and potential but neglecting binding directives from legislative organs.

...However, in pursuing this more active role in support of United Nations goals – be they economic and social or political – OPI must continue to draw a clear distinction between "active" and "activist". Thus, while it must expand its activities in such required fields as economic and social development, decolonization, the elimination of <u>apartheid</u> and racial discrimination, the expansion must be an activity which itself remains essentially objective and informational and does not cross...the "boundary" separating it from propaganda or promotion.[55]

Therefore the UN would only have an "active" public information program on topics defined as "universally approved causes and movements". Presumably these would be initiatives for which there was overwhelming support at the General Assembly. However, as will be revealed later in this book the numeric majority of African, Latin American and Asian states at the UN would mean that the passing of a number of General Assembly resolutions with very large majorities did not necessarily get the UN out of hot water. Famous cases of this include UN policies on Palestinian statehood and apartheid in South Africa, developed by popular support in the General Assembly but often contrary to the foreign policies of the small minority of states that were the UN's most powerful members by virtue of their economic and military power, particularly the US and the UK (see Chapter 4).

In the 1970s the Secretariat continued to describe public information work in a two-dimensional way. It was informational, and "active" only on select "safe" issues, i.e. those for which the UN had solid backing. These were called "universally approved causes and movements" in 1971, and "future of the world" issues in 1977 – "disarmament, food, health, environment, industrialization, trade, racial discrimination and meeting the basic needs of the poorest groups in developing countries within the framework of a new international economic order".[56] The UN's work on these issues had produced more world conferences and placed a greater strain on the organization's public information resources. In addition the public information services had to make changes and adjustments in response to an increased number of mandates from the legislative organs of the UN. More and more of these issues related to economic development, as a 1977 report explained:

As the need to restructure the world economy has emerged as a major preoccupation of the international community and consequently the United Nations system, a growing proportion of the efforts of the information services of the system have had to be directed towards general economic and social problems. Since these general problems are of concern to the international community as a whole as well as to international organizations individually, the latter have been seeking a common understanding of, and a common approach towards, the information aspects of these problems. Developmental issues, by the very fact that they have had to be dealt with in a co-ordinated way, have thus played the role of a catalyst.[57]

The 1970s was in fact a period in which broad transformations in the UN's work and image became very clear. The DPI's administrative response to the need to become involved in more global campaigns was to establish a number of "thematic task forces" to cover such topics as disarmament, decolonization, outer space, apartheid and human rights.[58] But as the UN became more involved in the problems of the developing world, its image in the richer countries waned. Reporting on the DPI's radio news, a 1977 Secretariat document said "there had been a decline of interest in developed countries, balanced by a growing receptivity in developing countries".[59] It reported a decline "in the acceptance by United States commercial stations" of UN documentary films.[60] "Political decisions of the United Nations receive by far the greatest attention from news media in Africa, especially those related to African problems," claimed the review's Annex.[61]

The UN was becoming aware of such changes in the receptivity to its messages because at the same time it was grappling with the problem of how to properly gauge the *impact* of its public information campaign. This is a particularly tricky problem for an organization that eschews propaganda and avoids offending member states while at the same time claiming to promote international causes. Assessing impact does mean research into whether or how attitudes, actions or policies have changed as a direct result of public information practice, and the UN walked this tightrope by interpreting "impact" as data on audiences and the extent to which DPI output was used. "Determining the impact of a subprogramme intended to create deep understanding and awareness of the United Nations is obviously an even more difficult undertaking than making systematic and comprehensive surveys of the news media," the 1977 report noted.[62] However, in the UN's defense such research on cause and effect is scarce even in other social areas, for example the relationship between advertising and consumer behavior or the relationship between the presence of floodlighting and the incidence of burglaries. In 1982 the UN did propose a system for monitoring and evaluating the effectiveness of the DPI, and as part of that effort it was suggested that communication scholars be asked to carry out an evaluation of DPI publicity for a "time-limited major United Nations event", such as an international year, and that this would "assess the impact of the Year on the various sectors of world public opinion".[63] But, an in-depth evaluation of the DPI published in 1983 still continued the trend of suggesting the "impact" of the DPI could be gauged by collecting data on its production and the demand for its output, not in looking at exactly how the DPI was a player in changing the course of international politics.[64]

It was not until the administration of Kofi Annan – the most media-savvy of all UN Secretaries-General – that a systematic attempt to define more clearly the DPI's role both within the UN and in international politics emerged. This might have been due in large part to historical circumstances. In 1997, when Annan assumed office, who could deny the tremendous impact of the media in international politics? The term "CNN factor" had joined the lingo of international relations to describe the capacity of international electronic media networks to be more efficient collectors and disseminators of information than government diplomatic channels (see Chapter 6). Hate radio and television were critical dimensions of genocide in places as different as Rwanda and Bosnia.

Shortly afterwards, in March 1997, Annan announced that the public information strategy of the United Nations needed to have a "reorientation" in three main ways: to better serve re-disseminators of information, utilizing the latest information technology; to have the "information capacity" of the Secretariat better serve the "substantive departments"; and to decentralize and refocus resources to make greater use of local resources.[65] A month later Annan appointed a nine-member Task Force[66] on the Reorientation of United Nations Public Information Activities. The body submitted its 34-page report, *Global Vision, Local Voice: A Strategic Communications Programme for the United Nations*, in August 1997. The investigation summed up the main weaknesses of the DPI as

> the inexplicable absence of an organizational communications strategy; the dispersion of responsibilities for communications across the four units without overall direction or coordination of activities; the commitment of the bulk of the communications' budget to disseminating institutional information – which in essence describes the work and priorities of the Organization – without adequately catering to strategic communication, which is designed to enhance the Organization's substantive capacities through strengthening its global leadership position and through building support among its crucial constituencies.[67]

The Task Force clearly felt that the DPI's problems went deeper than the Secretary-General had suggested in his charge. Changes in the administrative structure of the DPI were not enough on their own; there needed to be a change in the fundamental principles that guided UN public information work. The DPI had to cease being passive – disseminating institutional information – and become a real player in changing the character of international relations, producing what the Task Force called "strategic communication".

To implement such revolutionary change, the Task Force recommended a new set of principles for the UN's public information program. It suggested that public information be elevated to "the heart of the strategic management" of the UN, and that a "culture of communications" should exist in the whole organization. Public information campaigns should place less emphasis on abstract principles and focus more on the actual work of the agencies of the UN system. The image constructed should be that of the UN as a unique forum for creation of consensus about world problems and the channeling of that consensus into action. The Task Force also recommended that the principles behind the organization of the UN's public information program be changed. The Secretariat should be given more autonomy from the General Assembly and the Information Committee to determine public information practice. UN public information programs should focus more on the local relevance of the organization's work, and be flexible enough to adjust to changing priorities.

The Task Force explained the difference between the past "institutional" communication of the UN and the "strategic" communication it needed to produce:

> The key difference between strategic and institutional communications is that the former proceeds from a fully developed sense of the direction in which the organization wants to move opinion. Various communications techniques are then enlisted to that end. Strategic communications involves a process that begins with identifying the *what* (what is the vision of the United Nations' role and objectives that is to be promoted), the *how* (which vehicles such as press relations, public information and constituency-building are to be used in promoting this vision?), and the *who* (to whom are communications to be targeted; which NGOs, interest groups, parliamentarians, press organs, members of the policy community, elements of the general public?) of a concerted communications strategy. The guiding strategy is aimed at making the United Nations a more powerful and effective advocate for the programs, policies, and values its members seek to advance. Without such a strategy, institutional communications are likely to be fragmented, reactive, and to have little cumulative impact on public opinion. Strategic communications aim not just to affect but also to mobilize public and specialist opinion on behalf of the United Nations.[68]

On more than one occasion in the report the Task Force described the necessary strategic communication as "public diplomacy". In the study of international relations, and its sub-field of international communication, public or cultural diplomacy is one of the tools states use to conduct their external relations (see Chapter 1). Public diplomacy is never the only strategy used to extract results. Instead it is defined as the use of culture to directly support conventional diplomacy, or even to reach beyond governments and communicate with foreign publics where conventional diplomacy does not exist or has broken down.[69] Although public diplomacy is most often associated with US foreign policy practice, by the end of the twentieth century states as varied as communist China, Serbia and Syria were using what was called "public diplomacy" as part of their foreign relations.[70]

Methods of public diplomacy include international broadcasting, control of news flows, war propaganda, educational exchanges and even maintaining "information" centers to provide a ready supply of data to promote the sponsoring state's prestige and policies. It can be said that there is little difference between public information work and public diplomacy. However, there are major differences between the prospects of a state as opposed to the United Nations in conducting public diplomacy. Governments are more unitary entities that can more coherently determine their interests, devise policy and directly implement public diplomacy programs. In contrast, the policy-making process of the UN is much more complicated, and the will of the majority in the General Assembly will not necessarily be translated into UN policy because of the powers of the Security Council and the veto powers of its permanent members. Also, it has been the policy of the UN to avoid such strategic communication on most controversial international issues for fear that it might either anger some member states or violate its own principle against promoting propaganda. Some issues – such as the South African apartheid and human rights – have been considered so safe that the UN has had no qualms about devising and implementing very successful strategic communication programs related to them, but on a whole range of other international topics the UN has been gun-shy. This all begs the question of whether it is realistic to expect an international organization like the UN – with its power differentials and bulky organizational structure – to be able to implement a meaningful public diplomacy program. Public diplomacy assumes a unity and decisiveness that is often beyond the UN.

Although the UN's "Medium-Term Plan for the Period 2002–2005" was produced three years after the Task Force's report, there was little evidence that it was invigorated with the spirit of strategic communication advocated by the Task Force. The plan proposed that the UN's public information program aimed simply "to increase awareness and understanding of the work and purposes of the United Nations among peoples of the world".[71] The use of the term "culture of communication" was one indication of the influence of the Task Force, but the plan was in no way a strategy for launching the UN into public diplomacy or an international communication strategy that would mobilize instead of just inform. According to the plan, the public information strategy would be "based on the premise that public information and communications should be placed at the heart of the strategic management of the United Nations and that a culture of communications should permeate all levels of the Organization as a means of fully informing the peoples of the world of the aims and activities of the United Nations".[72]

The target audiences would be various components of "civil society" (such as the media, business and professional organizations, and educational institutions), and although it was projected that the DPI would devise "campaigns" and "mobilize support" for these, the language used to describe the indicators of objectives having been met was very timid, with nothing to suggest that the DPI wanted to rise to the challenge posed by the Task Force: there would be success if there was "an increase in the coverage of United Nations activities by newspapers, radio, television and relevant Internet sites worldwide and in the level of interest shown by the target audience; an increase in the number of requests for and enquiries about the promotional products and services; an increase in the number of visitors to the United Nations web site; and an increase in the number of visitors to United Nations premises under the guided tour programme".[73] Ironically, the list of tasks the General Assembly wanted the DPI to carry out was continuing to grow despite this obvious problem in evaluating its work. The 2002–2005 Medium-Term Plan listed 46 General Assembly resolutions as the basis for the DPI's legislative mandate, 36 of which were from the fifty-fourth session of the General Assembly alone! Also, following the Task Force's report there was renewed emphasis on a communication development role for the DPI. According to the plan:

> In order to contribute to bridging the gap between developing and developed countries in the field of public information and communications, particular attention will be given to areas of special interest to developing countries, and, where appropriate, to countries with economies in transition. In particular, attention will be given to the special needs of African countries and the least developed countries, keeping in mind that most developing countries are not fully benefiting from the information revolution and the information technology gap is widening.[74]

The Task Force on the DPI was a good example of what was taking place within the UN at the end of the century. There was no disagreement on whether there should be reform – the only questions were regarding how that reform would occur. This explains why Kofi Annan had declared that there would be reform at the DPI before he announced the Task Force, and not the other way around. Annan viewed the Millennium Summit of 2000 as a way to show the world a new United Nations. The JUNIC report for 2000 explained the link between this summit and the renovation of the UN's public information program:

> ... the main objective of the Millennium Summit [was] the repositioning of the United Nations at the beginning of the new century. Accordingly, the corresponding communications strategy needed to show the United Nations as a renewed and changing organization, relevant to the broad range of aspirations and concerns of the peoples of the planet and essential in the search for global solutions to global problems.[75]

In later years reviews and reports of the public information work of the UN would reveal that the organization continued to grapple with the past and what Annan and the Task Force felt should be its future. In 2000, members of the JUNIC "raised the issue of the distinction between public information and advocacy, and agreed on the need to discuss that matter in more depth".[76] More revealing still was the Secretary-General's "Millennium Report" issued in March 2000 in advance of the Millennium Assembly of the world's political leaders that took place at UN headquarters in New York later that year. The report made no explicit reference to the public information role of the UN in the three strategic priority areas identified, and this omission is striking because of the great attention the document paid to the role of public opinion and the communication revolution within global society. Secretary-General Annan noted that the communications revolution had three main impacts: (a) higher expectations of humanitarian intervention in places where there was human desperation; (b) a revolution in the nature of commerce; and (c) heightened global self-awareness.[77] He made reference to the largest ever survey of public opinion, which was conducted in late 1999 on a sample of 57 000 adults in 60 countries over six continents. Although the UN scored higher ratings than did governments, less than half of the respondents rated the UN as satisfactory.[78] Another indication that the DPI had its work cut out for it came elsewhere in the document, in Annan's comment that the UN was not fully exploiting the potential of information technology in "providing the world's people with information and data of concern to them".[79]

Having said all of the above, it could be argued that those who expect and advocate a rational, co-ordinated UN public information strategy are expecting the impossible in light of the nature of UN politics. Leon Gordenker's study of UN public information during the Korean War found that from as early as this period there was "no articulated program for the use of mass communications channels".[80] Gordenker also identified (several years before the UN's internal studies of the 1970s) the problem of trying to measure the effectiveness of the DPI in terms of "people reached" instead of "influence".[81] It is very doubtful that the DPI's contradictory mandate could produce order from what often resembled chaos. As far back as 1960 Gordenker concluded that:

> Contradictory instructions provide no rational basis for judging the work of the office. No one could estimate with any accuracy how closely the peoples of the world would approach full information on the United Nations, how much supplementary effort would be needed, what was propaganda and where or in what situations more rather than less effort might be needed – and above all how much money should be devoted to such efforts. The OPI nevertheless had to prepare a program and a budget. The General Assembly had to examine it. Without a clear standard, the examination inevitably fell into confusion.[82]

The hot seat

The story painted above indicates that the post of head of the DPI should be one of the least attractive positions in the UN Secretariat, and one of the most difficult to fill. It is.

During the first half-century of the UN, the job came with unwritten expectations that seemed almost impossible to fill. To competently run the UN's publicity requires a comprehensive knowledge of its vast bureaucracy or the sense to hire key staff with that knowledge. The head should also be not so engaged with UN culture that he or she is out of touch with world public opinion, and because of the communications revolution it is imperative that the DPI head be knowledgeable about the latest mass-media technologies in order to ensure the UN is using the best means possible to efficiently disseminate its message. Needless to say, the lucky candidate must also possess that rare skill of running a department deemed by the most powerful members of the General Assembly as a waste of money, and to which the General Assembly as a whole allocates more chores without committing the required resources.

As if the realities of the job are not enough, the DPI and its head had to deal with the occasional semantic downgrading of the place of public information within UN bureaucracy. From 1958 to 1978, as mentioned earlier the name was changed from *Department* of Public Information to *Office* of Public Information, a significant demotion within the UN hierarchy. Similarly, the person heading the department has not always held the title of Under Secretary-General (USG), but the lower ranking of Assistant Secretary-General (ASG). Ironically, although the tenure of Kofi Annan brought the "culture of communications" to the UN, his initial plans were to replace the DPI with "an Office for Communications and Media Services".[83]

The head of the DPI who lasted longest in the post was actually the first – Benjamin Cohen of Chile (see Table 2.1) – who was in office for eight years. When Cohen was appointed in 1946 he was paid the princely tax-free annual salary of $13 000 and up to $7000 in allowances.[84] Forty-one years later, the first and only woman to head the DPI – Thérèse Paquet Sévigny of Canada – assumed a job that paid well over $100 000, with allowances to match.[85]

The decision of who gets the job of Under Secretary-General in charge of public information is subject to the same political balancing act as all top-level UN posts, however the first 50 years show that it certainly helped to be Asian and Japanese if one aspired to the position. In the 54 years from 1946 to 2000, five of the heads of the DPI came from Asia and together ran the department for a total of 21 years. The only region that came close to this was South America, with three officials and a total of 14 years in the office, though Cohen accounted for eight of these years. Significantly, very rarely were North Americans or Europeans in the post, and when they were this was never for long. Thérèse Paquet Sévigny (1987–91) was the only North American to run the DPI in the twentieth century, and the only

Table 2.1   Assistant or Under-Secretaries-General for communications and public information, 1946–2000

1946–54	Benjamin A. Cohen (Chile)
1955–58	Ahmed S. Bokhari (Pakistan)
1959	Alfred Katzin (Acting Under-Secretary General) (Union of South Africa)
1960–65	Hernane Tavares de Sá (Brazil)
1966–67	José Rolz-Bennett (Guatemala)
1968–71	Agha Abdul Hamid (Pakistan)
1972–78	Genichi Akatani (Japan)
1979–86	Yasushi Akashi (Japan)
1987–91	Thérèse Paquet Sévigny (Canada)
1992	Eugeniusz Wyzner (Poland)
1993	Marco Vianello-Chiodo (Italy)
1994–97	Samir Sanbar (Lebanon)
1998–2000	Kensaku Hogen (Japan)

Europeans – Eugeniusz Wyzner of Poland and Marco Vianello-Chiodo of Italy – were in charge for only a matter of months.

This paucity of DPI heads from powerful, large countries that might have many enemies was due to the same reason why UN Secretaries-General did not come from such states. Their control of such high-profile jobs would only add to the power differential they already enjoyed in the Security Council and the existing perception that the UN is a tool of the powerful in the international system. Another significant factor was explained by UN scholar Leon Gordenker as far back as 1960, when he noted that over a period of a number of years the DPI's budgets and expansion were supported by a bloc that included the Latin American states and some mainly poor countries that supported the Latin Americans. Gordenker attributed this early backing to "the personality and popularity" of the fellow Latin American, Cohen.[86]

In contrast, Japan has been a state in search of power at the UN, and the position in charge of the DPI has provided a means to achieving that end. The lack of Japanese in UN service to match Japanese financial support of the organization was one of the best-known stories of the UN's first 50 years. The career diplomats Genichi Akatani, Yasushi Akashi and Kensaku Hogen were the only Japanese to be so highly ranked at the UN Secretariat. When Hogen was appointed, *The Nikkei Weekly* used the opportunity to report on why so relatively few Japanese were in international diplomatic service with international organizations. The periodical noted that despite Japan's contribution of "15.65%, or about 166.7 million dollars, of the U.N.'s 1997 budget, Japanese accounted for only 104, or 4.2%, of the U.N. Secretariat's 2,461 managers, technical experts and other ranking staff".[87] Reasons given to explain why there were so little Japanese in the field included: the difficulty of Japanese in learning foreign languages; the unattractiveness of UN salaries to Japanese; Japan's lifetime employment system that worked against labor mobility; and the fact that there were fewer people in Japan with Master's and doctoral degrees compared to in other industrialized countries.[88] However, by the end of the 1990s the situation did seem to be improving. Japanese won posts as heads of the WHO and UNESCO, and as UN High Commissioner for Refugees, though not without problems. For example, Hiroshi Nakajima left the WHO under a cloud of "accusations of highhandedness and incompetence",[89] Akashi's last years with the UN included a stint as Special Envoy to the former Yugoslavia, a failure, and Hogen's stay at the DPI was brief, unspectacular and marked by staff dissatisfaction. Hogen's next stop was not a position within the UN, but as Japan's Ambassador to Canada and to the International Civil Aviation Organization in Quebec.[90]

One benefit of having Japanese officials in the top seat at the DPI was that it provided an incentive for Japanese foundations to financially support some very significant public information projects. Akatani secured Japanese foundation money to underwrite a series of articles on world development that were published in influential publications, a project that would later prove to be controversial during his successor's term[91] (see Chapter 3). During Akashi's time in office the Soka Gakkai foundation gave $160 000 to the DPI to launch the UN's Oral History project, a series of interviews with prominent retired UN officials that was eventually conducted in collaboration with Yale University and lasted well into the 1990s.[92]

Figure 2.2 Yasushi Akashi of Japan ran the DPI for seven years (1979–86) before becoming famous in several more high-profile posts, such as UN Representative in Cambodia (1992), Special Envoy to the former Yugoslavia (1994–95) and UN Emergency Relief Coordinator (1997–98).

Unlike some other responsibilities at the Secretariat (such as peacekeeping), the position at the top of the DPI during the UN's first half-century did not often attract much controversy outside of the usual annual struggles over the department's budget. However, Hernane Tavares de Sá of Brazil, who ran the DPI from 1960 to 1965, published a book a year after leaving office in which he made it clear that he did not like much about the UN nor the people running it. He came out in support of the US government's vetting of American UN employees, which was permitted by the Secretaries-General of the time.[93] Tavares de Sá's racist rantings in the book against black people were ironic not only because for five years he was responsible for projecting the UN's message of world peace and harmony but also because he came from a country where the majority of the population has some kind of African ancestry. His discussion of Africans in *The Play Within the Play: The Inside Story of the UN* displayed a pathological hatred. He spoke of "underdeveloped Afro-Asians" and "sophisticated Europeans",[94] and said African delegations hosted the most expensive parties because they felt "inferior about their color".[95] According to the Brazilian, the wives of African delegates spoke "no civilized language" and knew "only an obscure African dialect".[96] However, he did identify one type of African that he did like, and that was the "tame African". "They have an indefinable family air about them," he said in explaining this African. "Well-dressed, urbane, articulate, and lazy, having a family connection with the prime minister or the president of their country, they are usually the African version of a Western playboy".[97]

For Tavares de Sá the large numbers of African states that got representation in the General Assembly in the wake of decolonization was clearly a negative occurrence. He described a General Assembly debate in which Africans were especially vocal as "dominated by countries without political maturity, economic significance, or civilized background", and questioned the value of having a "world forum dominated by scores of unimportant and irresponsible countries".[98] He summed up his opinion on how Africans were treated at the UN by declaring that no one "dares say anything resembling the truth about the black continent".[99] So presumably he was daring to do what lesser mortals could not.

Also surprising here in the case of Hernane Tavares de Sá and the power structure of his time is that before he was appointed by Dag Hammarskjöld, as Under-Secretary for Public Information, he was awarded (in 1959) Columbia University's distinguished Maria Moors Cabot Award for promoting friendship and understanding in the Western hemisphere in the field of journalism!

Ironically, however, it was not during the tenure of a Japanese that the DPI got negative press about the home government affiliation of its head. Soon after taking office, Thérèse Paquet Sévigny had to admit that she had erred in deciding to award $200 000 in short-term DPI contracts – over half of the total – to Canadians.[100] The error, in not being sensitive enough to the politics of the UN, was made by a communications executive who came to the DPI in 1987 with no background in diplomacy. All heads of the DPI before and after her, up to 2001, were career diplomats. Thérèse Paquet Sévigny came to the DPI from the post of Vice-President for Communications with CBC/Radio Canada, and before that she had been a journalist and advertising executive.[101] Secretary-General Javier Perez de Cuellar had broken with tradition and appointed a media professional because this was another one of the several occasions in the history of the DPI when it was felt the department needed an overhaul. A year into the job Paquet Sévigny said the plan was for her to "design a new structure for the organization's information and archive activities, as part of an overall reform of UN structures, staffing, and procedures".[102]

In the case of Paquet Sévigny there was clearly a vision of what someone with her background could achieve in the post. However, there were also cases where actual professional competence in the field of communications obviously took a back seat to the other criteria Secretaries-General used to fill top jobs, especially the factors of nationality and the intensity of lobbying by particular national or regional interests to get the position. Certainly

Figure 2.3 By the turn of the century, still only one woman had the distinction of running the DPI. Thérèse Paquet Sévigny of Canada is shown here, in a 1987 photo at the start of her four years in office, sharing a light moment with staff as she presents a plan to restructure the DPI.

sophistication, cosmopolitanism and a genuine commitment to the high ideals of the UN were not taken seriously when Brazil's Hernane Tavares de Sá was selected!

Instead of a renaissance following the tenure of the first woman and non-diplomat, there followed a decade of much instability at the helm of the DPI, a reflection of the doldrums within which the UN Secretariat as a whole found itself. The relatively successful two terms of Javier Perez de Cuellar as UN Secretary-General were followed by the one disappointing term of Boutros Boutros-Ghali, continued failure of the US and other states to pay dues, and the most famous UN peacekeeping debacles in Somalia, Bosnia and Rwanda. During the 1990s no one held the position of head of the DPI for more than three years.

Sadly for the department, critics of the UN continued to single out the DPI for criticism and associate its name with wasted resources. That was the case in the 1950s, and it was also that way in 2001. "The U.N. public information office is a swollen monstrosity and needs to be cut severely," the US Ambassador to the UN, Richard Holbrooke, said in a parting shot. "They are not up to date. The documentation services pile up documents nobody reads, in six official languages."[103] However, in the DPI's defense, taking cheap shots at the UN is much easier than fixing its problems. Also, it is highly unlikely that an organization designed to prevent another World War will escape criticism. The DPI's fortunes are intricately linked to those of the UN, and the UN's image before world public opinion is both a challenge for the DPI to manage as well as a problem that is bound to stigmatize the department as well. It is to this question of the DPI in relation to the overall image of the UN that this book will now turn.

3
Polishing the Tarnished Image

> Our world would be a better place if there was an unbiased organization that functioned as an arbiter of national interests, that acted according to principles rather than interests. In my younger days – an era that I realize ended when I first stepped foot in Bosnia – I had thought, like many others, that the United Nations might fulfill this role after the Cold War. We learned in Bosnia that the U.N. flag deserves no more trust than any of the national flags in front of its New York headquarters. Integrity is like virginity; you can't get it back once it is gone, and the U.N. lost it in Bosnia.[1]

Peter Maas, the author of the quote above, was actually wrong. The UN had lost its integrity, and its credibility, long before the debacle of peacekeeping in Bosnia. The honeymoon only lasted for about 20 years after the organization was established. By then, in the late 1960s, the core group of powers that created it was a tiny minority in an organization that they still controlled but whose rhetoric proclaimed that there was some semblance of equality among nations. In addition, the major event of international relations – the Cold War – served to show how circumscribed was the UN's power in relation to the states that ran it.

So these first 20 years saw the UN enjoying a relatively good reputation with the big powers. It was active in the resettlement of refugees displaced by the war, was seeking solutions in regional conflicts in places like the Middle East and Africa, and was a symbol of hope against the new threat of nuclear annihilation. However, by the end of the 1960s, entities that had been colonies when the UN was founded became states and were a majority of the members of the General Assembly. The UN devoted itself to social and economic development in many of these countries and its profile in those parts of the world rose while it declined in the wealthier countries. By the beginning of the 1980s, UN studies were already admitting that such a shift had occurred and were pondering how to resolve the problem. While it was good that it had public opinion on its side in the poorer countries, the UN needed to win over the publics of the richer states as well, as these countries were the other side of the equation for solving world inequality. Thus the evolution of the DPI and the UN's public information program is intimately connected to the ecology of the UN's role in international relations.

The task of defining the UN's reputation is, therefore, a complicated one. The UN does not mean the same thing to all publics; it has different levels of credibility and integrity across its panoply of issues. And its image can change drastically from one period to another. For most of the organization's first 50 years its collective leadership has never been satisfied with its image. A 1972 report even noted that there had been constant criticism of the state of the UN's public relations, coming from diplomats, statesmen, journalists, scholars and even the UN Secretary-General U Thant. In 1970 U Thant said that the UN was often criticized "for failing to make the organization – its achievements as well as its shortcomings – understood to the general public".[2] This provokes the question tackled in this chapter: Why does the public image of the UN remain distorted despite the fact that it has had an international public information program for all of its history – a program that often absorbs more than 5 per cent of its budget?

In this context the term "public image" refers to the kind of reputation the organization has. As has already been noted, this reputation varied among the different constituencies served by the UN. But it is often not difficult to find examples of how there is usually a great difference between perceptions of the UN and what the UN felt were the facts of what it actually did. One of the key objectives of the public information program was to achieve wide understanding of the UN and its work, so to the extent that such understanding was not achieved it could be said that there was a discrepancy between what the UN wished for and what was actually found in research on public opinion or media representation of the organization.

There are four dimensions of this chapter's response to this question. First is a chronological discussion of some of the most significant controversies involving the UN that have contributed to the image problem. Second is a case study of the UN's historical representation in Hollywood films – although by the end of the twentieth century India was the world's largest producer of feature films, the US was the largest exporter of such films and as such had greater access to world public opinion through one of the most popular forms of mass communication. Third is a critical analysis of the insight provided by the controversies and the case study into why the UN's reputation suffered. Fourth is a concluding discussion of how the image problems of the UN's first 50 years had an impact on the nature of the public information program at the end of the century.

Controversies

As the preceding section indicates, the UN's image problems could not be attributed to one or even a number of specific events. Rather there was gradual erosion caused by a confluence of factors related to the evolution of world politics. However, some specific controversies, and the UN's reaction to them, did provide further insight into its loss of standing and credibility. These controversies served to symbolize specific points of contention. In the case of the 1981 revelation that the UN Secretariat was paying newspapers to print articles on world development, the background issue at the time was the idea that the UN was hostile to liberal-democratic ideals. The 1986 revelation that fourth UN Secretary-General Kurt Waldheim was a Nazi fueled the fires of suspicion that the UN was never a fair dealer in international relations. And the failed peacekeeping spectacles of the 1990s collectively revealed suspicions that the UN was impotent in rising to the additional challenges it faced at the end of the Cold War. Each of these controversies will be examined in turn below.

The World Newspaper Supplement

When journalist Bernard Nossiter reported in *The New York Times* in late May 1981 that over the past two years the UN had been paying a number of publications around the world to publish a "World Newspaper Supplement" he sparked an international diplomatic controversy. At issue were a number of problems. Why did the UN have to pay for publicity that was (in effect) a form of propaganda? What did such a practice say about the UN's attitudes towards freedom of the press? Was not such expenditure a waste of scarce resources?

The World Newspaper Supplement had been appearing quarterly since 1979 in 16 newspapers, and the UN had been paying 15 of them for the favor, an expenditure that amounted to US$432 000 by 1981. The only participant to decline payment was *Jornal do Brasil* of Rio de Janeiro, but the list of periodicals that accepted included some of the world's most prestigious newspapers, such as *Asahi Shimbun* of Japan, *Le Monde* of France, and Spain's *El Pais*. The project was started with money from a Japanese businessman and once that initial funding was gone the DPI began to seek UN funding for the project to continue. The supplement consisted of a number of articles written by UN writers that promoted approaches to international development then popular within the UN, and was not always labeled as paid advertising. In addition, Nossiter's first report raised questions about the ideological angle of the articles:

> What the United Nations received for its money is unclear … In one issue, a long article by Bhaskar P. Menon of the United Nations' Division for Social and Economic Information, deplored the fact that the "new international economic order" had not been enacted. But Mr. Menon did not explain that this is the term used to refer to an enormous transfer of goods and services from rich to poor through the erection of commodity cartels, the printing of money by the International Monetary Fund, big increases in aid and similar devices. Mr. Menon simply described all this as the "decolonization of the world economy".[3]

When examined in the context of the ecology of world politics, it is not surprising that *The New York Times* reported on the World Newspaper Supplement in 1981 in the skeptical way that it did. This DPI project was at the intersection of two of the main controversies in which the UN was embroiled at the time: the proposed New World Information and Communication Order (NWICO) and the so-called "North-South Dialog", a later description of what started out as the proposal for a New International Economic Order (NIEO). The NWICO was actually an outgrowth of the NIEO. After the failure of the model of "dependent development" promoted by the UN in the 1960s, the Non-Aligned Movement (NAM) and the Group of 77 developing nation-states proposed the alternative of the NIEO. This was a plan to close the "development gap" between the rich countries of the North and the poor of the global South by returning the control over natural resources that had been taken away by colonialism, regulating transnational corporations and paying fairer commodity prices. One of the NIEO's 20 principles set out in a 1974 General Assembly resolution was: "The strengthening, through individual and collective actions, of mutual economic, trade, financial and technical co-operation among the developing countries, mainly on a preferential basis".[4]

The NAM and the Group of 77 proposed the NWICO as a logical necessity for achieving the NIEO because uneven information flows in areas such as transnational advertising, news and book publishing were seen as maintaining an ideological superstructure that justified international economic inequality. The NWICO was a proposal to reform the international system of communication (including the mail, telecommunication and intellectual property arrangements) in order to end inequality in the use of, and access to, communication technologies. UNESCO supported a number of initiatives in the name of the NWICO, such as a 1978 "Mass Media Declaration" and a 1980 report on the state of world communication that suggested governments should play a greater role in the media sector. The governments of the US and UK in particular criticized UNESCO for being hostile to a free press, and the organization's communication program received more coverage by the North American and European transnational media. In addition, press groups were formed in North America and Europe to defend the world from the perceived threat posed by UNESCO. UN General Assembly resolutions continued to voice support for the NWICO despite this kind of pressure, and although the NIEO had already died by the time the World Newspaper Supplement controversy occurred, it was still very much a live issue. Indeed, the US, UK and Singapore would use the NWICO as part of their pretext for leaving UNESCO a few years later.

So the revelation that the UN was paying for publicity in media around the world was, then, seen as yet further evidence that the organization was not committed to the principles of liberal democracy. "Why, in promoting its point of view, is the United Nations not content to print and distribute its own pamphlets?" *The New York Times* asked rhetorically. "Because it wants readers to believe they are getting not propaganda or the special pleading of advertising but a 'journalistic' product enhanced by the credibility and prestige of independent journals".[5]

By the summer of 1981 the controversy had blown over. The US abandoned its diplomatic posturing against the World Newspaper Supplement and in subsequent years the UN Information Committee openly admitted that the project was worthwhile and deserved support. The UN felt projects such as this were needed to guarantee "the best coverage of the realities of the third world in the media of the developed countries and in order to avoid risks of trivialization, sensationalism or insufficient journalistic coverage".[6]

The UN, like all other international actors who enter the propaganda game, does so from the belief that if it does not manage its image it can be hurt by misunderstandings of its policies and activities – or by others discovering the painful truth. For example, the UN General Assembly Information Committee's Chairman, Miguel Albornoz of Ecuador, in an address to the Committee in 1982, said that 80 per cent of UN activities were in the economic and social field, and that the other 20 per cent were political; however, most information about the UN carried in the news media ignored its achievements in the field of development, an unfair way of portraying its activities. Albornoz claimed he was not advocating propaganda, but a NWICO consistent with the mandate of the General Assembly.[7] At the time, the UN was considering investing in means of international communication of its own. The committee considered a report that put the cost of the UN having its own satellite system at $175 million, and another report examined the possibility of the UN having its own shortwave broadcasting system. It was estimated that it would cost about $28 million to build four regional production and transmission centers, and about $12.5 million annually to operate the system. UN satellites and enhanced broadcasting capabilities would have been an unacceptable strain on the UN's budget, therefore, as an alternative the committee recommended that the UN continue renting transmitters but that there should be daily broadcasts.[8] By the end of the century the pace of technological development had overtaken much of this planning. The UN was broadcasting to millions daily via the World Wide Web at a fraction of the cost of that required for the earlier plans for shortwave broadcasting.

Eventually, fears that the UN's proposed NWICO would poison the spread of liberal-democracy worldwide were put to rest by the policy change that the withdrawals of the US, UK and Singapore encouraged at UNESCO. The UN Information Committee continued to stress the necessity for a NWICO, but the actual policies of UNESCO and the UN shifted to giving more recognition to the importance of non-government-controlled media. Indeed, in Kofi Annan the UN would get a Secretary-General who openly courted transnational media moguls and succeeded in getting them to financially support UN social projects. Nevertheless, the very fact that there even had to be a World Newspaper Supplement to promote UN perspectives in the richer countries was testimony enough to the decline in support for the organization from the centers of world power, and the UN continued to look for ways to win public opinion in these areas.

Waldheim's Nazi past

When the story broke in 1986 that Kurt Waldheim had indeed been a Nazi (despite his denying such for several years), this was not in fact a direct public relations disaster for the UN because Waldheim had left the helm of the UN Secretariat in 1981. However, that a man with such a past had been able to achieve high office at the UN, and remain there for two terms, said much about how the UN conducted its business, how the world powers regarded the UN, and how the ability of the UN to be a more meaningful world actor might have been circumscribed during the Waldheim years (1972–81).

Waldheim had claimed that he had spent most of the Second World War studying law in Vienna, but investigations by the World Jewish Congress and the Austrian magazine *Profil* revealed that he had in fact been a German Army staff officer in the Balkans from 1942 to 1945. The news came to light whilst Waldheim was running for the post of President of Austria, a race that he won in June 1986. But the saga of revelation and controversy would last his entire term in office until he announced in 1991 that he would not seek re-election. The first stories about Waldheim's Nazi past reported that he was responsible for prison interrogations and "special assignments" – a euphemism often used by the Nazi's for murder, kidnapping or the taking of hostages.[9] Later it was reported that even before Waldheim was elected UN Secretary-General, the UN knew of his Nazi past because the UN War Crimes Commission had determined that there was sufficient evidence to prosecute him for murder, and that Yugoslavia had sent the UN additional evidence of his involvement in 1967.[10]

The governments of the United States, Israel and Austria all launched inquiries, though press reports stated that the French and Soviet governments had already known about Waldheim's war record for several years.[11] In 1987, after the US Justice Department found that Waldheim had participated in transferring civilians to slave labor, deportations to death camps, reprisal executions and anti-Semitic propaganda, he was barred from ever visiting the US again.[12] Contrary to this, a panel of military historians convened by the Austrian government reported in 1988 that Waldheim had known of war crimes being committed but that he had not actually committed any himself.[13] The Waldheim case even became an international television event when a mock trial was aired in the summer of 1988 on the Home Box Office (HBO) channel in the US and the UK's Channel 4.[14] Waldheim eventually apologized to the Israeli people for attempting

Figure 3.1 Kurt Waldheim, his wife Elisabeth and son Gerhard in a photo released by the UN in December 1971 at the time of Waldheim's election to UN Secretary-General. It was only after his term in office (1972–81) that the details of his Nazi military service were revealed, raising questions about his malleability by the powers that should have known the truth at the time he was elected to the post.

to conceal his role in the Nazi army but maintained that he had not mistreated Jews.[15]

There was speculation and outright assertion that the intelligence services of the major powers used Waldheim's Nazi past as a means to control him while he ran the UN. If Waldheim knew that he could be exposed at any time he would be as inoffensive a Secretary-General as possible, and according to American novelist Shirley Hazzard[16] that was indeed the case. Hazzard claimed this was the reason Waldheim had been selected as Secretary-General ahead of "several more substantial candidates".[17] After he was in office "honesty was at no time conspicuous in Waldheim, and his relations with the world's powers were never those of a disinterested mediator".[18] The American historian Robert Edwin Herzstein, who investigated Waldheim's Nazi record and wrote a 1988 book, *Waldheim: The Missing Years*, declared that "throughout the postwar period, including his tenure as UN secretary-general, Kurt Waldheim was a U.S. intelligence asset who expected to be – and always was – protected by his friends in the American intelligence community".[19] For Herzstein, the Waldheim debacle was "a cover-up without equal in modern history".[20]

This would not have been the first time that intelligence services were manipulating the UN. Beginning with the first UN Secretary-General, Trygve Lie, the UN maintained an agreement with the US government for 30 years in which all American candidates for UN posts had to be cleared by US intelligence. Shirley Hazzard reported that Byron Price, Lie's Assistant Secretary-General for Administrative and Financial Services, was actually "the secret agent of the United States government within the United Nations leadership".[21] She estimated that due to the "secret agreement", at least 40 Americans were fired from the UN during the years 1951 to 1953 despite having good work records and not committing any offense. The vetting was carried out to ensure that communists or communist sympathizers would not infiltrate the organization and undermine the UN, and it coincided with the period of so-called "witch hunts" led by American Senator Joseph McCarthy to uncover subversives in the US federal government. The practice of US government vetting of American UN staff continued until challenged in the courts in the early 1980s. According to Hazzard:

> In September 1983, as the result of a sustained challenge to its legality by Dr. David Ozonoff, a candidate for employment at the United Nations World Health Organization, the clearance was ruled unconstitutional by a United States District Court judge... An appeal of the court's ruling by the United States government was disallowed in 1984. And in 1986, following the upholding of a subsequent legal challenge to the procedure, the national-security-clearance requirement for American applicants to United Nations positions was at last withdrawn.[22]

For UN critics such as Shirley Hazzard the Waldheim deception was just the most recent example of how the UN had never really lived up to the high hopes pinned on it for creating and maintaining a completely new international order after the Second World War. Among the list of faults were gender discrimination, financial mismanagement and wasted resources, being a dumping place for incompetent civil servants who were not wanted in their home countries, and cronyism so extensive that top deputies of Waldheim (such as Brian Urquhart, the UN top official from 1946 to 1985 and one of the most prolific writers on the UN) were praising the ex-Nazi right down to the very end until the evidence of his past could no longer be denied.[23]

Intellectual responses to such negative publicity surrounding the UN were of two main types. Some shared Hazzard's outrage and supported calls for a change in business-as-usual at the UN or a complete abolition of the organization. "It's hard to imagine a greater mockery of an organization devoted to world peace than its leader turning out to have been a war criminal who based his career on a falsified past," a reviewer of Hazzard's *Countenance of Truth* declared in *The Boston Globe* newspaper.[24] On the other hand, there was the position of realpolitik, represented by the American journalist on the UN beat, Bernard Nossiter, who in his own review of the same book said it was perfectly understandable why Waldheim kept the top UN job for two terms. This was because the great powers knew of his Nazi past and used it as a resource to keep him in line if he ever dared to be an independent Secretary-General. From this position, those who were surprised and outraged at the UN's ineffectiveness were simply very naïve about world politics. According to Nossiter:

> The U.N. is no more and no less than its sovereign member states, particularly the five permanent and vetoing members of the Security Council – Britain, China, France, the Soviet Union and the U.S. They pay the bills, or don't, to block a policy or punish an agency. They vote for and supply the blue-helmeted troops that provide symbolic barriers between Cypriot Greeks and Turks, Indians and Pakistanis, Israelis and Syrians. Inevitably, the big five and the lesser 150 or so have a great deal to say about their nationals who fill jobs at the U.N. None is quite as brassy as the United States with its loyalty tests or the Russians who keep their citizens on short contracts, but the distinctions are minor.[25]

Failed peacekeeping

When the Cold War ended the UN became the world's leading peacekeeper. During the 43 years of the war the UN conducted only 13 peacekeeping operations, but between 1992 and 2000 it ran 25. Although a number of these were successes – such as El Salvador, the Central African Republic and Namibia – Secretary-General Annan had to admit in his Millennium Report that Rwanda and Bosnia had been failures.[26] International failures are better remembered than are successes, so at the end of the century the UN was trying to control the damage caused to its image by its failure to save lives in these two most well-known cases from Africa and Europe.

The UN's own estimates were that a total of about 820 000 people had been slaughtered in Bosnia and Rwanda – 800 000 in Rwanda and 20 000 in Bosnia and Herzegovina. In addition, 117 members of the UN's Protection Force in Bosnia and Herzegovina (UNPROFOR), and 10 Belgian peacekeepers of the United Nations Assistance Mission for Rwanda (UNAMIR) had been killed.[27] This was not the first time in the post-Second World War period that there had been mass slaughter. However, what made Rwanda and Bosnia different was the fact that the killings had happened in places where UN peacekeeping plans were already in place, and they were therefore glaring examples of UN impotence that led to questions from opinion leaders and members of the general public around the world as to whether the UN served any useful purpose. Just as interesting is the fact that these two cases of genocide occurred when Kofi Annan was Under Secretary-General for Peacekeeping

Operations. Yet this detail did not impede Annan's ascendancy to UN Secretary-General in 1997 and his winning the 2001 Nobel Peace Prize for (according to the Norwegian Nobel Committee) making it clear "that sovereignty cannot be a shield behind which member states conceal their violations".[28]

UNAMIR was set up in October 1993 to monitor the Arusha Peace Agreement between the Rwandan government and the Rwandese Patriotic Front (RPF). Brigadier-General Romeo A. Dallaire was appointed to head UNAMIR. From the start he encountered difficulties in getting the UN Secretariat to take a firm stand about how and when his soldiers should intervene with force. For example, the Secretariat never responded formally to his proposal (made at the start of the tour) that the mission be given powers to use force against those committing "ethnically and politically motivated criminal acts".[29] Similarly, in January 1994 Dallaire was not given approval to use force, even after he shared with Headquarters in New York intelligence that indicated the Rwandan government militia was training personnel to massacre and had started registering ethnic Tutsi for extermination.

When the President of Rwanda's plane was shot down on 6 April 1994 and he was killed, the incident sparked a breakdown of order in Rwanda and the initiation of mass killings. The civil war did not end until the RPF victory on 18 July the same year, the declaration of a unilateral ceasefire, and the swearing in of a national unity government on 19 July.

The UN's failure in Rwanda came not long after the UN peacekeeping debacle in Somalia. The UN's peacekeeping operations in Somalia (UNOSOM I and UNOSOM II) lasted from April 1992 until March 1995. The UN's initial role was to monitor a ceasefire in the Somali capital, Mogadishu, and ensure the safe delivery of supplies to thousands of Somalis who risked starvation. Civil war between several groups had left Somalia without a central government and the other aspects expected of a country with a civil society, such as a judiciary and a police force. Thus because the country was in disarray and it was impossible to have peace without national reconciliation and functioning government institutions, the UN's mandate expanded to include essentially the complete reconstitution of Somali civil society.

At the end of the three years the UN claimed an achievement in this area, although Somalia's problems were by no means over. Through UN help a Somali police force of 8000 had been created and there was a judicial system that included 46 district courts, 11 regional courts and 11 appeals courts.[30] However, the three years cost a total of 155 lives of personnel working with the UN effort. The most famous losses occurred in 1993. In June of that year Somali militia in south Mogadishu killed several Pakistani soldiers of UNOSOM. In October, 18 American soldiers were killed and 75 wounded when they launched an operation to capture those suspected of complicity in the June killings and later attacks on UN personnel and facilities. The global reach of American broadcast media meant that the scenes of American corpses being dragged by Somalis through the streets of Mogadishu were brought to the attention of world public opinion, a graphic illustration of failure. A short time later President Clinton announced the withdrawal of American troops from the country. The US troops had participated in Somalia under American command.

According to the UN-sponsored independent inquiry into what happened in Rwanda, the memory of Somalia made both the UN and its most powerful member, the United States, gun-shy about military engagement in Rwanda. The UN's report on Somalia had said that "the UN should refrain from undertaking further peace enforcement actions within the internal conflicts of states".[31] After Somalia, US President Clinton placed strict guidelines for US involvement in UN peacekeeping missions.

An additional embarrassment for the UN was that the Rwandan government that planned the genocide was, in 1994, a member of the UN Security Council!

Even before the UN-sponsored inquiry blamed the UN for essentially permitting the Rwandan genocide to occur, journalistic investigations had already done so. According to the Rwanda report:

> The Independent Inquiry finds that the response of the United Nations before and during the 1994 genocide in Rwanda failed in a number of fundamental respects. The responsibilities for the failings of the United Nations to prevent and stop the genocide in Rwanda lies with a number of different actors, in particular the Secretary-General, the Secretariat, the Security Council, UNAMIR and the broader membership of the United Nations. This institutional responsibility is one which warrants a clear apology by the Organization and by Member States concerned to the Rwandese people.[32]

But Rwanda was not the only place to which the UN would have to apologize for permitting genocide. Almost simultaneously with Rwanda was the case of Bosnia and Herzegovina.

The events that led to the UN's involvement in Bosnia began in 1992 when Bosnia declared its independence from the political entity that was known during the Cold War as Yugoslavia. The Bosnian Serbs – an ethnic minority in the region – rejected Bosnian independence, and received military assistance from the Serb-dominated Yugoslav Army. They "cleansed" Bosnian towns and villages of Muslims – who were a majority in Bosnia – and held siege the Bosnian capital of Sarajevo. This was just the latest in a series of conflicts in the Balkans caused by the end of the Cold War and the disintegration of Yugoslavia. In 1991, war had broken out in Croatia when Serbs there rejected that region's declaration of independence. The United Nations Protection Force (UNPROFOR), which was to become famous for its failures in Bosnia, was actually created to establish peace in Croatia, but its mandate had to be extended to Bosnia when fighting started there. While attempts by the European Union and other entities to negotiate a settlement failed, the percentage of Bosnian territory taken over by the Serbs continued to expand. Meanwhile, the UN's approach to peacekeeping in the region was that it was intervening to alleviate a humanitarian disaster. UNPROFOR sought to protect the Sarajevo airport, food and refugee convoys, and six UN-designated "safe areas" that included five Bosnian towns and the city of Sarajevo. It also monitored a ban on military flights in Bosnia and Herzegovina.

The war in Bosnia came to a climax in 1995 when the North Atlantic Treaty Organization (NATO) launched air strikes on the Serbs to force them to comply with the terms of a UN exclusion zone around Sarajevo. The Serbs retaliated by bombing the "safe areas" and taking hostage 370 UN peace-keepers. Later in the year the Serbs were forced to the bargaining table by offensives from NATO, Bosnia and Croatia. In November, in Dayton, Ohio, US, a political solution was worked out for the formation of an independent state. Federal and regional elections were held in 1996.

UNPROFOR was the largest UN peacekeeping mission ever launched. Between 1992 and 1996 it cost more than $4616 million, and had involved a force of military, police and civilians that numbered more than 40 000. But still 20 000 died and thousands more were displaced. The most glaring fail-ure was the UN policy of declaring "safe areas" to which people fled on the mistaken assumption that they would be protected. In fact, these "safe areas" were solely a UN creation, without the consent of the fighting parties and without any UN policy to provide military protection for the civilians. This meant that in the particular case of one of these areas – Srebrenica – there were systematic massacres of civilians when the town fell to the Serbs. After the fall of Srebrenica in 1995, and while the Serb's were at the bar-gaining table, genocide was taking place and thousands of bodies were being buried in mass graves.

There were two other grave contradictions in UN peacekeeping policy in Bosnia. The organization imposed an arms embargo on Bosnia and Herzegovina and then did not protect it from Serb aggression. Also, the UN deployed a peacekeeping force without the necessary conditions in place. According to the UN-sponsored inquiry of 1999, "there was no peace agree-ment – not even a functioning ceasefire – there was no clear will to peace and there was no clear consent by the belligerents".[33] Another costly failure was the UN's focus on defining its response to the events in Bosnia purely in terms of providing humanitarian relief, especially in the early stages of the fighting. The UN's 1999 analysis summed up the shortcomings of this policy by saying that:

> The problem which cried out for a political/military solution, was that a State Member of the United Nations, left largely defenceless as a result of an arms embargo imposed upon it by the United Nations, was being

dismembered by forces committed to its destruction. This was not a problem with a humanitarian solution.[34]

Another analysis of what went wrong in Bosnia pointed to the connection between this limited definition of the problem and the failure to mobilize sufficient international public opinion in favor of military force against the aggressors in Bosnia. According to the report by the International Commission on the Balkans: "This minimal definition – as if the conflict were a natural disaster unrelated to political strategies – had the effect of dampening public pressure for robust action in response to news of atrocities by Serb forces, and later by Croat forces as well".[35]

The failures in Rwanda and Bosnia were motivations for the UN to appoint a 10-member panel to look into UN peacekeeping. Former Algerian Foreign Minister Lakhdar Brahimi chaired the panel, and its recommendations became known as the "Brahimi Report".[36] This said that the Security Council should no longer authorize peacekeeping missions without first having the troops and resources to undertake the missions. It also recommended a revamping of the mechanisms of UN peacekeeping, such as increased and more reliable funding, better conflict-prevention strategies and "robust rules of engagement" for UN peacekeepers who had to deal with parties that sought to undermine agreements (as did the Rwandan and Yugoslavian governments).

In the mix of criticisms of international policy to avert genocide in Rwanda were allegations of religious and ethnic bias. If the persecuted in Bosnia were not Muslims or the slaughtered in Rwanda not black Africans, would the response have been so indecisive? Such questions were even being asked by the then Secretary-General of the UN himself, Boutros Boutros-Ghali.[37]

The UN image on film

The indecisive, inept, hypocritical image of the UN projected by its failures in peacekeeping in the mid-1990s stands in stark contrast to the representation of the organization in the world's most powerful image industry in that historical epoch. A critical examination of the representation of the UN in popular Hollywood movies and American television programs that was carried out for this book revealed a movement away from very positive representations early in the life of the organization to quite negative portrayals in later years.

Although Hollywood films are seen as trivial dimensions of low culture in the eyes of some observers, by the end of the century the UN could not ignore the importance of Hollywood in its struggle to win hearts and minds the world over. By 2000, India was producing more feature films than the United States, but the world market in films remained dominated by the

American industry. UNESCO's *World Culture Report 2000* reported that a majority of countries had the US as their favorite source of imported movies.[38] In all but three of the 30 countries sampled, US films accounted for more than 50 per cent of box-office receipts.[39] The US also accounted for 75 per cent of TV programs sold in the world. This meant that the ideological reach of the United States at the end of the century appeared to have been even greater than it had been when the UN was founded, because between 1980 and 1997 the number of television sets per 1000 population in the world had more than doubled, though most of this growth was in India and China.[40] Because of the capital-intensive nature of cinema and television production, countries that introduced television for the first time had to rely on the United States to fill their programming voids.

In the UN's early days, a few American showbusiness personalities – most notably Danny Kaye – used their celebrity status to help promote the UN's causes. But by the end of the UN's first 50 years the organization was actively trying to recruit stars to speak on its behalf and was even using Hollywood films in public information campaigns. In a 2001 speech in Australia, Under Secretary-General for Disarmament Affairs Jayantha Dhanapala reported that part of the UN's disarmament campaign was the screening of the Hollywood movie *Thirteen Days*, a film about the Cuban missile crisis. Dhanapala said this was "being shown to students and general audiences worldwide and it has surely opened people's eyes about the harsh realities of nuclear war".[41] The Department for Disarmament Affairs was originally a center, but the UN Secretary-General made it a department of the Secretariat in 1998. Despite being the Secretariat's smallest department and having an annual budget of "far less than what the UN spends on cleaning services" (in the words of Dhanapala), the Department devoted considerable resources to an international public information campaign for disarmament that included the production of a web site, posters and pamphlets. A prominent spokesman on its behalf was the Hollywood star Michael Douglas, one of scores of celebrities the UN appointed to the honorary positions of "Messengers of Peace" or "Goodwill Ambassadors" to use their celebrity to promote the UN. The list of these celebrities numbered 77 by late 2000, and in addition to Michael Douglas included the actors Danny Glover, Harry Belafonte, Susan Sarandon and Mia Farrow. It also included celebrities from other fields and countries, such as Britain's Geri Halliwell of the Spice Girls singing group, Brazilian soccer star Ronaldo, and South African writer Nadine Gordimer. However, though these celebrities attract attention to the causes, they are not always sufficiently knowledgeable about the issues as to avoid embarrassment, as Michael Douglas found out in 2000 during his talk on the evils of nuclear proliferation to the Oxford Research Group in London, when he could not engage with the question of whether the positions of President Reagan and Prime Minister Margaret Thatcher helped end the Cold War.[42]

Embarrassing situations such as that with Michael Douglas shed light not only on the limitations of the celebrities but also on the shortcomings of this practice of using celebrity to supposedly attract attention to international problems. William Over, in his *Human Rights in the International Public Sphere*, says that in such cases the media focus more on the celebrity than on "the causal connections between the human conditions of suffering and those social and political agencies affecting them". Over argues that this use of celebrity is an inherently shallow approach to solving the crises it purportedly intends to cure. He points out that the communitarian ethic of intellectuals, such as Cornel West (and Paulo Freire,[43] who is not cited by Over), emphasize "conscientization" of the oppressed to foster a sense of personal agency to act and solve their own problems. In contrast, the well-publicized media tours of celebrities "offer primarily a meliorative approach, giving succor to the incapacitated rather than hope for a better life through programs of education, consciousness-raising, and cultural affirmation".[44]

On 23 October 2000 the UN held a day-long event for its celebrity supporters that itself generated much international press attention. "You have the passion to inspire their faith in the principles on which the United Nations was founded," Secretary-General Kofi Annan said to them. "And you have the power to convince them of the importance of the United Nations' work in people's lives".[45] Some of the celebrities spoke at a forum the same day on the theme "The United Nations and Celebrity Advocacy in an Age of Cynicism".

Therefore, more than 50 years after its birth, the UN's leadership was courting celebrity – and American media celebrity in particular – to get its messages across. The UN was acutely aware that the powers of the international audio-visual complex were collectively one of the most formidable forces in international affairs – creators of the images that captured the hearts and minds of the world's people, more of whom were increasingly able to sit before television sets or were captive audiences in cinemas, evoking affective responses through media, and especially film. Because films engage so many emotions they often figure in the world of politics. Phillip L. Gianos, in his *Politics and Politicians in American Film*, illustrates this relationship by pointing to how the proposed Strategic Defense Initiative became known by the name of a popular film – *Star Wars* – and how politicians as different as Richard Nixon and Bill Clinton used particular famous Hollywood films as types of political aphrodisiacs – as sources of emotional inspiration and emulation necessary to confront the challenges of their political careers.[46] Films also engage the political world by what insight they provide into the representation of particular political sentiments at particular historical periods. For example, Deborah Gee's documentary on racial and gender stereotyping of Asian women in American motion pictures, *Slaying The Dragon*, focused on how representations of Asians varied throughout the century according to contemporary events and the disposition of American foreign policy.[47]

In the search to answer the central question of this chapter about why the UN's image remained distorted it is therefore very important to consider the representation of the United Nations in film. Because of expedience and the limitations of resources and time, the analysis has been limited to Hollywood films in English. However, although the American industry is the most powerful in the world, it should not be forgotten that the representation of the UN in fictional films has not been limited to Hollywood, and that there is work to be done to explore whether the findings here for Hollywood were also true for other film industries around the world.

As was noted in Chapter 2, concern regarding a decline in the UN's image in the powerful countries was emerging from as early as the turn of the 1970s. Research for this book was aimed at establishing whether Hollywood film discourse reflected in any way changed attitudes towards the UN. The research found that during the period 1952 to 2000, seven major feature films had plots that either revolved around the UN or incorporated assumptions about the organization as part of their plots. During the same period there were also two television series and one TV show (see Appendix VII).

If the three films from the 1950s and 1960s are our guides, the general sense of idealism about the UN project that characterized this period in the United States was reflected in the feature films from Hollywood. *The Glory Brigade* (1953), *A Global Affair* (1964) and *Gidget Grows Up* (1969) all depict a world of ethnic diversity in which the ability to resolve differences is both a challenge and an opportunity for positive change. Only the latter two films were actually set at the UN, however *The Glory Brigade* is a part of film discourse about the UN because it is set in the Korean War, the first major international conflict in which the UN played a key role.

The film was actually released the same year that the armistice that ended the three-year conflict was signed. The US led a "police action" undertaken by 16 United Nations member states to stem a North Korean attack on the south across the 38th parallel that divided the two Koreas. The war cost three million lives, but ironically resulted in no territorial gains for either side, and the Korean peninsula was to remain divided into two states for the rest of the century. The film is in the tradition of Hollywood war propaganda films, projects undertaken with the explicit intent of mobilizing American troops to achieve specific goals. In the case of the Korean War, the aim was to foster the respect of the American soldiers for the cultural differences of the men alongside whom they fought. The film's plot chronicles how an American platoon overcomes its prejudices towards Greeks when it is assigned to escort the Greeks behind enemy lines. Although being generally unimpressed by the film, *The New York Times* reviewer said in 1953 that it was a "frank, sincere plea for true democratic understanding and harmony, in appraising the friction of a United Nations unit of Americans and Greeks".[48]

A Global Affair is a propaganda movie on the behalf of the UN if there ever was one. From the very start of the film there is imagery of internationalism and this theme is never abandoned and indeed nailed home at ever opportunity. The opening credits are run to the tune of Vic Dana's "So Wide The World", with a background of a world map, photos of people of various ethnicities, the UN building and its interior. The plot revolves around a controversy at the UN over what country should have custody of a baby who is abandoned at the UN. "I can no longer take care of my baby," a note left with the child says. "I want her to be raised in a place she can be free from fear, want and prejudice. I heard a man named Larimore speak on the radio. He said some day these things will be guaranteed by the United Nations to all babies everywhere. That's why I am leaving her here."

The then very famous American comedian and actor Bob Hope plays the UN's Frank Larimore who made the idealistic speech referred to in the note. He is collecting data on children everywhere and trying to get the UN Secretary-General interested in a proposal on "the universal rights of the child". The task of taking care of the baby until the UN decides what to do with her falls on Larimore's shoulders, setting up a very simple plot that allows the film to preach the virtues of internationalism and the values of the UN. To the suggestion of a friend that he quit the "UN malarkey", Larimore declares that: "The UN happens to be one real hope of the future... At least I am part of something that's keeping the world from blowing itself up".

The work betrays the Cold War preoccupations of the time with an almost obligatory sub-plot in which Larimore must protect the child from a cold Russian female diplomat who promises the threat of a "state orphanage" and sabotage of international co-operation on a variety of issues. But even the Russian has to melt in the face of the American's humanity.

After the International Court of Justice and the General Assembly fail to resolve the matter, Larimore brings the film to its climax with a platitudinous speech before the General Assembly on why he will raise the child himself. The baby girl will be raised free of nationalism, he explains. He will raise her as a true international citizen, exposing her to the cultures of the world.

No Hollywood movie has been as boldly in favor of the United Nations as 1964's *A Global Affair*. Although in the period some American groups opposed the UN for racist or isolationist reasons – most notably the John Birch Society – public opinion polls and opinion leaders were generally favorable to the UN project that, after all, was largely an American creation. The note left with the abandoned baby echoed the hopes of President F. D. Roosevelt's "four freedoms" in the 1941 Atlantic Charter, and the movie's internationalist politics is so unsubtle that it is heavy handed. Ironically, some of the work's fiction would actually become a reality within 25 years: a Peruvian did become UN Secretary-General (Javier Pérez de Cuéllar), and in 1989 the General Assembly did adopt a Convention on the Rights of the Child that became binding international law a year later.

Gidget Grows Up manifests the same internationalist politics of *The Glory Brigade* and *A Global Affair*, but its pro-UN message is subtler than that of the Bob Hope movie even though in the earliest minutes the main protagonist – Gidget Lawrence (played by Karen Valentine) – declares that the UN is "one of humanity's noblest achievements". The basic plot is that Gidget learns lessons of life while working for the UN: during her time away from her native California she has a failed romantic relationship with an Australian international civil servant before she returns to her childhood sweetheart Jeff (Moondoggie) and gets engaged on 4 July, US Independence Day. The movie is a remarkable historical artifact because of the way it depicts a world in which multiculturalism and internationalism are portrayed as the norm; however the historical reality outside the world of the movie (especially in the United States) was anything but that.

The movie was released just a year after the Reverend Martin Luther King was assassinated in the midst of a struggle to achieve basic civil rights for African-Americans, such as the right to vote, the right to live anywhere, and the right to equal access to social services. European powers were still dismantling generations of formal imperialism and colonialism in locations as far apart as Africa, the Caribbean and Asia. It was the period of 1968's "Czech Spring" in which the Soviet Union crushed dissent in Czechoslovakia. However, that world does not exist in *Gidget Grows Up*. Gidget returns to the United States after two years as an exchange student in Italy and France, and goes to work for the UN as a guide having being inspired by a speech by the US Representative to the UN. She thinks nothing of having a Chinese-American and a Ugandan as room mates in an apartment in the East Village, and their landlord is more interested in being flattered about his history as a child filmstar than in the race of his prospective tenants. Gidget even becomes the romantic interest of an "Arab" (with the stereotypical dress to make the point) who wants to make her his twelfth wife. He is very wealthy and Gidget has to admit that he is handsome, though she has no interest in joining his "happy harem".

A Global Affair and *Gidget Grows Up* suggest a naïve enthusiasm for the UN ideal. However, this Hollywood version of internationalism is without complications. The UN is not an American tool but an innocent organization promoting international peace and tolerance. But of course the UN (as has already been shown in this book) was never that even-handed a player in world affairs. Also, reality outside the movie made the world a much more challenging place in which to sustain even that simplistic Hollywood version of internationalism.

The cultural politics of American television with regards to the UN seems to have been of a similar type during the 1950s and 1960s. This message of internationalism with an American bias was present in a 1952 episode of the "Lucky Strike Theatre" series of weekly shows on the NBC channel and a TV project sponsored by the Xerox Corporation in the 1960s.

Those In Favor (1952) is set at the United Nations and depicts the Cold War rivalry between the US and the USSR that was then in its infancy. A Soviet diplomat at the UN writes a letter to his wife in which he reveals the USSR's strategy at UN talks and complains about Soviet intelligence. The letter also says that the UN is of "great value" as a "propaganda platform" for the Soviet Union. The damaging letter gets into the hands of his American adversaries who, instead of exploiting the situation, offer to help the diplomat defect. But the Soviets kill their man when they get wind of his sloppiness, and this leads the US representative to the UN to conclude in the last scene that the United States respects personal privacy – unlike the Soviets. The United States was not in favor of "arbitrary interference with privacy, home or correspondence".

Those In Favor was not so much a pro-UN propaganda show as it was a warning that the then infant UN would be used by the USSR for its own propaganda ends. As is the case with the movies discussed above, the full meaning of the work cannot be grasped without putting it into historical context. The show was produced during the Korean War, which pitted the Soviet Union and Communist China on the side of the North against an alliance of states that fought under the UN flag, including the United States, South Korea and others. The Security Council's 1950 resolution that condemned the North Korean invasion of the South and authorized the UN "police action" had been passed only because the Soviet delegate was then boycotting the council to protest the UN's seating of nationalist China instead of the People's Republic of China. *Those In Favor* presented an American spin on what would be at stake in the new organization. Indeed, when we consider that the US was then at war against communists in Korea, we can place the show in the category of war propaganda, produced to simplify war aims for a mass audience and mobilize the home front behind them. The Americans abided by the rules of fair play and the communists did not. The communists would even kill their own diplomats for political expedience. But the real-life context of the television fiction was not that simple; the same United States had just finished fighting a world war in which it had relegated its black citizens to fighting in segregated units, interned its Japanese citizens and still maintained a system of legal segregation and discrimination even in such areas as marriage and education.

The politics of representation were somewhat different in a series of programs funded by the Xerox Corporation and broadcast by the American Broadcasting Company over 12 years later. For the purposes of this book, the story of how the series of fictional shows came about and the controversy surrounding it are more interesting than the content of the shows themselves. Managing Director of the United Nations Special Fund, Paul G. Hoffman, came up with the idea when a 1963 violent attack on the American Ambassador to the UN by a right-wing demonstrator in Dallas reinforced his belief that Americans were very uninformed about the UN. Hoffman, *TV Guide* reported, was convinced "that great masses of people in the U.S. had only the flimsiest notion of what the UN was all about; that the UN's peace-keeping and parliamentary functions were understood in a general way but the extensive activities of the UN and its associated agencies, which make up 85 per cent of the UN's business, were little more than a blur to many Americans".[49] Hoffman found a sympathetic ear from the CEO and President of the copy-machine company Xerox, Joseph C. Wilson, because Wilson was a believer in the UN and had even started the first chapter of the United Nations Association in Rochester, New York.[50] Wilson committed $4 million to the project, an amount that was then twice the annual advertising budget of the company.[51] Xerox explained the action by putting the series in the context of its role as a company that helps people communicate; international understanding was one of the most profound means of communication.[52] Another explanation was that the UN was then viewed as the prime institution capable of maintaining the social and economic health that would nurture the global expansion of transnational corporations such as Xerox.[53] It was not the first time that a large American corporation had backed the UN in a controversial way. When Xerox announced its plans, the *Saturday Review* reminded its readers that United Airlines had put the UN insignia on its planes "a few years ago" but had taken them off after protests from the right-wing John Birch Society.[54]

The fact that the Xerox project was controversial suggests that there was never a naïve acceptance of the UN in the United States. CBS refused to broadcast any of the programs on the grounds that such an action would violate its principle of not broadcasting political propaganda. A CBS executive noted that although "most men of goodwill wholly approve of the United Nations", there was still "a substantial segment of the American population which is opposed to the U.N".[55] Soon after the project was announced in April 1964, the John Birch Society launched a letter-writing campaign to stop it. Xerox had received 2100 of these negative letters by October. The *Saturday Review* reported that the tone of the letters varied from "scrawled invective to serious exposition of the far right's argument that the U.N. is a Communist-dominated front out to destroy the sovereignty and freedom of the republic".[56] After the first show was aired a group in San Jose, California, the Santa Clara Citizens Committee to Promote the Truth About the United Nations, asked for equal broadcasting time under US broadcasting regulations on the grounds that the show contained "pro-United Nations propaganda".[57] Individuals and organizations that supported the project wrote letters or publicly commended Xerox, as did the Protestant Council of the City of New York and the American Jewish Committee.[58]

The foundation that was set up to supervise the shows made only two stipulations: the shows should be of good taste and should not make a hero or villain out of any particular country.[59] Telsun was the name given to the foundation because it was a compressed way of saying "Television Series for United Nations".[60] Within two years Telsun funded four shows all of which were broadcast on ABC: "Carol For Another Christmas" (broadcast on

Figure 3.2 Joseph C. Wilson, CEO of Xerox from 1946 to 1966, poses in the early 1960s with the then new Xerox 914 copier. Wilson committed $4 million of the company's money to fund the Telsun (Television Series for United Nations) project on the grounds that "the highest interests of the corporation are involved in the health of the earth's society".

28 December 1964); "Who Has Seen The Wind" (19 February 1965); "Once Upon A Tractor" (9 September 1965); and "The Poppy Is Also A Flower" (22 April 1966). All tried to propagate the importance of the UN by illustrating through drama why the international organization was important. The hour-and-a-half-long "Carol For Another Christmas" is a take-off on Dickens' *A Christmas Carol*; in it a disbeliever in internationalism finally gets an epiphany after he is introduced by the ghosts of Christmas Past (war), Christmas Present (extreme global inequality), and Christmas Future (selfishness and global chaos). "Who Has Seen The Wind" (90 minutes) attempted to build support for the UN High Commissioner for Refugees (UNHCR) by depicting the squalor onboard a tramp steamer filled with stateless persons and on which the crew had not had shore leave for 12 years. In this case the epiphany comes not through a ghost but through the intervention of the UNHCR that compassionately finds the protagonists new lives in new countries. "Once Upon A Tractor" (60 minutes) makes its case for the UN as the body that literally turns swords into ploughshares with the story of a farmer who successfully argues

his case before the UN. His home state reneged on a promise to provide him with a tractor because of an expanded military budget, but his argument is that the state has an obligation to the individual as much as the other way around. The UN agrees and he gets his tractor. "The Poppy Is Also A Flower" (90 minutes) is the story of how the UN was on the ball with another world problem, illegal drugs, and follows the tribulations of two UN agents who trace a shipment of opium from Iran to Italy and France.

Telsun was able to enlist the services of distinguished actors, directors and musicians of the day who all participated not for money but to show support for the UN cause. The director of the first show was none other than Joseph L. Mankiewicz of *Cleopatra* fame; Nancy Wilson sang the title song of "Who Has Seen The Wind"; and some of the stars involved in "The Poppy Is Also A Flower" were Princess Grace of Monaco (who introduced the show) and E. G. Marshall. The galaxy of stars did not stop *The New York Times* television critic from panning all four productions, however. For example, of "Carol For Another Christmas" he said: "it was a pretentious and wearing exercise in garrulous ineptitude, one of the more dismaying TV disappointments in several seasons".[61] But the Hollywood stars were even willing to risk their reputations with bad art to promote an organization that they saw as hope for a better future. Mankiewicz communicated an insight into this mood in an interview with *The New York Times* that was published the day before the first show was broadcast. For Mankiewicz, internationalism was an antidote against the looming threat of nuclear annihilation and a repeat of the communist witch-hunts of Senator Joseph McCarthy. "Anti-U.N. feelings are attitudes of hate", he declared. "I wanted to expose them as anti-everything I believe in. It's no longer a question of one country killing off another – we can destroy the universe. The necessity of self-involvement is something every man has got to face".[62]

Almost exactly 20 years later the ABC network would again attract controversy when it aired a series of programs that featured the UN, but, perhaps reflecting how drastically attitudes towards the organization had changed, the series was regarded as crude, anti-United Nations propaganda. The show was a "mini-series" called "Amerika", a fourteen-and-a-half-hour production that ran for seven successive nights, beginning on 15 February 1987. It depicted a United States ten years into occupation by the Soviet Union. It cleverly exploited a view popular in some sectors of American society that the UN was a Soviet puppet by depicting the UN as complicit in the new colonialism, with UN peacekeeping troops portrayed as part of the military domination. The news that this type of show was being planned provoked a controversy several months before it actually aired, prompting an ABC publicist to quip that never "has so much been said about something of which so little has been seen".[63] Media reports said the idea for the series originated three years earlier after American conservative columnist Ben Stein had criticized another ABC mini-series, 1983's "The Day After", that represented what life in the US would look like in the aftermath of a nuclear war between the US and USSR. For Stein, "The Day After" was too left-wing and ABC was challenged to produce a show that would balance the score.[64]

So 20 years after the Telsun project the political economy of American television was much different. The increased industrialization of the media meant that media discourse about "Amerika" was as much about how the show would improve ABC's low audience ratings as about the ideological controversy. In terms of ratings, ABC did not get much in return for its $40 million investment. Although the first episode beat out the other two competing networks (NBC and CBS), the show did not maintain high ratings and was not enough to lift the network out of third place.[65] As some had feared, Americans did not warm to the propaganda message. In retrospect, the storm over the series was very anti-climatic.

The fervor of opposition to "Amerika" from those who disagreed with its ideological line was as devoted as was the protest to the Telsun project from the right 20 years earlier. ABC and companies that planned to advertise on the show received a total of over 4000 letters,[66] and various interest groups demanded broadcast time to respond with alternative opinions. The Chrysler Corporation committed $5 million worth of advertising but then changed its mind in the wake of the controversy.[67] The Soviet newspaper *Pravda* declared: "One cannot help thinking that the television serial 'Amerika', though fiction, is a deliberate act of psychological warfare intended to scare the Americans and to make them believe 'the Russians are coming' so as to whip up hatred for the Soviet people and the Soviet Union".[68] The UN was so upset by the damage that "Amerika" would do to its image that it hired former special counsel to President John F. Kennedy, Ted Sorensen, to get a disclaimer from ABC and time for a UN response. The UN also hired an advertising firm to produce a 30-second public service announcement to promote it.[69] The disclaimer was shown at the start of each episode: "The institutions and organizations depicted are not intended to bear any resemblance to today's counterparts".[70] But in defending the UN, Sorensen himself revealed that he was not entirely happy with all the UN's work. The *Los Angeles Times* quoted him as saying: "I think that the (real) U.N. peacekeeping forces constitute one of the bright spots in the disappointing history of the U.N. ... and to see them trashed this way, I felt, was offensive".[71]

The contemporary international political context of "Amerika" was even more complex than during the TV shows and movies of the 1950s and 1960s. The defeat in the Vietnam War and the Carter administration's failure to end a hostage crisis in Iran was powerful evidence for the American right-wing that the US had lost its standing internationally. Ronald Reagan promised to change this, and came to office at the start of the 1980s with a foreign policy agenda that would restore the country's standing by being tougher on the Soviets and their clients. Right-wing governments around the world that were seen as bulwarks against the spread of communism – such as the apartheid government in South Africa, and various dictatorships in Latin America – were maintained in power by American support. Meanwhile, anti-communist insurgents who fought civil wars against socialist regimes – most famously in Nicaragua – were hailed as freedom fighters and supported militarily by the United States. This passion to fight the global spread of communism led to one of the biggest debacles of the Reagan presidency.

The "Iran-Contra Affair" (as it became known) was a political scandal in which it was revealed that between 1985 and 1986 the US National Security Council was involved in selling arms to the government of Iran and diverting part of the proceeds to the "Contra" rebels in Nicaragua. The arms sales were made in the hope that American hostages being held in Lebanon would be released. However, the revelation was a serious blow to the US government's credibility because both the Contras and the Iranian government were considered sponsors of terrorism and US government policy was not to support such entities. Ironically, about the same time the political changes that would eventually lead to the disintegration of the Soviet Union and the collapse of the communist bloc started to occur when Mikhail Gorbachev came to power in 1985. In 1987 the Soviet war in Afghanistan – a defeat as devastating for the USSR as the Vietnam War had been for the United States – was coming to an end.

The ideological contradictions of the timing of the release of "Amerika" were pointed out in the American left opinion journal *The Nation*, which noted that world events had made the US look more the villain than the USSR. On the depiction of the suppression of free speech in "Amerika", it noted that "many of the meanest policies of the conquerors, such as banning the patriotic flag and outlawing resistance organizations, refer directly to Israel and South Africa [two countries supported by the US], rather than to the Soviet Union".[72]

Despite the great concern of the UN and its supporters regarding the damage "Amerika" would do to the image of the organization, the UN was still portrayed as a surrogate of a state power, the Soviet Union. This makes it ironic and puzzling that a movie released 13 years later that directly identified the organization as a corrupt world-power on its own did not attract any protest or even concern. One must go back to 1964's *A Global Affair* to find a movie that makes the UN the center of its plot as 2000's *The Art of War* does.

In *The Art of War* the African-American actor Wesley Snipes plays Neil Shaw, a UN special operations agent who is framed in the murder of the Chinese Ambassador to the UN. The murder occurs on the eve of the signing of a historic trade agreement between China and the United States and it is believed that it is part of a plot to derail the pact. In the movie the UN is portrayed as a very powerful actor in international politics. It hires Snipes to blackmail corrupt governments in order to get back to the negotiating table, and maintains an arsenal of sophisticated arms and surveillance equipment that Shaw uses. They bug ambassadors and listen to their personal conversations. They can break into the computers of the US government and remove videotaped evidence. As if this kind of power is not enough, Douglas Thomas – the UN Secretary-General played by Donald Sutherland – expresses the hope at the beginning of the movie that the UN could and should become even more powerful. Thomas' deputy is Eleanor Hooks (played by Anne Archer) who is in charge of sending Shaw on all his covert operations for the UN. Hooks turns out to be one of the villains of the plot. She colludes with a Chinese businessman to try and derail the trade agreement by murdering the Chinese ambassador, and is the one who manipulates one of Shaw's mercenary colleagues to frame him for the murder. The climatic moment of the movie is the fight between Shaw and his treacherous "friend" at UN Headquarters that ends in the death of the villain – lanced through the neck by the broken glass of a panel with the UN's insignia. Eleanor Hooks is motivated by the fear that China will eventually dominate the United States. Her ploy to defeat them is to manipulate them against each other. But the Chinese get wind of her deception and assassinate her. The funeral of the UN official is so important that it is broadcast live on television. The movie gets its title from Hooks' modus operandi. She had resolved to deal with the Chinese according to their own definition of "the art of war" – you win by destroying your enemy from within. Hooks also delivers another key line of the plot: "Appearances are everything ... Politics and deception are built on it".

Perhaps *The Art of War*'s negative depiction of the UN did not arouse the anxiety that "Amerika" did because the international context was drastically different from that of the mid-1980s. The Soviets, the Cold War, the Reagan presidency and the threat of "mutually assured destruction" had all disappeared. There was no longer a need to shore up the UN as the last hope for saving humanity. Besides, the UN's failures in Somalia, Rwanda and Bosnia probably cost it not only its credibility but also defenders in the United States. Indeed, 1997's *Welcome To Sarajevo* (a story about a British journalist covering the war who adopts a child from Bosnia) mixed drama with actual news footage to represent the UN's ineptitude in the Balkans. Early in the movie, when news footage shows UN Blue Berets escorting Britain's Prime Minister John Major and France's President Francois Mitterand on a visit to Bosnia, one of the protagonists jokes about how clean they all look, a clear reference to how the UN and the world powers seemed so divorced from Bosnia's nightmare. Later the movie features a video clip of UN Secretary-General Boutros Boutros-Ghali saying: "I believe it will take time to find a solution to the problem, thus we must have patience".

By the end of the century the UN had become a film villain. *Welcome To Sarajevo* suggested that the film makers just had to look at the news to find out why.

Another feature evident in the representation of the UN by the end of the century was the idea that the organization's power exceeded that of the governments. For example, in the 1990 comedy *Operation Condor* (in which Jackie Chan goes in search of lost gold) the US Ambassador to Spain declares that: "the United Nations has ordered me to find the gold for them" in order to avoid an international incident. Chan's guide is Ada, "an attaché to the UN", who is an expert on the African desert and environments. *Austin Powers: International Man of Mystery* (1997) also gives the UN powers that were previously reserved for governments. In the film it is the UN that is about to receive a nuclear warhead from a breakaway Russian republic.

The UN has therefore had a complicated relationship with the most powerful entertainment industry in the world. While public information strategies such as the "Messengers of Peace" and "Goodwill Ambassadors" have been growing, the industry's representation of the UN has not always been flattering, especially in the later years of the century. Also, a striking feature of many of the shows surveyed here was the tendency to portray communists as villains and to have the UN as, if not complicit, certainly a world force liable to be corrupted by communists. However, something positive for the UN is that the industry never joined with the far-right in urging a complete abandonment of the organization by the United States. Even while being the star of "Amerika", the Rhodes Scholar and musician Kris Kristofferson went to Moscow to participate in a peace forum and donated his services for a 30-second film promoting the UN.[73] Similarly, media mogul Ted Turner broadcast on his WTBS station a series of shows to promote international understanding at the same time that "Amerika" was being shown. He also inaugurated the "Goodwill Games" in 1986 to promote peace between the East and West.[74]

Loss of credibility

The changes in perceptions of the UN's reputation and credibility over time – based on public opinion research and government postures to the organization – are not easy to explain. There are three main categories of explanation. One focuses on the demographics of UN membership, noting that as the UN got a majority of non-white "Third World" members, the Western white states felt more alienated. Another emphasizes the part played by UN inefficiency and failure, and the third places emphasis on the failure of the UN's public information program itself.

The first explanation was evident as early as the beginning of the 1970s. Chairman of the US Senate Foreign Relations Committee, J. William Fulbright, said in 1972 that: "Having controlled the United Nations for many years as tightly and as easily as a big-city boss controls his party machine, we had got used to the idea that the United Nations was a place where we could work our will".[75] In a 1974 speech, US Permanent Representative to the UN, John Scali, explained that: "when the rule of the majority becomes the tyranny of the majority, the minority will cease to respect or obey it".[76]

In a 1993 review of United States public opinion poll data on the UN, sociologist William J. Millard reported that:

> In the 1950s and 1960s there was more positive evaluation than negative. But through the 1970s and 1980s, most poll ratings were net negative. A clue to the reasons for change in public opinion is found in the history of that period. In 1971 Communist China was admitted to the UN over objections by the United States. In 1973 the OPEC nations raised the price of oil. There followed a period of confrontation with economic demands from Third World countries. In the UN General Assembly a number of resolutions were passed by Third World countries voting as a bloc, opposed strongly by the U.S. and some of its allies. Budgets were approved by the General Assembly, which met with disapproval of the countries providing the major funding, including the U.S. The United States even withdrew from UNESCO for reasons related to management and to policy – specifically the new world information order that appeared to legitimize governmental action to suppress freedom of the international press. Negative opinions about Third World countries appear to have been transferred to the UN.[77]

An example of the second explanation is that given by Thérèse Paquet Sévigny, the only woman to have headed the DPI in the UN's first 50 years, who noted in a 1988 interview with the *World Press Review*:

> Original expectations for the UN were unrealistically high. The Cold War and the nuclear arms race undercut the effectiveness of UN Charter security provisions. Decolonization brought a sudden surge in membership; and resolutions, even when passed by large majorities, are not implemented. The UN bureaucracy became perceived as inefficient and top-heavy.[78]

In contrast, the writer Shirley Hazzard blamed the failure to properly cultivate world public opinion, which is the basis of the third explanation. In 1989, in two long articles critical of the UN that were later turned into a book, Hazzard noted that:

> Despite the constitutional authority – embodied in the opening words of the Charter – of world citizenry over the nature and direction of the United Nations, intelligent public engagement has been the least nurtured element of the organization's latent potential. The public has been regarded as a passive and uniformly unenlightened audience for U.N. proclamations, and as a sounding board for the vanity of U.N. officials. The possibility of progress toward durable resolution of disputes rests, nevertheless, with the active enlistment of what Dag Hammarskjöld called "the final, least tangible, but perhaps most important new factor

in diplomacy: mass public opinion as a living force in international affairs ... the expression of a democratic mass civilization that is still in its infancy, giving to the man in the street and to group reactions a new significance in foreign policy".[79]

Explaining the problem

What the analysis in this chapter makes clear is that no one of these explanations accounted on its own for the UN's image problems. It could be said that the very political and bureaucratic arrangements that were put in place when the UN was established in 1946 guaranteed that the organization would have image problems in the years to come. Although the General Assembly provided a semblance of democracy among states, the control of the organization remained firmly in the hands of the great powers, both overtly in the form of the Security Council, and covertly by other means, as the Waldheim case revealed. Although the Secretariat and the "UN System" as a whole suffered image problems as a direct result of controversial General Assembly resolutions caused by its expanded membership in the last 30 of its first 50 years, the UN also won friends as some states found it a convenient means through which their grievances could be aired. In addition, to understand the damage caused by UN inefficiency and failure – especially the peacekeeping debacles of the 1990s – a fair assessment of the UN must put the organization's weaknesses within the historical context of its origins, development and political role. Somalia, Rwanda and Bosnia were as much about the inadequacies of the stewardship of the international system by the world powers as they were about the particular shortcomings of the UN. Indeed, it is remarkable that such a contradictory organization managed to survive for so long despite having such moral selectivity, political hypocrisy and bureaucratic ineptitude.

Of course, the UN's public information program failed. However, to focus just on the public information program would be like counting the proverbial placement of deck chairs on the sinking *Titanic*. No public information – regardless of its slickness – can shore up the image of such a contradictory body. Also, as Chapter 2 has already shown, the UN labored for many years – and had the paper trail to prove it – on trying to find ways of improving its public image and promoting its causes. Kofi Annan's clever courting of American corporate and entertainment celebrity at the end of the century was just the latest stage of that search. The organization's resort to propaganda was actually a contradiction itself, and it is to that question that the next chapter will now turn.

4
Good Propaganda, Bad Propaganda

Although in some Romance languages the word "propaganda" means "advertising" and does not necessarily have the pejorative meaning it has in English, the concept is the type of problem in international relations that encourages sarcasm. "One man's 'truth' is another man's 'propaganda'", the saying goes, and the implication is that propaganda is an issue that will most likely never be satisfactorily resolved. However, as was discussed in Chapter 1, propaganda became a standard means of conducting international relations in the twentieth century, spurred on by technological developments in psychology, mass media and in the conduct of war. And because something described as "propaganda" has been blamed for provoking conflict, it was declared illegal under international law even before the UN was established. For this reason questions about how the DPI should avoid being propagandist were a consistent feature of bureaucratic ruminations over policy during the first half-century of the department's life. The Technical Advisory Committee that recommended the creation of the DPI in 1946 actually said the department "should not engage in 'propaganda'", even though it did not define the concept.[1] So this book must pay substantial attention to the question of propaganda because from the start it was evident that the DPI could play some role in international political and legal discourses on the subject.

The specific question is: How do we resolve the contradiction between the UN's prohibition of propaganda as a threat to world peace and its own "public information" activities that seem in many cases to be examples of propaganda? This is a very important question because the UN (like all international organizations) has never enjoyed unquestioned global acceptance, and for many its public information program is a propaganda scheme. This chapter will tackle the question by first exploring the international legal discourse on propaganda. It will then examine how the UN has defined propaganda. Based on that foundation will be an analysis of the UN's assumptions that led it to believe that its public information work is not propagandist. From there will be a comparison of two public information

93

campaigns – on human rights and anti-apartheid – to show how these assumptions about propaganda operate in actual policy. The chapter will conclude by explaining how the contradiction should be resolved based on the preceding analysis.

Propaganda and international law

From its origins in the "Congregation of the Propaganda", a committee of cardinals in charge of foreign missions, founded by Pope Gregory XV in 1622, right up to the time of the modern states system, propaganda was not a pejorative English term. Its pejorative connotations did not begin until the First and Second World Wars. However, Martin identifies two international treaties in the pre-First World War period, at the bilateral level, that specifically proscribed behavior that could be described as propagandistic – an 1801 treaty between Russia and France, and an 1881 treaty between Austria–Hungary and Serbia.[2] But in the twentieth century there was considerable multilateral attention to propaganda and efforts to create international laws against it, as propaganda became an increasingly more critical dimension of international relations for the reasons discussed in Chapter 1. William Preston has identified a number of the multilateral measures taken during the period between the two World Wars to deal with the increasing problem of propaganda.[3] For example, group libel became a recognized aspect of international law; the Kellogg-Briand Pact of 1928 that outlawed war also implied that incitement to war was criminal; an international right of reply was favored by the International Juridical Congress in 1929 and by the International Federation of Journalists in 1934; and the League of Nations established "Radio Nations" to foster mutual understanding and good will.

Ploman's seminal collection, *International Law Governing Communication and Information: A Collection of Basic Documents*,[4] does not identify international law regarding propaganda as a topic in its own right in either the table of contents or the index. It is subsumed under laws regarding "Security and Disarmament" and "Media Regulation". This is symbolic of how propaganda has generally appeared in international political and legal discourses – as a phenomenon subsidiary to larger problems, usually maintaining the peace, and usually considered a factor promoting international friction.

The "International Convention Concerning the Use of Broadcasting in the Cause of Peace" was the closest the League of Nations came to creating a body of international law that attempted to specifically proscribe international propaganda. This was signed by 28 states on 23 September 1936, and went into force on 2 April 1938.[5] The three Axis powers and the US did not sign the convention, on the grounds that their media were private and media houses could only be asked to volunteer. Article 1 said the signatory states "mutually undertake to prohibit and, if occasion arises, to stop without delay the broadcasting within their respective territories of any transmission which to the detriment of good international understanding is of such a character as to incite the population of any territory to acts incompatible with the internal order or the security of a territory of [another signatory state]". Article 2 further stated that the states would "ensure that transmissions from stations within their respective territories shall not constitute an incitement either to war against another [signatory] or to acts likely to lead thereto". The subsequent articles endorsed the principle of prior restraint, and undertakings to correct errors, broadcast the truth and collaborate in the exchange of positive information. The convention recognized that not all international broadcasters were state run, and in Article 6 the signatories agreed to put in place domestic policies that would ensure compliance with the obligations of the document by both state and non-state broadcasters. Article 7 identified a number of means by which disputes arising from the convention could be settled, including through the Permanent Court of International Justice, an arbitral tribunal, and the International Committee on Intellectual Cooperation (see the full text of the convention in Appendix I).

The shortcomings of the convention began with its inadequate definition of what actions would "incite the population of any territory to acts incompatible with the internal order or the security of a territory". Presumably that would be the task of the institutions settling disputes. Another weakness of the convention was that it did not have any penalties for violators. Also, as Finland pointed out at the time of signing, it was likely that the document would not have a very practical impact on international relations because those signing and ratifying it would be those most likely not to violate its principles even if there were no convention.[6]

Indeed, Germany did not sign the convention, and it was Nazi propaganda use in the Second World War, under the direction of Hitler's propaganda minister Josef Goebbels, that solidified the pejorative connotations to the term "propaganda".[7] It is understandable, therefore, why there was some sentiment at the new United Nations to curb the practice.

The foundation for the UN's approach to propaganda was laid by General Assembly Resolution 110(II), of 3 November 1947, that echoed the 1936 convention's prohibition of hostile propaganda – still without defining it but at least using the explicit term "propaganda" (see Appendix III). The resolution condemned "all forms of propaganda, in whatsoever country conducted, which is either designed or likely to provoke or encourage any threat to the peace, breach of the peace, or act of aggression". But most significant is the resolution's espousing of the idea that has been the most characteristic of post-Second World War political and legal discourses on the subject – the recognition that some types of propaganda could actually help to preserve international order and should be promoted. It requested:

> ... the Government of each Member to take appropriate steps within its constitutional limits:
> (a) To promote, by all means of publicity and propaganda available to them, friendly relations among nations based upon the Purposes and Principles of the Charter;
> (b) To encourage the dissemination of all information designed to give expression to the undoubted desire of all people for peace ...

The resolution was passed with the explicit intention of it being communicated to the 1948 United Nations Conference on Freedom of Information. In its Final Act, this conference not only specifically endorsed UN Resolution 110(II) but repeated verbatim the description of bad propaganda being information "either designed or likely to provoke or encourage any threat to the peace, breach of the peace, or act of aggression" (see Appendix IV).

In the Final Act, the discourse on propaganda was expanded in four ways. First, the labeling of what I call "bad propaganda" was lengthened to include false or distorted news, and the idea of how such bad propaganda threatened the international order was made more explicit. So Resolution 2 of the Final Act condemned "all propaganda either designed or likely to provoke or encourage any threat to the peace, breach of the peace, or act of aggression, and all distortion and falsification of news through whatever channels, private or governmental, since such activities can only promote misunderstanding and mistrust between the peoples of the world and thereby endanger the lasting peace which the United Nations is consecrated to maintain".

Second, the discourse on propaganda was made more specific by the Final Act identifying the news media – not just government-owned broadcasters or other media – as being the most important in the battle against bad propaganda. And Nazi and fascist propaganda were specifically identified as being particularly offensive. So Resolution 2 said the conference:

> [a]ppeals vigorously to the personnel of the Press and other agencies of information of the countries of the world, and to those responsible for their activities, to serve the aims of friendship, understanding and peace by accomplishing their task in a spirit of accuracy, fairness and responsibility;
> Expresses its profound conviction that only organs of information in all countries of the world that are free to seek and to disseminate the truth, and thus to carry out their responsibility to the people, can greatly contribute to the counteracting of nazi, fascist or any other propaganda of aggression of racial, national and religious discrimination and to the prevention of recurrence of nazi, fascist, or any other aggression; and
> Therefore recommends that all countries take within their respective territories the measures which they consider necessary to give effect to this resolution.

Third, the Final Act paid special attention to propaganda instilling racial hatred. This theme would become a constant feature of United Nations political and legal discourse in later years, especially in the late 1970s and 1980s when the propaganda of the South African apartheid regime was condemned and the United Nations Department of Public Information was mobilized to counteract it.

Fourth, as did General Assembly Resolution 110(II), the Final Act recognized a role for what I call "good propaganda". But the language of the Final Act made explicit the idea that good propaganda fit into the liberal-democratic notion that a free and open flow of information fostered a marketplace of ideas in which the good would be accepted and bad rejected. Therefore, Resolution 4 said that:

> Considering that there are in some countries media of information which disseminate racial and national hatred,
> The United Nations Conference on Freedom of Information
> Recommends that the Governments of such countries should:
> (a) Encourage the widest possible dissemination of free information through a diversity of sources as the best safeguard against the creation of racial and national hatred and prejudice;
> (b) Encourage, in consultation with organizations or journalists, suitable and effective non-legislative measures against the dissemination of such hatred and prejudice; and
> (c) Take, within their constitutional limits, appropriate measures to encourage the dissemination of information promoting friendly relations between races and nations based upon the purposes and principles of the United Nations Charter.

The four points identified above formed the kernel of ideas about propaganda at the United Nations, and these were not modified in the succeeding 50 years. All significant UN treaties, resolutions and other sources of international law either referred to General Assembly Resolution 110(II) explicitly or repeated ideas about good and bad propaganda found in the 1948 Final Act. All that changed in the subsequent 50 years was that the ideas were directly applied to specific desiderata, such as the maintenance of human rights, ending apartheid in South Africa, and in the development of rules governing transnational television broadcasting via satellite.

The International Covenant on Civil and Political Rights (1966) mentions propaganda in Article 20 where it says:

> 1. Any propaganda for war shall be prohibited by law.
> 2. Any advocacy of national, racial or religious hatred that constitutes incitement to discrimination, hostility or violence shall be prohibited by law.

The 1967 Outer Space Treaty (officially called the "Treaty on principles governing the Activities of states in the Exploration and use of Outer Space,

Including the Moon and Other Celestial Bodies") mentions the 1947 resolution by name in its preamble, saying it is "applicable to outer space". This approach to propaganda was also implicit in the principles governing the operation of direct broadcast satellites set out by the General Assembly in 1982 because those principles were based on the Outer Space Treaty (see Appendix VI). Number four of the Principles was as follows:

> Activities in the field of international direct television broadcasting by satellite should be conducted in accordance with international law, including the Charter of the United Nations, the Treaty on Principles Governing the Activities of States in the Exploration and Use of Outer Space, including the Moon and Other Celestial Bodies, of 27 January 1967, the relevant provisions of the International Telecommunication Convention and its Radio Regulations and of International instruments relating to friendly relations and co-operation among States and to human rights.[8]

The recognition of good propaganda is implicit in the second and third paragraphs of the list of the principles, which say DBS broadcasting:

> should promote the free dissemination and mutual exchange of information and knowledge in cultural and scientific fields, assist in educational, social and economic development, particularly in the developing countries, enhance the qualities of life of all peoples and provide recreation with due respect to the political and cultural integrity of States.
>
> 3. These activities should accordingly be carried out in a manner compatible with the development of mutual understanding and the strengthening of friendly relations and co-operation among all States and peoples in the interest of maintaining international peace and security.

UNESCO's Mass Media Declaration of 1978 not only mentions Resolution 110(II) by name, but identifies "racialism" and "apartheid" in its official title as evils to be countered by the media.[9] According to Article III:

> In countering aggressive war, racialism, apartheid and other violations of human rights which are *inter alia* spawned by prejudice and ignorance, the mass media by disseminating information on the aims, aspirations, cultures and needs of all peoples contribute to eliminate ignorance and misunderstanding between peoples, to make nations of a country sensitive to the needs and desires of others, to ensure the respect of the rights and dignity of all nations, all peoples and all individuals without distinction of race, sex, language, religion or nationality and to draw attention to the great evils which afflict humanity, such as poverty, malnutrition and diseases, thereby promoting the formulation by States of the policies best able to promote the reduction of international tension and the peaceful and equitable settlement of international disputes.

The prospect of regulating international propaganda by multilateral agreement was particularly contentious because it required a delicate balancing act between two significant principles of the post-Second World War order – the free flow of information, and national sovereignty. A number of international instruments proclaimed freedom of information regardless of frontiers, such as Article 19 of the Universal Declaration of Human Rights, Article 10 of the European Convention on Human Rights, Article 4 of the American Declaration on the Rights and Duties of Man, and the Declaration of Principles in the Final Act of the Helsinki Conference on Security and Co-operation in Europe. But, as the UK pointed out during the deliberations of the Committee on the Peaceful Uses of Outer Space, the absolute right to freedom of information does not exist. In all countries the right is moderated by "rules and regulations, and these rules and regulations not only vary from country to country but sometimes also vary from province to province within the same State, because what is acceptable in a given community might not be acceptable in a neighbouring community, depending on variations in moral and cultural patterns".[10] These legal realities notwithstanding, the idea of regulating propaganda seemed more unviable as new technologies, such as satellites and the Internet, obviated territorial borders and national legal enforcement.

Propaganda and the UN

Although there will always be disputes over what exactly is an example of propaganda, the international legal discourse described above makes it clear that the post-Second World War peace system – of which the UN is the centerpiece – views propaganda as a form of information dissemination that involves a specific intent in relation to the publics of the international system. Communication that the UN (or those in charge of deciding international law) views as having benign intentions is what I call "good propaganda", but it is often not called propaganda at all by the UN. Communication that those parties view as threatening the values of the order they maintain is deemed propaganda – what I call "bad propaganda".

Because the UN was established to promote principles that would actually be antidotes to the racist and other types of inflammatory propaganda that helped ignite and encouraged the Second World War it has always been very sensitive to conducting propaganda of its own or being perceived as doing such. Therefore even though the infant organization made a de facto department of propaganda one of its very first main functional parts, the document that set out the department's purpose said it "should not engage in 'propaganda'". This contradiction was so immediately obvious that one of the first assessments of the UN's public information program sought to make clear that the prohibition on propaganda did not mean the DPI would not engage in communication work with a specific intent. It was just that UN public information work would be based on "impartiality" and "objectivity." According to the 1952 report:

> ...the prohibition against engaging in "propaganda" as stated in the open-ing paragraph [of the Technical Advisory Committee's 1946 recommen-dations] should not be interpreted as in any way limiting the Department's mandate actively to promote public understanding and knowledge of the aims and activities in the United Nations. It is intended, rather, to refer to propaganda in the commonly accepted sense of the term as implying a bias in contradistinction to a policy of strict impartiality and objectivity in the presentation of news and information.[11]

In depicting its propaganda work as somehow not being biased and as common-sense ideas for running the world, the UN was not unlike all pro-pagandists. Propagandists would prefer that everyone see their approach to events as normal and what they disseminate as mere "information". So, as was noted in Chapter 2, Secretary-General U Thant described the DPI as nothing more than an "international information service". A 1971 report from the Secretary-General said the DPI produced "programmes aimed at explanation and clarification and not exhortation", and the DPI promoted only "universally approved causes and movements" and would be careful to not cross "the 'boundary' separating it from propaganda or promotion".[12] In the same vein, a 1972 document from the UN's leadership said the public information policy would concentrate on problems that required interna-tional co-operation, and would "adhere strictly to the principles of 'univer-sality' and 'objectivity'", and target opinion elites, such as "specialist press, schools, universities, professions, non-governmental organizations".[13]

But even while the UN was making such contradictory pronouncements on its public information policy, an evaluation by UN outsiders was express-ing incredulity and exasperation at the lengths the UN was going to in order to avoid being labeled a propagandist. A 1972 study of the UN's relations with the news media, carried out for the United Nations Institute for Training and Research (UNITAR), raised the question of whether the UN would even suffer an image crisis from being more forthright about its propaganda pro-gram. According to the report, the UN was less accused by reporters of being propagandistic than of issuing useless press releases characterized by vague bureaucratic language. The UNITAR report criticized the vagueness of the prohibition on propaganda in the DPI's guiding principles:

> They give no guidelines whatever with regard to those positive informa-tional activities in which the United Nations simply has to engage in order to propagate – or if another word is preferred – in order to promote many constructive ideas, programmes, and resolutions *approved* by its membership. The success of such ideas, programmes and resolutions

often depends quite directly on the widest range of popular understanding and support which can only be achieved by the most purposeful and effective promotional activities. United Nations programmes and projects in the field of socio-economic development, human rights, health and welfare, etc., provide many pertinent examples, and the number and scope of such programmes and projects in need of active promotion (often undertaken for the sake of acquiring voluntary contributions for their financing) is steadily growing.[14]

The UNITAR study said the task of promoting specific causes while at the same time supplying objective information was not as difficult as it might seem. It pointed out that "there is no reason why the United Nations cannot, as a newspaper does in its news columns as distinguished from its editorial columns, carry out both roles".[15]

This inability to admit and declare that the UN was maintaining a propaganda program to fashion world public opinion had two severe consequences for the organization. First it compromised the very policy-making process of the DPI because the only type of evaluation of policy impact the department was allowed to do was the collection of data on its information production and the demand for its output, not an assessment of exactly how the DPI was a player in changing the course of international politics[16] (see Chapter 2). Second it left the Secretariat vulnerable to controversies similar to that over the "World Newspaper Supplement" described in Chapter 3; when the UN needed to promote policies that were controversial it was reduced to paying prestigious newspapers to publish articles without the warning label that they were paid advertising.

The 1997 Task Force on the Reorientation of United Nations Public Information Activities called on the DPI to abandon a strategy of passive "institutional communication" for "strategic communication" that would "mobilize public and specialist opinion on behalf of the United Nations".[17] The Task Force even used the term "public diplomacy" – a euphemism for the propaganda work of states (see Chapter 1) – to describe the type of policy needed. However, in the few years following the Task Force's proposals there was plenty of evidence of the fear that still existed at the UN about associations with propaganda, and the UN still could not bring itself to embrace "strategic communication". As has already been pointed out in Chapter 2, the Secretary-General's "Millennium Report" that was issued in March 2000 for the Millennium Assembly of the world's political leaders made no explicit reference to the public information role of the UN in the three strategic priority areas identified, despite its focus on the role of public opinion and the communication revolution in global society. That year, members of the Joint United Nations Information Committee (JUNIC) "raised the issue of the distinction between public information and advocacy, and agreed on the need to discuss that matter in more depth".[18] The UN's *Medium-Term Plan for the*

Period 2002–2005 (a document published in 2001) said the UN's public information program aimed simply "to increase awareness and understanding of the work and purposes of the United Nations among peoples of the world".[19]

UN propaganda: two case studies

So although the full range of the DPI's work can be described as a propaganda campaign – not all members of international society embrace the UN's principles and practices for maintaining world order – it has only been in the case of "universally approved causes and movements", or "future of the world" issues that the UN would declare its hand on propaganda. In 1971 these types of topics were listed as "economic and social development, promotion of human rights, decolonization, elimination of racial discrimination and ... protection of the human environment".[20] The list in 1977 was "disarmament, food, health, environment, industrialization, trade, racial discrimination and meeting the basic needs of the poorest groups in developing countries within the framework of a new international economic order".[21] These are all issues around which the UN has been able to build a fair amount of rhetorical consensus. The qualifier of "rhetorical" is used because while many states have supported resolutions on these issues in principle, they have often made exceptions in practice; for example the Soviet Union's tolerance of anti-Semitism, or the United States' support of the South African apartheid regime. Economic development and the fight against racial discrimination appear on both lists, a testament to how long they have been a focus of UN propaganda campaigns. However, by the end of the twentieth century some issues had receded due to the evolution of international politics. This was the case with decolonization. With others – such as trade and disarmament – the international discourse had evolved to the point where an array of new questions and institutions were created by the end of the century. For example, a World Trade Organization (WTO) was created, and by 2000 was the focus for much of the criticism of "globalization" and "neo-liberalism".

The most basic propaganda strategy used by the United Nations to rally opinion around a cause is to name a day, year or month after the issue and conduct a number of activities during that time period. Tables 4.1 and 4.2 are listings of how the UN has used this particular type of what I call "calendar propaganda". The list is not only an indication of the kinds of issues the UN has considered important to the welfare of humanity but also relatively safe topics for it to tackle. In the attempt to illustrate how the UN's assumptions about propaganda manifest themselves in actual policy, this chapter could have examined several of those on the list, but the cases of human rights and anti-apartheid have been selected because the two campaigns spanned almost the entire history of the organization in the twentieth century.

Table 4.1   UN-designated International Years

Starting in 1959 the UN designated International Years to draw attention
to major issues and to encourage international action to address concerns
that have global importance and ramifications. This is a chronological list
of years designated by 2000.

1959/60	World Refugee Year
1965	International Cooperation Year
1967	International Tourism Year
1968	International Year for Human Rights
1970	International Education Year
1971	International Year for Action to Combat Racism & Racial Discrimination
1974	World Population Year
1975	International Women's Year
1978	International Anti-Apartheid Year
1979	International Year of the Child
1981	International Year of Disabled Persons
1982	International Year of Mobilization for Sanctions Against South Africa
1983	World Communications Year
1985	International Youth Year
1986	International Year of Peace
1987	International Year of Shelter for the Homeless
1990	International Literacy Year
1992	International Space Year (endorsed, not declared)
1993	International Year for World's Indigenous People
1994	International Year of the Family
1994	International Year of Sport & Olympic Ideal
1995	United Nations Year for Tolerance
1995	World Year of People's Commemoration of the Victims of the Second World War
1996	International Year for the Eradication of Poverty
1998	International Year of the Ocean
1999	International Year of Older Persons
1999	Centennial of the First International Peace Conference
2000	International Year for the Culture of Peace
2000	International Year of Thanksgiving
2001	International Year of Volunteers
2001	United Nations Year of Dialogue among Civilizations
2001	International Year of Mobilization against Racism, Racial Discrimination, Xenophobia and Related Intolerance
2002	International Year of Mountains
2002	International Year of Ecotourism
2005	International Year of Microcredit

Table 4.2   UN-designated International Decades

1965–74	International Hydrological Decade
1970–80	International Decade of Ocean Exploration
1973–83	First Decade to Combat Racism and Racial Discrimination
1976–85	United Nations Decade for Women
1980s	Second Disarmament Decade
1981–90	International Drinking Water Supply and Sanitation Decade
1983–92	United Nations Decade of Disabled Persons
1983–93	Second Decade to Combat Racism and Racial Discrimination
1988–97	World Decade for Cultural Development
1990–99	United Nations Decade of International Law
1990–2000	International Decade for the Eradication of Colonialism
1991–2000	Fourth United Nations Development Decade
1991–2000	Second Transport and Communications Decade in Africa
1991–2000	United Nations Decade Against Drug Abuse
1990s	International Decade for Natural Disaster Reduction
1990s	Third Disarmament Decade
1993–2002	Second Industrial Development Decade for Africa
1993–2002	Asian and Pacific Decade for Disabled Persons
1993–2003	Third Decade to Combat Racism and Racial Discrimination
1995–2004	International Decade for the World's Indigenous People
1995–2004	United Nations Decade for Human Rights Education
1997–2006	United Nations Decade for the Eradication of Poverty
2001–2010	International Decade for a Culture of Peace and Non-Violence for the Children of the World

The long track-record of the UN in these two cases provides fertile ground for a more comprehensive analysis than might be the case with campaigns of shorter duration. Also, the nature of the issue areas presents contrasting types of propaganda campaigns. The UN's human rights agitation was based on a contested project of universality and had a global focus, while the anti-apartheid campaign had an almost singular focus on the pariah state of South Africa and was to a large extent a counter-propaganda campaign.

Propagating human rights

It has been common to mistake internationalism (a concept that was introduced and examined in Chapter 1) with the related concept of universality. However, while universality is the baby of internationalism, not all internationalism is a project in universality. It is therefore important to note that the advocacy of universal human rights is both a project of internationalism and universality.

Universality is the idea that the values promoted by a specific set of interests, states or entities (that are only part of the world, or even a minority of it) can be held by, and applied to, all members of the international system of states. Writers on this issue often use the term "universalism" to mean universality.[22] But the term "universality" that is preferred by some writers on the subject[23] should be used to make clear its distinction from Universalist Christian beliefs, a doctrine that predated the UN and refers to a different system of beliefs.

The more decolonization progressed and the membership of the United Nations expanded, the more its pretensions at universality were challenged and became a problem. Two cases in point were the controversies at the United Nations Educational, Scientific and Cultural Organization (UNESCO) over a proposed New World Information and Communication Order (NWICO), and the international discourse on human rights.

In explaining the problem at UNESCO, Pierre de Senarclens described the scene in 1945 when the Conference of Allied Ministers of Education agreed to create UNESCO. He then explained why the universality promoted in 1945 became besieged later. Of 1945 he said:

> Never were the beliefs and hopes underpinning the birth of the UN system more completely shared. Never before at an intergovernmental conference was there such fervor or were intellectuals and governmental delegates gathered together in such single-minded harmony. The East–West rift had not as yet taken on the form of the cold war, and the fact that the Soviet Union stood aside favored unanimity at the Conference. Representatives of the colonized peoples were almost totally absent. The political universe appeared to be identical with the values and the social and political aspirations of the Western world. The liberal order had been restored by the Allied victory. It seemed more secure than ever. Progressive ideology, having triumphed over fascism, appeared to be so dominant that it was believed to be universal.[24]

But of the later controversies that led to the US, the UK and Singapore quitting the UNESCO, de Senarclens said they were a reflection of

> ...the universal ambitions that underlie the entire UN system. If liberal civilization continues to dominate the world through the strength of its economy, its science, and its technology; through the preponderance of its values and objects of consumption; and by its political and military power as well; its ideology and the order of legitimacy it presents are everywhere suspect and in decline. In several spheres of international society, the principles of political and social organization – legitimated by ideologies of the secular liberal-democratic sort founded on the separation of powers and the rule of law and the preponderance of individualistic, if not actually hedonistic, values – have become unacceptable and clash profoundly with traditions and established cultural norms. They are considered all the more intolerable in that they seem to be subversive to those systems of authority and power that exist in the majority of member states

of the UN system. In the majority of Third World countries – in Africa especially – the representative institutions and the systems of public administration bequeathed by Western colonialism were very rapidly relinquished and rejected in the decolonization process.[25]

On the specific issue of human rights, Renteln has pointed out that the literature on how human rights are actually conceived has been very slim. The presumption of universality

> ... is the belief that human rights exist independent of culture, ideology, and value systems. This absolutistic perspective is found particularly among philosophers and legal theorists. Even when scholars acknowledge that human-rights norms appear to be Western, they nevertheless assert their universality. This is a peculiar form of ethnocentrism insofar as Western ideas are presumed to be ubiquitous.[26]

Examples from Articles 16 and 21 of the Universal Declaration of Human Rights (UDHR) illustrate how, upon closer examination, the specifics of what is meant by "human rights" in the various parts of the international bill of human rights are a source of controversy. Article 16 states that everyone has "the right to marry and found a family" regardless of race, nationality or religion, and that "the family is the natural and fundamental group unit of society". However, this suggestion that the Western-type nuclear family is the norm flies in the face of perhaps most societies around the world where extended families are customary. The Article's assertion that there should be marriage "only with the free and full consent of the intending spouses" also runs counter to cultures where there are arranged marriages. In addition, at a time when homosexuals in various parts of the world have become more vocal in asserting their "rights", this Article of the UDHR seems out of date because it suggests a preference for the traditional institution of heterosexual marriage.

Article 21 states that people have a right to participate in the governments that rule them, and that their will "shall be expressed in periodic and genuine elections which shall be by universal and equal suffrage and shall be held by secret vote or by equivalent free voting procedures". This is a prescription for a Western European or North American form of liberal democracy. Even in countries that are strong allies of the United States, France and the other members of the Western alliance, such forms of government do not exist. Some examples are monarchies, such as Jordan and Saudi Arabia, communist governments, such as the People's Republic of China, and have various different electoral systems, such as Australia where the electorate is compelled to vote by law (so the voting procedures are not necessarily "free"). Renteln summed up the problems with this Article by noting that: "it is ethnocentric to assume that Western electoral procedures are unanimously favored".[27]

This ethnocentrism and Eurocentrism in international human rights law also appears in intellectual discourses on the topic. The problem can be illustrated by the example of how American communication scholar William H. Meyer discusses the ecology of the concept of "human rights". Meyer asserts that "many human rights emerged first in the West". However, later in his paper he points to scholarship that argues that precolonial African societies had recognized several categories of rights.[28] Similarly, he concentrates exclusively on what happened in Europe during the Second World War to explain why there was "the rapid growth of the postwar rights campaign". The failure to consider resistance to imperialism and colonialism is stunning, in light of the fact that Meyer notes later in the paper that both international human rights covenants in the international bill of human rights (see below) begin "by recognizing the right of all peoples to self-determination", a right that is not even in the Universal Declaration of Human Rights.[29] What actually happened was that between 1948 and 1966 (when the covenants were adopted by the General Assembly), UN membership had been greatly expanded due to decolonization. These new states (with their very recent histories of imperialism and colonialism) and the Soviet Bloc, lobbied for making self-determination a right through which peoples (according to the texts of both covenants) "freely determine their political status and freely pursue their economic, social and cultural development".[30] Of course, the Soviet Union's own history of denying that "right" is a contradiction that is self-evident.

The UN has been the actor in international politics most responsible for promoting human rights as perhaps the most prominent dimension of the broader project of universality. It has done this through legal, bureaucratic and propaganda means. The legal measures centered on the creation of an international bill of human rights (IBHR) and then getting recognition of those principles by all members of the international system. The IBHR is made up of the UDHR, the International Covenant on Civil and Political Rights (ICCPR) and the International Covenant on Economic, Social and Cultural Rights (ICESCR). The UDHR is not legally binding on states, but the two covenants are for all the states that accede to them, even though they allow derogations. The UN seeks compliance with the international law of human rights. The bureaucratic measures have been the construction of institutions for propagating the notion of human rights, investigating human rights abuses and facilitating the continuing international discourse on human rights. By the end of the century the most well-known part of that bureaucracy was the United Nations High Commissioner for Human Rights, a post established following 1993's World Conference on Human Rights in Vienna. The High Commissioner is part of the top brass of the UN and reports directly to the Secretary-General. Basically, he or she co-ordinates the organization's activities in the field of human rights and is the voice of the UN on the subject. The two other key parts of the UN's human rights bureaucracy at the end of the century were the UN Human Rights Committee and the UN Commission on Human Rights. The committee – a group of experts in the field – was created to monitor the implementation of the International Covenant on Civil and Political Rights and its protocols. The commission – a political body comprised of states – existed to monitor and report on human rights compliance in individual countries and on threats to human rights globally.

The UN's activities in relation to the issue have been described as nothing less than a "global human rights campaign".[31] American scholar William Over says that what the UN has tried to do in relation to human rights is create an international culture that "must be inherently pluralistic and universal, with, for the first time in human history, a vision of global harmony based on a shared communicative understanding". Over explains that the UN

> ...functions largely as a symbolic theatre where human rights are researched and analyzed, taught, broadcast, and monitored (every Member State must present a human rights progress report and answer charges against it). Although this approach has been attacked regularly as a mere "debating society," and certainly its enforcement arm would be more significant if the powerful Member States chose to support it, the UN has from its beginning explicitly called for persuasive means to change the underlying causes of human rights abuse...[32]

Since the passage of the UDHR in 1948, this campaign has included the negotiation, drafting and passage of the two covenants; promoting and assisting in the creation of regional human rights treaties; developing methods of securing human rights compliance; and focusing world attention on victims of human rights abuse. In addition, Article 55 of the UN Charter says that all members of the UN must "promote universal respect for and observance of human rights and fundamental freedoms". So whenever a state becomes a member of the United Nations it in effect signs up to the UN's idea of human rights and pledges to respect those rights.

The DPI's specific role in the international discourse on human rights comprises two main functions: to explain what the rights are, and to tell the world what the UN is doing in relation to these rights. It carries out these two basic tasks in a number of ways:

- publishing the texts of the various components of the International Bill of Human Rights;
- promoting activity around various UN days, years and decades, through posters, media programs and conferences;
- exploiting the prominence of celebrities, such as through the UN Goodwill Ambassador program;
- developing programs for young people so that they can be exposed to these ideas at a young age; and
- facilitating wide coverage of instances when interest groups appeal to the UN for help in promoting and protecting their rights.

A traditional view at the Secretariat of regarding non-governmental organizations (NGOs) as being most useful for propagating the UN's position on issues also meant that the DPI, from 1968, was given the task by the Economic and Social Council of managing the daily relations between the Secretariat and NGOs. As will be discussed in detail in Chapter 5, attitudes towards NGOs at the Secretariat became more complex in the 1990s. However, the DPI continued to devote much resources and attention to interfacing with NGOs on the premise that they are key dimensions of the expanding international civil society. Indeed, in the 1990s NGOs (such as Amnesty International and the Committee to Protect Journalists) were arguably often more prominent in advocacy and educational work to promote respect for human rights around the world than was the UN itself.[33]

To mark the adoption of the UDHR by the General Assembly on 10 December 1948, that date every year is promoted by the UN as "Human Rights Day". In addition, the UN has also celebrated the "International Year for Human Rights" (1968), and it has declared a "United Nations Decade for Human Rights Education" (1995–2004).[34] In 1993, the UN held an international conference on human rights. In an address for Human Rights Day 2000, the General Assembly President, Harri Holkeri of Finland, said the UDHR had been translated into more than 300 languages, "making it the most translated document in the world".[35]

The program for Human Rights Day 1997 was an example of the kind of events run by the UN and publicized by the DPI, and was meant to focus media and public attention on human rights. The UN held a special program in New York to launch a year of events celebrating the fiftieth anniversary of the UDHR. Giving speeches were the United States First Lady Hillary Rodham Clinton; Executive Director of the UN Population Fund (UNFPA) Nafis Sadik; UN Secretary-General Kofi Annan; UN High Commissioner for Human Rights Mary Robinson; then General Assembly President Hennadiy Udovenko of the Ukraine; and Assistant Secretary-General for Public Information Samir Sanbar. Sanbar presented Mrs. Clinton with a photograph of Eleanor Roosevelt holding the original UDHR. The same day an exhibit on human rights was opened in the public lobby of UN headquarters, and there was a panel discussion on human rights at the UN, which featured Nobel literature prizewinner Wole Soyinka who was a victim of harassment by the Nigerian government. Earlier that week, UN headquarters was also the venue for a two-day roundtable on human rights.[36] In April that year the DPI had organized "The Roundtable on Communication for the Promotion of Peace, Development, Democracy and Respect for Human Rights and Fundamental Freedoms in the Global Village", a conference at Columbia University, New York. About 40 media practioners, industry executives, communications theorists and policy-makers from several countries attended. There were panels on such topics as expanding independent and pluralistic media, and the role of mass media in improving the human condition.[37] Two years later the Human Rights Day program at UN headquarters featured a "Student Conference on Human Rights and the Culture of Peace of the New Millennium".

By the end of the century, the UN's activities in relation to human rights could be described as threefold: legal (creating international human rights law); bureaucratic (creating an infrastructure for discussion and documentation); and propagandistic (working with NGOs and governments at making the world aware of the concept and shaming those who did not recognize human rights). The propaganda role was perhaps the most successful of the three. It had succeeded in making human rights part of the common-sense of international affairs by the end of the century. Ethnic minorities, indigenous peoples, women, the economically exploited and other oppressed groups used the international law and various UN documents to support their claims to fair treatment. Human rights seemed as natural as the physical environment, one of the basic parts of any domestic or international society that claimed to be "civil" or "civilized". This was so despite the notable reservations made by Asian countries. Asia was the only area not to have a regional human rights convention by the end of the century, and in response to the 1993 UN World Human Rights Conference in Vienna some Asian states issued the Bangkok Declaration that took exception to universality on the question of human rights. However, this action was indication in itself of how powerful the propagation of human rights had become, because even those who disagreed with the UN's approach could not ignore it and still felt obligated to respond to it.

Human rights also became woven into the fabric of international politics as a particularly effective tool to exert pressure on certain states or non-state actors. For example, in 2000 the Organization for Economic Cooperation and Development (OECD) revived its guidelines on multinational business, including a section on the need for transnational corporations to respect human rights, including eliminating child labor and forced labor.[38] Similarly, the government of the People's Republic of China was under pressure (especially from the United States) to improve its human rights record before it was finally approved for admission to the WTO in 2001.[39] The rhetoric on human rights was often similar to that of Mexican President Vicente Fox when he explained his administration's support of a UN Commission on Human Rights resolution urging Cuba to allow greater political rights. Fox declared that human rights "are universal and are above political and ideological interests", that they "should be respected by all governments, by all societies and by all countries", and that they were "one of the bases of human civilization".[40]

Seen in the context of this book's analysis, the UN human rights campaign is by no means a project in safeguarding a set of rights that are self-evident. It originated in the power politics that founded the UN and is still a reflection of that power dynamic. It is tempting to think of the human rights project as internationalist, but the universality of its internationalism is vital to properly conceptualizing its place in international politics.

The public information program has been essential to the UN's human rights project because – in lieu of the ability to enforce compliance with international law – the production of human rights propaganda is the essence of the UN's role with respect to human rights.

When we look at the UN's human rights program as a propaganda campaign, it is easier to interrogate its relationship not only to the preservation of world peace but also to the creation of world conflict. Of course, this is a possibility that the UN might be reluctant to investigate, but it is a critical step in better understanding the UN's role in international politics and in refining its own policy formulation and planning.

Counter-propaganda: apartheid South Africa

Although the pace towards creating an apartheid system in South Africa did not speed up until after the 1948 elections in that country, in which the National Party gained a parliamentary majority, the question of racial discrimination in South Africa was raised by India at the very first session of the UN General Assembly. The apartheid regime never really had a prolonged period of peaceful relations with the UN because it resented the UN's attention to its racial policies, expressed that displeasure by maintaining only token representation at the General Assembly from the mid-1950s, and finally found itself expelled from the UN General Assembly in 1973.[41] It was only after non-racial elections and the taking of power of a majority government in 1994 that South Africa was welcomed back to the UN General Assembly. However, although anti-apartheid was one of those "universally approved causes and movements" that the DPI was given full license to propagate, the UN's counter-propaganda war against the minority regime was often foiled by support the white government got from allies on the Security Council. So even though the defeat of apartheid has been hailed as one of the major achievements of the UN, the case study provides insight into the international politics of "good propaganda" and its limitations as a means of international reform.

The UN's propaganda war with South Africa was over the two main issues of racist government and South Africa's occupation of Namibia. In the new international order of the post-Second World War period, South Africa's blatantly pseudoscientific racist explanations for white domination were illegal according to international law and international support diminished as time went on. Also illegal was its occupation of the territory it called South-West Africa (named Namibia by the UN). South Africa was defending its rule over the territory in the face of a guerrilla war from the South-West Africa People's Organization (SWAPO) that was fighting for Namibian independence. It had also been put on the defensive when the International Court of Justice ruled in 1971 that South Africa's occupation was illegal, and in 1978 the UN Security Council had called for Namibian independence in Resolution 435.

The South African government insisted on the withdrawal of Cuban troops from neighboring Angola as a precondition to Namibian independence. The years of military conflict in Namibia (that involved UN non-military support for SWAPO) and the international propaganda war between South Africa and the UN, culminated with a plan agreed to by SWAPO, Angola, Cuba and South Africa in 1988. This required the withdrawal of Cuban forces from Angola and black majority rule in Namibia. Namibia became independent on 21 March 1990.

The opposition to apartheid was the classic safe issue for the UN to tackle because anti-apartheid sentiment had been expressed in General Assembly resolutions even before the mass decolonization of black African and Caribbean states in the 1960s and 1970s. Therefore, it could never be said that opposition to the racist government was solely a reflection of the special concerns of a bloc of non-white countries in the General Assembly because resolutions from the early 1950s stated that South Africa's policies were a clear contravention of the UN Charter because they violated human rights and were also a threat to international peace.[42]

The UN took two bureaucratic steps that were significant moves in the enhancement of its organizational ability to disseminate counter-propaganda on the issue. In 1962 the General Assembly created what eventually became known as the Special Committee Against Apartheid with the two main goals of: "(a) [t]o keep the racial policies of the Government of South Africa under review when the Assembly is not in session; [and] (b) [t]o report either to the Assembly or to the Security Council or to both, as may be appropriate, from time to time".[43] The second measure was the establishment in 1966 of a propaganda outfit within the Secretariat to focus directly on South Africa. The Unit On Apartheid, as it was called, was expanded into the Centre Against Apartheid in 1976. In 1973 the Unit's war chest was given a boost when the Trust Fund For Publicity Against Apartheid was created as a means of pooling voluntary contributions dedicated to the fight against apartheid.[44] Since 1965 the UN had also maintained a Trust Fund for South Africa to help those persecuted by the racist government in South Africa and Namibia. By 1988 that fund had attracted $32.4 million since its inception.[45]

UN anti-apartheid propaganda was almost of every conceivable type: daily programs in several South African languages produced by the DPI's radio service; posters; films on apartheid; exhibitions of art against apartheid; the promotion of the then-imprisoned Nelson Mandela as an international hero; records of freedom songs; events related to various parts of its calendar propaganda (such as the International Day for the Elimination of Racial Discrimination).[46] The UN also gave money to groups outside the UN that were involved in the effort to eliminate the racist government. For example, a $10 000 grant in 1988 gave life to "South Africa Now", a weekly counter-propaganda TV show in the US that ran from 1988 to 1991. The program

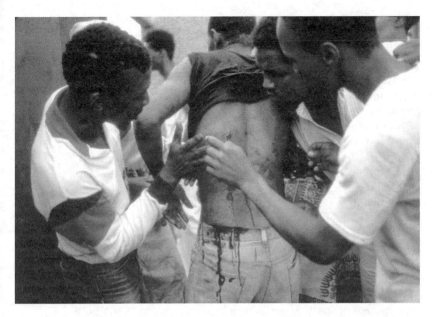

Figure 4.1 In 1985 this was one of the photos released by the United Nations to publicize the atrocities of the South African apartheid state. A black man displays the wounds he received after being attacked by police during a funeral for those killed by the same police force during an event to mark the International Day for the Elimination of Racial Discrimination.

sought to provide an alternative source of information, from the perspective of the oppressed in South Africa, to counter the racist government's propaganda and the reactionary coverage of the US network media.[47] The UN and its Specialized Agencies also included in their campaign against the racist government a program of recognition and assistance for the black organizations fighting against the apartheid regime, most notably SWAPO in Namibia, and the African National Congress (ANC) and Pan-Africanist Congress (PAC) of South Africa.

For most of the UN's existence in the twentieth century there was also a UN-led program to isolate the apartheid government as much as possible through sanctions and boycotts. The first economic sanctions were in 1962 when the General Assembly said UN member states should break all diplomatic and trading relations with South Africa. Various General Assembly resolutions condemned apartheid as a "crime against humanity", and the sanctions movement was expanded over the years. A voluntary arms embargo instituted by the Security Council in 1963 was made mandatory in 1977. The General Assembly adopted the international Convention Against Apartheid in Sports in 1985 that obliged states not to have sporting contacts with countries practicing apartheid.[48]

The counter-propaganda strategy most easily available to the General Assembly was the resolution condemning the apartheid government and its various practices. By the 1980s the passage of such resolutions became a ritual, and often the same resolution was passed in successive years. For example, General Assembly resolutions set out in great detail how the UN used every means available to counter South Africa's version of events in Namibia, and each one of these resolutions contained a section entitled "Dissemination of information and mobilization of international public opinion in support of the immediate independence of Namibia". That section of the resolutions passed by the 41st (1986–87), 42nd (1987–88) and 43rd (1988–89) General Assemblies used almost the same language each year.[49] Each resolution mentioned the word "propaganda" only once, and then only in reference to "the hostile propaganda and disinformation campaign of the racist regime of South Africa". Each explained how the UN would use the DPI to produce, inter alia, booklets, exhibitions, radio and television programs, advertising, news releases, posters, "media encounters", and even maps to counteract the South African government. But never was the term "propaganda" used as a label for the UN's activities.

The General Assembly resolutions on the "Policies of Apartheid of the Government of South Africa" were all passed between 1986 (the 40th General Assembly) and 1989.[50] This was the period during which events relating to the eventual demise of apartheid escalated. The resolutions condemned apartheid on human rights and security grounds, saying apartheid was "a crime against humanity and a threat to international peace and security". The resolution passed at the 43rd General Assembly in 1989 included an entire section describing UN counter-propaganda against apartheid. Radio programs were a prominent part of the campaign because broadcasting into South Africa could be done from neighboring countries and radio could reach a very large audience by overcoming the problem of illiteracy. Beginning in 1978, the UN collaborated with neighboring countries and broadcast into South Africa daily in the main languages spoken by South Africans – English, Afrikaans, Sesotho, Setswana, Xhosa and Zulu. According to the UN:

> The major theme of the programmes was the worldwide condemnation of apartheid, as well as the steady intensification of the international campaign against it. Within this framework, the programmes aimed at educating supporters of apartheid concerning their growing isolation, and at encouraging and reassuring the oppressed people and other opponents of apartheid about international solidarity with their cause. Well over 1,000 programmes were produced annually and sent to interested broadcasting organizations in many countries for broadcast to South Africa, where they could be heard throughout the country.[51]

By the 1980s the General Assembly was calling for the struggle against racist propaganda to take place at the level of domestic law as well, in line with the international law that was already in place. This posture was reflected in the General Assembly resolutions condemning "Nazi, Fascist and Neo-Fascist Activities and All Other Forms of Totalitarian Ideologies and Practices Based on Racial Intolerance, Hatred and Terror". Five of these resolutions passed during the 1980s mentioned propaganda explicitly. The 1986 and 1987 resolutions said propaganda by such intolerant groups was to be dealt with at the national level through national judicial systems. The resolutions invited member states to "adopt, in accordance with their national constitutional systems and with the provisions of the Universal Declaration of Human Rights and the International Covenants on Human Rights, as a matter of high priority, measures declaring punishable by law any dissemination of ideas based on racial superiority or hatred and of war propaganda, including Nazi, Fascist and neo-Fascist ideologies".[52]

The propaganda pressure on the South African government to change was also levied by various prestigious organizations honoring the opponents of apartheid. For example, prior to 1993, when the Nobel Peace Prize went to Nelson Mandela and South African President F. W. de Klerk for their work to finally end apartheid, the Nobel Committee had already honored in a similar way two other South Africans: ANC President Albert Luthuli (1960) and Archbishop Desmond Tutu (1984).

In its official history of its experience with apartheid the UN has acknowledged that despite such concerted action by the General Assembly, it was up against strong resistance by governments that wielded considerable power over South Africa and in the international system in general, most notably the US and the UK. For example, a number of predominantly white countries did not become members of the Special Committee Against Apartheid, robbing that body of debate between those who wanted the complete end of apartheid and those states that urged moderation.[53] In the 1980s the administration of President Ronald Reagan maintained a policy of "constructive engagement" with South Africa. So, although one of the last nails in the coffin of South African apartheid was the 1986 Comprehensive Anti-Apartheid Act, it only became US federal law after a veto by President Reagan was defeated.[54] The law banned all significant trade between the US and South Africa; it outlawed US government purchases of South African goods and services and denied landing rights for South African Airways.

For many years the racist government had to fight off attempts by opponents of apartheid to have it isolated through boycotts and sanctions. That is why it pursued both covert and overt strategies to manipulate world public opinion, especially opinion in the rich, powerful countries. Its propaganda was aided by existing prejudices in Western culture against Africa and Africans in particular, and blacks in general. For example, the stereotype of blacks as a lazy race was exploited to suggest that a black-led South Africa would never achieve its true economic potential. The generally poor economic condition of black Africa was also used as a standard of what to expect when majority rule came to South Africa. It also exploited the idea that ethnic divisions among South African blacks would eventually destroy the country.

The nature of the international news system also worked for years in favor of the South African government. The powerful international news organizations often reproduced the ethnic and government biases of their home countries. Danny Schechter was motivated to start the "South Africa Now" show for broadcast on American public television in the late 1980s to provide an alternative source of information to counteract the bias of US media coverage. In contrast to the UN's long-standing recognition of the black South African opposition groups, by the late 1980s the American media's reporting on groups like the ANC still reflected suspicion and the US government's geopolitical preoccupations of the time. According to Schechter:

> They were frequently tainted in our media the same way they were tainted in South Africa's pro-government white press as communists, frequently labeled "Moscow-backed" without much background offered about their histories or political goals. Liberation movements in other parts of the Third World received similar treatment although dissident movements in Eastern Europe and the Soviet bloc were usually treated much more sympathetically. Perhaps that is because network news programs, like the U.S. government, have always been more focused on East–West issues than North–South concerns.[55]

Of course there were some exceptions to this historical pattern of coverage, most notably when the South African security forces committed mass murder. The two most famous incidents were at Sharpeville in 1960, and Soweto in 1976. In the former over 60 were left dead when the police opened fire on a group of unarmed blacks who had gathered by a police station for a PAC-led protest against pass laws. The latter left hundreds dead over a period of months. It started when the police fired on school children protesting inferior "Bantu" education.[56] Actions such as these brought negative news coverage and drew international condemnation of the racist government.

In the so-called "Muldergate" scandal of 1978 it was revealed that the South African government maintained a slush fund of over $74 million to propagate its views, win friends and influence public opinion across the world, especially in the United States.[57] Included in this propaganda project were secret funds to a favorable South African newspaper, *The Citizen*, and financial assistance for an unsuccessful attempt by an American publisher to buy the then beleaguered *Washington Star* newspaper, the smaller of the two dailies published in the US capital, Washington DC. They also reportedly tried to buy into the international video news service UPITN.[58] The scandal got its name from the then Information Minister, Connie Mulder, whose Department of Information directed the campaign of covert and illegal activities that were reported to number in the range of between 150 and 200. Despite the revelations of financial impropriety, the National Party government was not brought down and no person implicated in the scandal went to jail.

Another propaganda strategy of the regime was taken in the late 1980s in response to Schechter's "South Africa Now" program. The racist government produced its own show of a similar half-hour news magazine format with a black host, called "Inside South Africa". It presented the government line to counter "South Africa Now" 's alternative version.

The South African government's propaganda campaign also continued well up to the demise of the minority government in the early 1990s.[59] Journalists from other countries were given free trips to South Africa and expected to write favorable reports; lobbyists and public relations firms were hired in Washington DC to maintain a good image of South Africa with the US government and public; and the white racist government even recruited a black cricket team from the West Indies to break the international sporting ban and play a national South African team.

The sign that the racist government was losing the propaganda war came when its most famous and influential political prisoner, Nelson Mandela, the de facto leader of the ANC, was finally released from prison in 1990. Mandela was formally installed as President of South Africa in early 1994 after he led the ANC to victory in non-racial elections.

This discussion puts us in a better position to provide an informed direct answer to the central question that was posed at the start of this chapter. There is no doubt that there has been a contradiction between the UN's prohibition of propaganda as a threat to world peace and its own propagandistic "public information" campaigns. The organization admitted this much in a number of the documents cited earlier. However, the UN engaged in a kind of doublespeak most of the time when describing its public information program. This has ranged from outright denial that it was in the business of propaganda to saying that even though it disseminates propaganda it is the type of propaganda the international system needs. Throughout the UN's first 50 years this cowardly posture has seriously hampered the policy-making process at the DPI. This is because (as has been noted earlier) the only type of evaluation of policy impact the department was allowed to carry out was the collection of data on its information production and the demand for its output, not an assessment of exactly how the DPI was a player in changing the course of international politics. In contrast, if the DPI boldly embraces the "strategic communication" the 1997 Task Force recommended, it would be able to set clear propaganda objectives and develop methods to evaluate how best to achieve them. This point notwithstanding, it must be noted that propaganda campaigns to sell public policy have been notoriously difficult to evaluate even at the domestic level. For example, in the United States, after the government had spent $930 million on a national anti-drug campaign over five years, it was still not possible to say whether the campaign had been effective in keeping young Americans away from drug abuse.[60] Some research has suggested that such propaganda campaigns must last several years before they are seen as actually changing behavior.[61] However, a more reflexive and honest approach by the DPI to its international propaganda is much more preferable than what appeared to be the duplicity of the World Newspaper Supplement campaign that was described in Chapter 3.

In reality, the UN has never been against propaganda per se but against a particular type of propaganda – the "bad" propaganda that undermined the post-Second World War order of which the UN was at the center. This is the type of propaganda that sought to deny human harmony by promoting racism, sexism, xenophobia and other forms of hatred. From the UN's perspective, "bad" propaganda was also that which undermined its approach to universality, a universality that is best exemplified by the UN's view of human rights. So if we understand the issue this way the UN's stance on propaganda has never been contradictory on a general level. However, there have been contradictions in how the UN has selected the safe issues for the focus of its campaigns. For example, in the early years of the UN, apartheid in the United States was just as evil as apartheid in South Africa. National self-determination (another value promoted in DPI propaganda campaigns) was just as relevant to the UN's consideration of the situation in the USSR and the eastern bloc as it was to colonial Africa. The civil rights movement in the US and the anti-communist movement in the Eastern bloc achieved what they did without significant involvement from the UN. In contrast, the UN was a bold and proud player in the "safe" campaigns to promote international human rights and against the pariah state of South Africa.

A number of developments in the 1990s and at the turn of the century helped to significantly refine the UN's discourse on international propaganda. Some of the most bloody religious and ethnic conflicts in human history – particularly those in Bosnia and Rwanda – occurred at about the same time the technological means for disseminating propaganda became much cheaper and efficient. In Rwanda, Radio Mille Collines was "vital in steering the [Hutu] militia and calling direct hits [on Tutsi]", reported *The New York Times*, and the station "broadcast the names and addresses of people who were targets along with their vehicle license plates and the hiding places of refugees".[62] Radio-Television Serbia (RTS) played a similar role for the Milosevic government in the former Yugoslavia. *NATO Review* reported that since the outbreak of war in that region NATO and other countries had to spend millions to counteract RTS propaganda:

> RTS and other media under Milosevic's control created the conditions that made war possible, spreading fear among peaceful neighbours and persuading many Serbs that the ghosts of the Second World War had

returned to slaughter them. RTS constructed a bizarre universe in which the Bosnian capital Sarajevo was never besieged and the devasted Croatian town of Vukovar was "liberated". The media onslaught launched in Belgrade helped spawn similar hateful propaganda elsewhere in other Yugoslav republics and its legacy will be felt for years to come.[63]

That "old" media of radio and television was supplemented by the "new media" of the 1990s, an even more potent weapon in the hands of international hate-mongers. Telematics – the convergence of digital computing with telecommunication – dated back to the late 1960s when the US military developed ARPANET, a communication network that could survive a nuclear attack, but the technology did not get into the hands of the general public until the 1990s. The Internet facilitated communication via computers and telephone lines between individuals and organizations in remote international locations. Electronic mail obviated the delays of days and weeks caused by regular mail. An individual could post a page on the World Wide Web to be read by millions in literally all parts of the globe. Individuals and organizations promoting hate used these tools to organize themselves more efficiently and to recruit new followers. In the space of five years – from 1995 – the number of hate sites on the Web went from one to more than 2000, according to some accounts.[64] West European hate-groups avoided prosecution under their countries' anti-Nazi propaganda laws by using United States Internet service providers (ISPs) to publish and sell Nazi memorabilia.[65] A British racist nail-bomber discovered his bomb recipes on the Internet, and American racist groups maintained web sites to help find romantic partners who shared their racist sentiments.[66]

The response to this new generation of propaganda by both state and non-state actors was primarily legal in character and of four main types.

The first was to try to criminalize hate propaganda in new media by creating new domestic and international law. For example, Germany and France extended their existing anti-Nazi laws to the Internet.[67] The European Union passed a European Convention on computer crimes that also outlawed hate propaganda. However, although the US congress passed a Communications Decency Act in 1996 its focus was on Internet pornography and it was soon struck down by the courts. Indeed, the First Amendment rights enjoyed in the United States made that country a useful alternative base for European hate groups wishing to circumvent their local and regional laws.

A second strategy was to sue Internet service providers to force them to make the technical changes necessary to block access to racist websites. The French court actually ordered the American ISP, Yahoo, to block access to neo-Nazi sites by French users.[68]

The latter two strategies required a more direct role by the UN. Jamie F. Metzl, a former UN human rights officer, proposed that the UN "establish an independent information intervention unit with three primary areas of responsibility: monitoring, peace broadcasting, and, in extreme cases, jamming radio and television broadcasts".[69] According to Metzl, such a proactive policy by the UN against bad international propaganda would be justified under Chapter VI of the UN Charter that allowed the Security Council to take action short of military intervention against a threat to world peace. It should be noted, however, that this interpretation of the UN Charter is rather simplistic. Chapter VI set out a number of steps states should take to peacefully resolve disputes using the mechanisms of the UN. But while Chapter VII laid out the procedures to be taken in cases of armed action, it also explained that the Security Council could approve measures short of armed force before resorting to military violence. "The Security Council may decide what measures not involving the use of armed force are to be employed to give effect to its decisions, and it may call upon the Members of the United Nations to apply such measures," said Article 41 of Chapter VII. "These may include complete or partial interruption of economic relations and of rail, sea, air, postal, telegraphic, radio, and other means of communication, and the severance of diplomatic relations."

As will be discussed in the next chapter, by the end of the century the UN had recognized that something needed to be done as part of its peacekeeping strategies to deal with disruptive, hateful propaganda forces. However, the most visible strategy taken by the UN was not the administrative move suggested by Metzl but the prosecution of propagandists as war criminals. This is what happened at the United Nations war crimes tribunal for Rwanda when Ferdinand Nahimana, Jean-Bosco Barayagwiza (founders of Radio Mille Collines) and Hassan Ngeze (who published a pictorial newspaper called *Kangura*) were tried for their roles in the Rwandan genocide.[70] This was not the first time such action was taken against this brand of propagandist. In 1946 Julius Streicher, who ran the anti-Semitic weekly *Der Stürmer*, was executed after being found guilty by the International Military Tribunal at Nuremberg of committing a crime against humanity through his Nazi propaganda work.[71]

The main argument for the establishment of the DPI in the first place was the need to construct the ideological superstructure of a new world order in the wake of the Second World War hate propaganda, and it follows from that logic that the new era of cyber-hate means that there should be a renewed obligation for the UN to counteract this propaganda with its own "good" propaganda. In other words, the coming of telematic technologies, such as the Internet, provided more of a justification for the maintenance of a UN public information program. Instead of denying and engaging in double-speak on the issue of propaganda, the UN had more of a reason to declare its propaganda program and give the reasons why such a program was critical for maintaining international peace.

5
Lubricating the Wheels

> Thus the "American" secretary-general has acquired a supremely American faith in publicity campaigns. Annan appears to revel in the role of the U.N.'s master pitchman. But the decision to take this road suggests again that Annan genuinely has not understood why the reputation of the U.N. has declined, and deservedly. He seems to view all the criticism of the United Nations as a matter of public relations.[1]

In Kofi Annan's defense, there is plenty of evidence to suggest that he did not try to solve all the UN's problems through attention to PR alone. Decisions already discussed in this book – such as the Brahimi Report and measures taken to improve UN peacekeeping – suggested that the UN's seventh Secretary-General attempted to make significant changes at the organization. His election to a second term would not have been justified if he had only a shallow focus on PR. However, one can understand why an external observer of UN affairs at the end of the century could conclude that public relations seemed to be playing a much greater role in the organization's affairs than before. Annan had the good fortune – or curse, depending on your point of view – of taking over the UN's reigns of power at the center of the "information age". His attention to PR was as much a consequence of the times as it was part of a deliberate strategy by the Secretary-General. Annan could ignore the imperatives of the media age only to his peril.

The enduring lesson that Annan would provide for the UN was that it is absolutely essential that those running UN public information policy be intimately in tune with the media currents of their time. That is the first response to the central question explored in this chapter: How can UN public information policy and strategy be refined to keep pace with the evolution of the international system and communication technology? Actually, Annan's attention to PR is quite remarkable when seen in the context of how UN public information policy evolved. Although early UN rhetoric mentioned the need to keep the "peoples" of the world informed about the

UN, what this chapter will show is that the model of public information employed by the UN was historically elitist in nature. However, the evolution in the nature of international politics, changes in the nature of diplomacy and the coming of the "information age" meant that the model had to be changed.

This chapter begins with an exploration of the specific sociopolitical and technological changes to which the UN's public information program has had to adjust, in particular the so-called "communications revolution" and the related concepts of "globalization" and "international civil society". It then critically examines the "two-step" model of communication the UN has historically employed to show how this model was particularly inadequate by the end of the century. The chapter ends with a focus on the one area of UN work where reform of public information policy and practice were considered by UN policy-makers to be very critical to UN success – peacekeeping.

International change

It has already been noted in this book that public information owes its very existence as a practice in international relations to revolutionary changes in the nature of international politics, specifically the decline of secret diplomacy and the expansion of the arena of war. These changes in the nature of diplomacy and war would continue apace in the second half of the twentieth century and meant that public information itself would have to change. Beginning at the end of the nineteenth century, the practice of war went from being essentially conducted by mercenary armies to an activity practiced by entire nation-states. Civilians stood to lose more from war. Hence it became imperative that governments needed to mobilize their publics to make the required sacrifices. This necessity helps to explain why so many resources were devoted to the study and manipulation of public opinion in the twentieth century. According to Finch:

> While the key features of psychological warfare were employed before the twentieth century, the scale of its use and the central place it came to occupy in national strategy, first during World War One and then, at a greatly increased level in the Second World War, locate psy-war as one of the defining features of the century. From Pope Gregory, through the American War of Independence and the atrocity fabrications of the First World War, to the totalitarian pseudo-environments of the Second World War – through these campaigns, the modern story of propaganda in warfare has emerged. The social sciences, developing throughout the nineteenth century, are crucial to the story of propaganda because questions about the human mind, about how groups will behave, and about how people will react to messages are the questions shared by social science and propagandists alike.[2]

The need to involve public opinion more in the construction of international politics was also spurred by the new breed of internationalists who were behind the setting up of the League of Nations. Article 18 of the League Covenant sought to end the practice of secret diplomacy by calling on member states to register their international treaties and agreements with the League Secretariat and publish them. "The heart of this so-called old diplomacy, known as international anarchy to its critics, was secrecy and elite decisionmaking (sic)," Millen-Penn has explained. "League internationalists argued that peace was dependent on the elimination of secrecy, fraud, and elite decisionmaking (sic), and the implementation of a new League diplomacy based on open covenants, democratic control, and an activist public opinion."[3] However, this new approach to diplomacy was not adopted without resistance. As Millen-Penn has observed: "the League depended on public opinion for its diplomacy to function, while at the same time nation-states, still wedded to the old diplomacy, found democratic control and an informed public opinion to be both a detriment and a danger to perceived state interests".[4] The trend of states establishing permanent public diplomacy agencies (such as the Japan Foundation and Spain's Instituto Cervantes) that became most pronounced after the Second World War was evidence of how states were finally convinced of the utility of this new diplomacy. In effect they were catching up with what the League of Nations and the UN were already preaching. Public information is one of the most enduring legacies of the League of Nations at the UN.

In addition to changes in the nature of war and conventional diplomacy, by the end of the twentieth century the list of transfigurations of international politics that affected public information policy and practice would also include an apparent wholesale reordering of the global dynamic. This profound shift has been labeled "globalization", or the triumph of "neo-liberalism".

The earliest work in globalization theory was carried out by sociologists, and this fact illustrates a greater sophistication by that field in understanding what was happening than was the case with the political scientists. By 1993, *The Wall Street Journal* was reporting that "[a]n estimated 15 million people in 50 countries" were using the Internet, "and the traffic seems to be rising as much as 15% a month";[5] Nelson Mandela's 11 February 1990 release from 27 years' imprisonment in South Africa had been viewed live on TV by millions around the world; and by 1994, Music Television (MTV) – a medium that had come to symbolize the global representation of American pop culture – was available in 250 million homes in 64 countries.[6] The revolution in communication and transportation that had caused Marshall McLuhan to spawn the term "global village" had been apace for more than 30 years before the 1990s. The first space satellite, *Sputnik*, had been put in orbit in 1957; between that year and 1979 over 2000 satellites had been launched, helping to make such practices as international telephone calls and live TV broadcasting a normal part of daily life for much of the world's population by the end of the 1970s. In the mid-1990s came the Internet, a global network of interlinked computers that obviated the inconveniences in international communication caused by geography and the slowness of the traditional mail. The Internet made interpersonal and mass communication almost instantaneous through such features as web pages, email and electronic chat rooms. To the extent that images, words and ideas could be relayed in limitless volume so rapidly and efficiently across the world we had arrived at the most global system known to humankind.

The UN had to play catch-up with the technological change and challenges of globalization. In 1999 Under Secretary-General Kensaku Hogen lamented that the UN's web site operation was launched in the 1990s without being "a budgeted activity" of the Department of Public Information.[7] But in the space of six years from 1994 the organization made revolutionary moves in terms of public information dissemination. For example, all public UN documents since 1993 and all UN resolutions in history were available through the World Wide Web. UN press briefings and radio programs were also accessible through the Web to anyone anywhere in the world with Internet access and the necessary technology.

The UN used public information policy and practice strategically to engage with the type of changes globalization represented. By the end of the century political and intellectual discourse on what these changes would actually mean for the future of the international system left more questions than answers. But one factor was clear: the number of organized entities acting in world politics had rapidly increased. More striking than the increase in the number of states was the increase in the number of non-governmental organizations (NGOs). The number of NGOs with transnational interests was more than 15 000 by the end of the century, and there had been just a handful of such organizations in 1900.[8] In 1948 there were only 41 NGOs with consultative status at the UN Economic and Social Council (ECOSOC), but this number was 1350 by 1998.[9] This did not mean that the ECOSOC actually consulted with this large number of NGOs but it did mean that there were many more NGOs than before using their consultative status as a means of gaining access to the UN. In popular political discourse this was just part of the rise of "social movements", the spur of "the universal movement towards greater citizen action".[10] At the UN, and in other parts of the international system concerned with global governance, this all heralded the coming of transnational "civil society", a global phenomenon that meant that not only was there more transparency and democracy in national politics but also greater accountability by international governmental organizations as well.[11]

The evidence used to argue this position was persuasive: the communications revolution curtailed the ability of governments to censor information from their populations; within the space of 20 years between 1980 and 2000 not only did the communist bloc collapse, but the military dictatorships that had characterized Central and South American politics also gave way to civilian governments; and those being awarded the Nobel Peace Prize started to be activists and international non-governmental organizations (INGOs) that were held up as good examples of agency in international civil society, such as International Physicians for the Prevention of Nuclear War (1985), Rigoberta Menchú Tum (1992), the International Campaign to Ban Landmines (1997) and Médecins Sans Frontières (1999).

Some of the scholarly literature produced in the wake of the increasing usage of the term "civil society" pointed out that – in a fashion similar to terms such as "propaganda" and "political correctness" – the meaning of the concept had a complicated ecology and it was by no means clear that the creation or expansion of civil society meant greater democracy. Hegel, Thomas Paine and others used the term to describe a "domain parallel to, but separate from, the state – a realm where citizens associate according to their own interests and wishes".[12] In the 1930s Antonio Gramsci expropriated the term to describe the realm of ideas and institutions of society in which class struggle takes place. According to John Keane, Gramsci viewed civil society as: "Wedged between the state and class-structured economy ... these 'fortresses and earthworks' normally protect the 'outer ditch' of state power and shield the ruling class from the shock waves produced by economic crises".[13] Alejandro Colás argued that, rather than being departures from international capitalism, globalization and international civil society were actually phases in the ecology of international capitalism. For Colás, international civil society was no more likely than capitalism to usher in greater democracy because many of the agents of international civil society were themselves unaccountable and run undemocratically.[14]

In light of the term's ecology, therefore, another international relations scholar was careful to define international civil society without the ideological particularity that colored UN propaganda about it when the label of civil society was resurrected in the 1990s. For Craig Warkentin, "it is a socially constructed and transnationally defined network of relationships that provides ideologically variable channels of opportunity for political involvement".[15]

Promptly upon assuming office, Kofi Annan organized his administration in such a way as to reflect his conviction that the UN had to make a special outreach to civil society. He appointed Gillian Martin Sorensen as Assistant Secretary-General for External Relations to undertake the task. In an interview for this book in late 2001, Sorensen explained what Annan saw as the key components of international civil society and the UN's perception of why they were important:

> Beyond the traditional non-governmental organizations, he wanted to see what he can do with the academic world, with the business world, with the foundation world, the world of religious leaders. He thought there was much more that could have been done. As we know, civil society is the

rapidly expanding universe and they have expertise. They have the capacity to mobilize, to lobby, to raise funds, to dramatize and publicize, and he felt I could add something to that.[16]

Sorensen's appointment was another significant stage in the development of a relationship between the UN and bodies other than governments that originated with the UN Charter itself. She was asked to do a public information job but under a different title. At the same time, the DPI – the part of the Secretariat that had handled the UN's relationship with non-governmental actors – was changing its relationship with these actors.

For most of the UN's first 50 years, the UN considered non-state actors that were partial to the UN as useful extensions of its public information program. They would spread the word about the UN and win more followers for it. However, this would all take place within limits defined by the member states who would have to be consulted first before any kind of relationship could be established between the UN and a particular non-state organization. From the very establishment of the UN a place for NGOs was set out. According to Article 71 of the UN Charter:

> The Economic and Social Council may make suitable arrangements for consultation with non-governmental organizations which are concerned with matters within its competence. Such arrangements may be made with international organizations and, where appropriate, with national organizations after consultation with the Member of the United Nations concerned.

The exact nature of the relationship that would exist between the UN and NGOs was made more specific by recommendation 12 of the Technical Advisory Committee that conceived of the DPI. It said:

> The Department and its branch offices should actively encourage national information services, educational institutions and other governmental and non-governmental organizations of all kinds interested in spreading information about the United Nations. For this and other purposes it should operate a fully equipped reference service, brief and supply lectures, and make available its publications, documentary films, film strips, poster and other exhibits for use by these agencies and organizations.[17]

However, there was no formal working relationship between the DPI and NGOs until 1968 when the Economic and Social Council (in Resolution 1297) said there should be institutional ties between the DPI and these organizations as a means of propagating information on economic and social affairs. However, the DPI had to screen applications from NGOs to exclude those "whose aims or practices tend to contribute to the propagation of nazi ideology and racial and/or religious discrimination". Special attention had to be given to getting the participation of NGOs from "inadequately represented regions of the world", especially Africa. There also had to be a special attempt to have "racial groups" – especially those "representing people of African descent" – affiliated with the DPI "because of the diversity of the experience they may have both in the field of human rights and in that of economic and social affairs".[18]

Over the years, the number of NGOs accredited to the DPI expanded and its bureaucratic arrangements to accommodate them also became more elaborate. In 1968 there were 200 NGOs associated with the DPI, but by 1998 the number was 1550.[19] An NGO Section was created within the DPI as a central point to which the NGOs could come for information and UN documents. An annual three-day DPI/NGO Conference at UN Headquarters in New York was started to foster dialog between UN officials and the NGOs, and in 1975 a UN Non-Governmental Liaison Service was started as an information link between the Secretariat, specialized agencies and the NGOs on development, humanitarian emergencies and human rights matters.

Rhetoric at the UN about NGOs fostering democracy, transparent governance and something called "civil society" was notably absent for much of the first 50 years. The NGOs were considered as little more than propaganda extensions of the UN, and this was a main reason why the ECOSOC and DPI were the parts of the Secretariat assigned to deal with them. As will be discussed in Chapter 7, the DPI–NGO relationship for most of the first 50 years was "asymmetric" (in terms of public relations theory) because a mutual exchange of ideas between the two sides was not fundamental to it. The rhetoric about civil society was more a product of the 1990s. The Millennium Declaration specifically stated that the UN needed to partner with the "private sector" and "civil society organizations" to achieve development and "poverty eradication". The UN openly admitted in 1998 that it was changing the old asymmetric relationship for a symmetrical one. NGOs were "no longer seen as disseminators of information but as shapers of policy and indispensable bridges between the general public and the intergovernmental processes".[20] A series of UN-sponsored international conferences became media spectacles partly because of the large presence of NGOs at them and the feuds that sometimes erupted with and among these groups. Perhaps the most famous of these meetings were the 1992 "Earth Summit" in Rio de Janeiro, the Global Conference on the Sustainable Development of Small Island Developing States in Barbados in 1994, and the 1995 Fourth World Conference on Women in Beijing.

Interestingly, it was soon after the Earth Summit that the UN Secretariat revamped its procedures governing its formal relationship with NGOs. The ECOSOC maintained three categories of consultative status for NGOs that had been in place since 1946, and these hierarchical categories of status would determine NGOs' rules of participation in future UN conferences.[21]

At the same time, although the UN framed differently the participation of NGOs within the discourse on international civil society, the criteria used to determine formal affiliation of NGOs with the DPI still reflected the previous "asymmetric" times. The 1500-plus NGOs accredited to the DPI by the end of the century had to:

- Share the ideals of the UN Charter;
- Operate solely on a not-for-profit basis;
- Have a demonstrated interest in United Nations issues and proven ability to reach large or specialized audiences, such as educators, media representatives, policy makers and the business community;
- Have the commitment and means to conduct effective information programmes about UN activities by publishing newsletters, bulletins, and pamphlets; organizing conferences, seminars and round tables; and enlisting the cooperation of the media.[22]

This role of the DPI and ECOSOC as gatekeepers to participation in UN affairs is critical to conceptualizing the UN's relationship with international civil society. By the end of the 1990s it was common to hear statements from the Secretariat to the effect that NGOs and civil society were "contributing to a process of enlargement of international cooperation and spurring the United Nations system and other intergovernmental structures towards greater transparency and accountability".[23] A well-known theorist on civil society, John Keane, described the thinking about civil society at the time in terms of a dichotomy: "Civil society is pluralism, participation, purity, reflexivity. The state is conformity, directives, corruption, blind compulsion".[24] However, as Colás has pointed out, it is questionable whether international civil society is as revolutionary to world politics as the UN and others would have us believe because the terms of the relationship between international civil society and entities of authority and power in international relations are not determined by civil society. Although admitting that global conferences do facilitate networking by the accredited NGOs and promote awareness through media coverage, Colás notes that "the form, content and eventual outcomes of such gatherings are so heavily circumscribed by the interests of states that it is difficult to see how the agents of global civil society can be said to be genuinely representative of an autonomous and undifferentiated 'global citizenry'".[25] Colás argues that "international social movements bring about change in international relations when they challenge the structural basis of state sovereignty".[26]

Academic work on the relationship between NGOs and the United Nations has helped to refine considerably our understanding of this phenomenon of expanded civil society. For example, books by Weiss and Gordenker, and by Willetts, have tried to provide a basic definition of who are the components of international civil society.[27] They have also engaged with this tension that exists between states and international governmental organizations, on the one hand, and NGOs on the other. "In contrast to the conventional Roman wisdom of divide and conquer, UN officials concerned about the proliferation of nongovernmental entities have responded with the attitude: 'If you can't beat 'em, organize 'em'," explained Weiss and Gordenker. "The efforts by the World Bank, UNHCR and the UNDP to structure project relationships are probably the best known".[28] John Sankey, the former British Permanent Representative to the UN in Geneva, has pointed out that "Bearing in mind the old adage 'if you can't beat them, join them', some 'governmental' NGOs are funded or controlled by governments in order to infiltrate, inform on or otherwise disrupt the work of genuine NGOs, particularly in the field of human rights".[29]

Therefore, the expansion of international civil society is more complex than the slogans of "barefoot revolution" and "people power" suggest. However, the *image* of an expanding and transforming international civil society is itself an important part of the *problematique*. So a study such as this into an entity that propagates ideology is that it refines our understanding of international politics. Such a more nuanced approach is especially critical in the so-called postmodern, post-industrial era when so much of politics (at both the domestic and transnational planes) is representational. This means that strategic success can be determined almost as much by image and appearances as by actual action. Seen from this perspective, it can be argued cynically that the propagation of international civil society and the UN's engagement with that construct serves both reactionary and progressive purposes at the same time.

This macro level of UN public information policy is not the only area where the question of reform in the later years of the century has been ripe for critical analysis. There are also provocative questions to be tackled at the micro levels. The issue of "two-step" flow, to which we now turn, is directly related to the discourse on international civil society because a public information program built on the assumptions of this paradigm cannot be in sync with the declared promise of international civil society.

"Two-step flow" and public information policy

The correlation between advances in social science research and the increased importance of propaganda in both domestic and international relations has been highlighted from the very start of this book, and the set of assumptions about exactly how UN public information propaganda would work is a case in point of the role played by a specific social theory on the issue. The UN was established at the very time when the social science establishment in the United States was grappling with the central problem of how to theorize the role of mass media in society. In the early years of mass media it was tempting to theorize media in a hypodermic fashion: media would inject the public with ideas in an almost mechanical way, and great emphasis was placed on the power of the new media. Later scholars would question the impartiality and credibility of this research. The leading American scholars at the time who carried out this research (such as Lasswell and Lazarsfeld, to name just two) were often funded by government and industry, and even though they claimed scientific neutrality, their research often served to buttress the status quo.[30] The shortcomings of this era of research notwithstanding, this did help to theorize mass communication at a time when little theory of this type existed, and even later theorists who found that generation of research to be seriously reactionary and intellectually bankrupt could use it in a contrapuntal manner to advance social thought.

One legacy of this period that relates directly to the work of the DPI is the "two-step flow" model of social communication. It was formulated based on a study of voting behavior by Paul F. Lazarsfeld, Bernard Berelson and Hazel Gaudet, first published in the mid-1940s under the title *The People's Choice*.[31] Based on the findings of their research, Lazarsfeld and his collaborators departed from the grain of the time when they suggested that mass media would not be the all-powerful key to social communication as was previously thought. They said the influence of mass media on the larger society was more indirect than direct. Mass media first influenced "opinion leaders" who then passed on this information and ideas to those who followed them (the second step in the two-step flow). In that study of how voting decisions were made, a key factor was said to be "personal influence". *The People's Choice* found that personal influence affected voting decisions more than the mass media, especially when voters changed their minds during the course of a campaign. It also claimed that these key opinion leaders could be found in all walks of life, in all social categories. And the study also argued that opinion leaders were more exposed to mass media than those who followed them.

A decade after *The People's Choice* was published, one of Lazarsfeld's disciples, Elihu Katz, published an update in which he argued that other studies had reinforced the findings of the original hypothesis. Katz refined the conception of "personal influence" by arguing that interpersonal relations worked in three main ways: "(1) channels of information, (2) sources of social pressure, and (3) sources of social support".[32] In summarizing the importance of the hypothesis proposed by the authors of *The People's Choice*, Katz said: "It was a healthy sign, they felt, that people were still most successfully persuaded by give-and-take with other people and that the influence of the mass media was less automatic and less potent than had been assumed".[33]

The two-step model was a contribution to theory not only in the then budding field of "communications research" but also to the study of cultural diffusion in sociology. It is actually as a model of diffusion that two-step flow is relevant to the study of the DPI because (unlike the study of voting behavior on which the original hypothesis was based) the field of diffusion research explores how culture and ideas spread internationally from one area to another. Diffusion scholars ask questions about such factors as the agents of diffusion (e.g. opinion leaders), the stimuli for diffusion (e.g. prestige), and how we account for differential rates of diffusion (for example one view is that it is easier to diffuse material or religious traits of a culture than "elements of social structure").[34]

Fifty years after *The People's Choice* was published, scholars in sociology and advertising (to name just two fields) were still making reference to the two-step model and the contribution of Lazarsfeld in this area. For example, Strang and Soule noted that: "Diffusion processes play a central role in contemporary explanations of the incidence of collective action and the spread of protest symbols and tactics".[35] Conversely, Muncy and Eastman drew on the two-step model to explain the impact of the *Journal of Advertising* on the advertising industry. "Considering the subscriber list of the Journal of Advertising, we believe the knowledge being developed and published in the Journal is unlikely to be following a one-step model of communication," they explained. "People who are using advertising knowledge in the realms of advertising practice or public policy are not the ones who appear to be reading the Journal of Advertising. However, they are likely to be influenced by people who are reading the Journal."[36]

It is important to note that the two-step strategy was being used even before the term was coined to describe the practice. For example, Michael S. Sweeney explained that the US government used respected personalities in the publishing industry as a means of getting the American news media as a whole to practice censorship during the Second World War.[37] But the field of development communication blossomed in the years after the Second World War and the UN Secretariat and other parts of the UN System consciously employed the two-step model in their strategies to take the newly decolonized regions from "traditional" to "modern" societies. In a classic text from the period, *Communications and Political Development*, Lucian Pye (then Chairman of Political Science at the Massachusetts Institute of Technology) declared that traditional societies were characterized by a lack of "professional communicators" and as such were less democratic than modern societies. "Information usually flowed along the lines of the social hierarchy or according to the particularistic patterns of social relations in each community," Pye explained. "Thus the process in traditional societies was not independent of either the ordering of social relationships or the content of communication." In contrast, Pye suggested that modern societies were more democratic because they were characterized by the two-step flow:

> A modern communications system involves two stages or levels. The first is that of the highly organized, explicitly structured mass media, and the second is that of the informal opinion leaders who communicate on a

face to face basis, much as communicators did in traditional systems. The mass media part of the communications process is both industrialized and professionalized, and it is comparatively independent of both the governing and the basic social processes of the country...

The critical feature of the modern communications system is that orderly relationships exist between the two levels so that the total process of communications has been aptly characterized as involving a "two-step flow." Political communications in particular do not rest solely upon the operations of the mass media; rather, there is a sensitive interaction between professional communicators and those in influential positions in the networks of personal and face-to-face communications channels. Above all, the interactions between the two levels take the form of establishing "feedback" mechanisms which produce adjustments in the content and the flow of different forms of messages.[38]

A wealth of critical communications research produced later – especially during the latter stages of the century in the wake of the increased concentration of ownership of the media in capitalist societies – now makes Pye's assertions seem simplistic, naïve and very unsophisticated.[39] There is nothing that makes modern mass media systems inherently immune to the social classes or political parties (in the case of communist countries) that control them.

However, the paper trail on UN public information policy during the first 50 years of the DPI leaves no doubt that the two-step flow model guided the practice. This has already been discussed in some detail in Chapter 2, where it was also pointed out that over the years there was much confusion and disagreement at the UN over who should constitute the opinion leaders – or "target audiences" – on whom the DPI should focus. A report on the DPI produced just eight years into its existence (in 1954) said that:

There is reason to believe that at this stage of the Organization's existence the task with which the Department should be mainly preoccupied is that of encouraging a more selective interest in the information disseminated, with relatively less emphasis than hitherto on volume and the processes of general dissemination. If this hypothesis should be accepted, it would seem to point to the need for a general reorientation of information activities and services as they have been developed, in terms of a wider "thematic" approach to the task to be performed. It would seem to imply also that without prejudice to that minimum of constant factual coverage essential to any information service, a more *intensive* and less *extensive* information operation is called for in the future.[40]

The Secretary-General's review and reappraisal of the DPI in 1971 recommended that the department identify and cultivate "target audiences". Twelve years later an evaluation of the DPI said the department had made "little progress" in reaching the objective, apart from an Editor's Roundtable that had been started and the work with the NGOs. The 1983 investigation's criticisms began with the very formulation of the objective. It noted that the target audiences would be "selected groups throughout the world with a high opinion-building potential".[41] But it went on to note that: "The target audiences mentioned in the [1971] reappraisal report included specialist press, schools, universities, professions and non-governmental organizations, but there was no indication of how the relevant groups would be defined and identified at the programme implementation stage".[42] This problem of carefully defining target audiences was critical because, as the number of languages used by the DPI increased, there was a tendency to confuse particularly language audiences with the target audiences needed to amplify the DPI's messages. The 1983 report explained:

> Indeed, it is apparent that although references to particular audiences are found in various documents of the Department, the concept of target audiences has been diluted from that of audiences with a high opinion-building potential to simply recipients or audiences. If audiences are identified only by the characteristic of language, there is now a significant broadening of audiences as compared to 1971, when virtually all of the Department's output, except radio, was restricted for the most part to English. The use of more languages is a necessary and welcome development; however, to cite it as serving the needs of target audiences is to misconstrue the original intent of the objective.[43]

From the premise of the two-step flow model and the assumption that ignorance is a cause of war, the UN and UNESCO have devoted large portions of their resources to such programs as scholarships, student exchanges and public information campaigns. For example, in early 1999 the DPI hosted a total of about 5000 students at UN headquarters for the National High School and National College Model United Nations. Also, in the late 1990s the UN started using the Internet to host question-and-answer sessions with students in various parts of the world on such issues as UN peacekeeping operations.

Throughout the DPI's first 50 years there was also a contradiction between this two-step strategy and the DPI's use of popular mass-media technologies as dissemination tools. For 50 years the UN considered the idea of setting up its own international radio station, and the organization was one of the first to exploit the popular communication potential of the Internet in the 1990s. Indeed, by the end of the century the UN used the Internet to provide international audio and video broadcasts to anyone anywhere in the world with World Wide Web access, essentially circumventing the authority of governments and providing a less elite form of popular communication than in the previous technological era.

Historical and social science research and real-life historical events have provided plenty of evidence that social and intellectual elites are not necessarily the leaders of the types of progressive social change that are at the heart of the UN's internationalism. James Loewen makes the point by reporting American poll results on attitudes towards US intervention in Vietnam. A 1971 Gallup poll found that twice as high a proportion of college-educated adults (40 per cent) were hawks (against withdrawal of US troops), compared to 20 per cent of adults with only grade school education. Loewen carried out surveys that found people likely to believe the opposite – the college-educated would be more likely to be for withdrawal of US troops than the less formally educated. Loewen's audiences justified such assumptions by giving such reasons as: "Educated people are more informed and critical, hence more able to sift through misinformation and conclude that the Vietnam War was not in our best interests, politically or morally", and "Educated people are more tolerant. There were elements of racism and ethnocentrism in our conduct of the war; educated people are less likely to accept such prejudice."[44]

The era of "globalization" and "international civil society" was actually a contradictory epoch that provided more reason to be skeptical of assumptions about a positive relationship between educational attainment and enlightenment and commitment to progressive internationalism. Neo-Nazis quickly took advantage of the new technology of the Internet to organize internationally and obviate European anti-fascist propaganda laws. Violence by these right-wing groups made certain parts of Europe dangerous places for people of color to be. Radio was used by Hutu fanatics in Rwanda to goad people of like minds into genocidal killings. In countries as far apart as Australia, Austria, France and the United States, resentment over immigration fueled racist support for such leaders as Pat Buchanan, Jean-Marie Le Pen, Erich Heder and Pauline Hanson. Sadly, activists for such hate often had home bases in universities. This point was poignantly illustrated in the United States in 1999. On Independence Day weekend Indiana University student Benjamin Smith, a follower of the racist World Church of the Creator, shot and killed former Northwestern University basketball coach Ricky Byrdsong and Korean student Won-Joon Yoon. Another case in point was that months before the famous Tiananmen Square anti-government demonstrations in China in 1989, Chinese universities were the scene of hateful, anti-Black demonstrations. According to media reports, what began in December 1988 as a dispute in Hehai University over the refusal of an African student to register with authorities the name of his Chinese date at a party soon escalated into violence, false rumors, and then Chinese student mobilization in several cities against African exchange students in general. Then there were reports that the African students were victims of police brutality in the days following the initial incident. Several African governments and the Organization of African Unity (OAU) protested to the Chinese authorities.[45] British and American news analyses said at the time that the demonstrations manifested the severe racism in Chinese culture towards Africans and people of African descent.[46] Another explanation was that (Chinese racism notwithstanding) an underlying current revealed by the demonstrations was the impatience by ordinary Chinese with their material lot in life. The African students on Chinese government scholarships were said to be living better than their Chinese counterparts and even their university teachers.[47]

As the years go by this image of universities and students being the leaders of progressive social movements is reinforced by news and documentary film depicting campuses as places of protest. Also, the people most likely to be recorders of history either work or spend some of their most impressionable years in universities. Similarly, such myths continue to influence UN policies because UN policy-makers are themselves intellectual elites with strong ties to formal education as students and, in many cases, teachers. Complicating the problem is the fact that universities are often contradictory places. While openmindedness and liberalism is often professed, "high culture" and the curricula that promote it are often alienating to groups marginal to centers of power in society.

Peacekeeping and public information reform

Concurrent with the growing discourse on international civil society and target audiences for UN propaganda described above was the revolution in the UN's role as peacemaker and peacekeeper. The UN defines peacemaking as a "diplomatic process of brokering an end to conflict, principally through mediation and negotiation, as foreseen under Chapter VI of the UN Charter; military activities contributing to peacemaking include military-to-military contacts, security assistance, shows of force and preventive deployments". In contrast, peacekeeping is "hybrid politico-military activity aimed at conflict control, which involves a United Nations presence in the field (usually involving military and civilian personnel), with the consent of the parties, to implement or monitor the implementation of arrangements relating to the control of conflicts (cease-fires, separation of forces etc.), and their resolution (partial or comprehensive settlements) and/or to protect the delivery of humanitarian relief".[48] By the end of the 1990s the UN was best known as a peacekeeper than as a peacemaker but this was a notoriety that the UN wished it might have achieved by other means. In the two most famous cases of Rwanda and Bosnia, thousands were massacred despite the presence of UN peacekeepers. In both cases the perpetrators used the mass media to instigate genocide. There were not only military failures on the part of the UN but failures to integrate public information policy into peacekeeping.

The end of the Cold War was both a blessing and a curse for the UN. After years of being marginal to many of the most serious conflicts around the world – a situation by design of the great powers, according to some observers (see Chapter 3) – the UN suddenly became relevant as a peacemaker and peacekeeper. Three times more peace agreements were negotiated and signed under UN auspices during the 1990s than in the previous four decades combined.[49] There were 13 operations during the 43 years of the Cold War, but that number of operations was launched in just three years of the 1990s.[50] And not only were there more UN peacekeeping missions, the nature of UN peacekeeping operations had become more complex. They were no longer of the "traditional" type, where troops monitored ceasefires; they had become "multi-function", involving such tasks as the creation of police forces, running elections, resettling refugees and demobilizing former fighters to reintegrate them within society.[51]

But what should UN peacekeepers do in situations where mass media and propaganda have been perfected as instruments of war? What happens when these multifunction peacekeeping missions do not account for the fact that warring factions might replace their weapons with hate propaganda meant to provoke genocide?

In Rwanda in 1994, Radio-Television Libre des Mille Collines (RTLM) was used by elements in the ethnic Hutu community to mobilize their followers to massacre the minority ethnic Tutsi. Although the Hutu controlled the government, they feared that the Rwandese Patriotic Front (RPF), with whom the government had signed a ceasefire under UN supervision, would restore Tutsi hegemony in the country. RTLM not only advocated wholesale ethnic genocide but also broadcast propaganda and threats against individuals and the Belgian peacekeepers stationed in Rwanda. Ten of the Belgians were eventually part of the 800 000 massacred in Rwanda in 1994. At the height of the conflict the RPF wrote to the UN Security Council appealing for the adoption of a resolution that would endorse the jamming and destruction of RTLM. The UN's own review of the Rwandan debacle admitted that

> ... a more determined effort should have been made to provide the United Nations with its own radio facility in Rwanda. Moreover, the political will and financial means should have been mustered to jam the notorious inciting radio station Radio Mille Collines. In the future, however, counteracting hate radio may not be enough. Attention must also be paid to the distribution of genocidal messages.[52]

In the Balkans, all sides were accused of using vicious media propaganda. On the Serbian side the media instrument that gained notoriety was TV Belgrade and a special propaganda unit within it called the Centre for Information for Foreign Public Opinion.[53] One tactic the Bosnians and Croatians used was to hire the American PR firm Ruder-Finn to help sway opinion in the United States in particular.[54] Although the collapse of the former

Yugoslavia came to a head in the late 1990s with NATO bombings to force the Serbs to accept a truce in Kosovo, it was not at all clear during the years of conflict whether the Serbs or their opponents were the most guilty of using propaganda to advance their war aims. In the same year the British government and the UN were accused of conducting a systematic disinformation campaign against the Bosnian Muslims[55] but at the same time the Bosnian Muslims and Croats were accused of successfully propagating world public opinion to view the Serbs as totally evil.[56] In 1997 *The Times* of London, in an editorial, appealed to NATO to shut down biased television and radio stations – a move that would be "the last frontier of disarmament".[57]

Public information policy posed two main challenges to UN peacekeeping. First, policy and methods had to be devised to effectively counter what has been described already in this book as "bad propaganda" (propaganda that seeks to provoke hatred and war). Second, public information had to be made an intrinsic part of every peacekeeping operation.

With regard to the first dimension, the Security Council did have authority under the UN charter to take measures against any party responsible for threats to the peace, breaches to the peace or acts of aggression. Chapter VII, Article 41, said such measures could include "complete or partial interruption of economic relations and of rail, sea, air, postal, telegraphic, radio, and other means of communication, and the severance of diplomatic relations". Article 41 could be invoked to jam or destroy offending broadcasters. The increased use of propaganda in some of the most infamous cases of genocide in the 1990s convinced some observers that the UN was not doing enough in this area of peacekeeping and that it needed to adopt such proactive actions, variously called "information intervention"[58] or "information diplomacy".[59] But of course the dilemma faced by the UN on this matter is that a key component of its universality is the doctrine of free expression which is part of the baggage of liberal-democratic social philosophy. However, one observer, writing in the American magazine *The Nation* in mid-1994, argued that "when a government severely restricts or prohibits opposition voices, the manipulation of public opinion by government-controlled media is itself a means of denying the free exchange of information and ideas", so "the most ardent defenders of freedom of expression may advocate jamming radio broadcasts in such circumstances".[60] NATO actions in the late 1990s to squelch propagandists harmful to the 1995 Dayton Accords to end conflicts between Bosnia and Herzegovina, the Republic of Croatia and the Federal Republic of Yugoslavia were an illustration of what UN peacekeepers could do in the future.[61]

The second dimension of the problem is a more involved matter. In the "information age" a key priority at the start of any peacekeeping mission was the efficient dissemination of information to the news media to ensure that the operation was framed before world public opinion in a fashion favorable to the UN. This is a task made all the more complicated by the nature of "news values" (the factors used by the media to determine what is news). The powerful international media tend to focus on the negative and ignore the positive. The uncontroversial is not news. Peacekeeping, human rights protection and humanitarian aid were listed as the most important functions of the UN by respondents to the Millennium Survey conducted worldwide by Gallup International in 1999.[62] But although there was more public awareness than before about peacekeeping it was not evident that the media did a competent job of explaining to world publics what peace-keeping actually entailed. "Bad news makes the headlines particularly when equated with a serious threat to national interest," Colombian journalist Lina Maria Holguin reflected in 1998. "For that reason zones where the killing has stopped and where peacekeepers are working in reconstruction (UNAVEM III, Angola), democratization (UNTAS, Slovenia), or prevention (UNPREDEP, Macedonia) are not seen as big stories that deserve broadcast-ing air time."[63]

Another full-time task of all peacekeeping operations is the countering of hostile propaganda against the UN. What the UN learned in the 1990s is that not all parties to peace agreements would view it as an honest broker, and when the mission encountered difficulties the UN itself and its repre-sentatives would be the targets of disinformation. One case in point used to illustrate this was in Bosnia where Muslim media accused the head of the peacekeeping operation there of having a Serbian wife and of being guilty of rape and murder, claims that the UN was accused of ignoring and not acting to refute.[64]

An even more complicated challenge for UN public information policy and practice was the obligation that came with the new multifunction peacekeeping – the construction of almost entirely new societies through "public service" mass communication about such topics as civil rights, civil institutions, voting, law enforcement and public health. Former UN Human Rights Officer Jamie Metzl has cited Namibia, Cambodia and eastern Slovenia as places where UN radio stations have been used successfully in this way. Metzl also noted that similar initiatives by NGOs worked in Liberia, Burundi and Bosnia.[65] According to Holguin: "The UN radio station estab-lished in Cambodia, for instance, was successfully used to counteract nega-tive perceptions of United Nations Transitional Authority in Cambodia (UNTAC) within the local population and to bring 90% of the Cambodian population to vote in that country's first democratic election".[66]

Although the Brahimi Report on UN peacekeeping did not once mention the word "propaganda", it did suggest that the UN needed to integrate public information policy and practice as an intrinsic part of peacekeeping operations. It recommended that "additional resources" should be put into mission budgets for public information to "get an operation's message out and build effective internal communications links". It also said "a unit for operational planning and support of public information in peace operations

Table 5.1 Public information tasks in support of peacekeeping operations[67]

- Organize and oversee pre-deployment field surveys of public information, media and public outreach requirements
- Advise on public information related requirements to be included in the status of mission/forces agreement
- Develop deployment timetables, equipment requirements, draft budgets and staffing tables
- Identify and recommend the appointment of qualified and experienced public information personnel for mission service, including the spokesman, and establish a roster of such personnel
- Ensure the early deployment of appropriate public information staff and all necessary equipment, including a rapidly deployable start-up kit
- Maintain regular contact with the missions' public information components and provide assistance and guidance in carrying out the operational plan
- Liaise with the Military Adviser's office and the Civilian Police Division to ensure that a military spokesman and a civilian police spokesman are identified for missions where these functions are appropriate, and that they work closely with the civilian spokesman
- Develop ongoing training procedures for mission personnel whose work entails significant public information activity, including the Special Representative of the Secretary-General, the Force Commander, the military spokesperson and the civilian police spokesperson
- Enhance standby capacity through co-operative arrangements with Member States, non-governmental organizations and United Nations Volunteers
- Translate overall the political and strategic information requirements of each mission into operational public information plans
- Develop concepts for programming packages during the pre- and post-deployment stages of peace missions, taking advantage of DPI's ongoing relationships with regional broadcasting partners
- Facilitate coverage of peacekeeping operations by the media
- Develop standard operating procedures and guidelines for the public information components of peace missions, and familiarize mission information personnel with these procedures and guidelines
- Monitor internally and externally the effectiveness of the public information campaigns in peace operations, and propose appropriate responses for shortcomings.
- Liaise with United Nations agencies on overall public information strategies and advise field public information components on the ground on the co-ordination of messages with humanitarian agencies
- Work with United Nations agencies active in the mission area on the shared use of information assets in field operations
- Preparation, production and dissemination of promotional materials on peace operations and disarmament, including books, information kits, timeline wall charts, the *Year in Review*, monthly background notes, newsletters, posters, press releases and features
- Create and maintain pages on the United Nations website about peacekeeping, as well as other peace operations (e.g. peacemaking; peace-building)
- Organization of promotional events, media encounters, press conferences in close collaboration with the Office of the Spokesman and substantive offices, and preparing memorial panels for United Nations peacekeepers and staff members who have lost their lives in the service of peace
- Handling media relations for DPKO and working with the Office of the Spokesman for the Secretary-General on peacekeeping-related issues
- Assist peacekeeping operations in managing media relations during crisis

should be established, either within DPKO [the Department of Peacekeeping Operations] or within a new Peace and Security Information Service in the DPI, reporting directly to the Under-Secretary-General for Communication and Public Information".[68]

Within months of the Brahimi Report being submitted, the Secretariat was able to identify 21 specific roles of public information in peacekeeping operations (see Table 5.1). The new philosophy was that "[p]ublic information specialists must be part of the mission from its inception".[69] However, the DPI was making it clear that it was not receiving the resources necessary to do a competent job in support of peacekeeping operations.[70] Peacekeeping was clearly another avenue of the UN's work where there was growing recognition that public information policy and practice was even more important than it was before. However, the traditional institutional ambivalence towards it continued.

Evolution and meaning

This chapter began with the question of whether UN public information policy and strategy could be refined to keep pace with the evolution of the international system and communication technology. It ends with the cautionary advice that we can provide a more dispassionate reply to the question if we do not become too passionate about the so-called revolutions in both communication technology and the nature of the international system. In the path to understanding UN public information policy and practice we must interrogate carefully the meaning of terms coined to give popular meaning to processes that are by no means uncomplicated in nature nor simple to understand.

The record is very clear that UN public information policy and practice did evolve as the international system changed, but the change did not necessarily take place for the professed reasons. What has been argued here is that "international civil society" is a contested concept. It does not always mean a simple movement to greater participation, democracy and accountability in world politics caused by the growth of "social movements". But UN rhetoric at the end of the century depicted it as such, while maintaining public information practices that were aimed at controlling the terms under which these social movements would participate in international politics. The discussion of the "two-step" paradigm also served to point out that UN public information policy and practice was traditionally elitist and exclusionary, all be it based on the grounds that it had to be that way because of a lack of resources needed to conduct more mass-oriented propaganda.

UN public information policy evolved, especially in the "media age" of the 1990s, because of the critical role media practice came to play in the nature of international politics. In order to be successful, an actor in international relations by the late 1990s had to pay as much attention to how it was *represented* as to what it did. Focus had to be placed on what it *meant* as much as to what it was. Public information policy and practice are the critical nexuses in this dynamic. As the book has noted in more than one place, the evolution of international relations to that stage was due to changes in the nature of diplomacy, war, communication technology, and the understanding of mass psychology. The League of Nations and the United Nations were innovators in international relations from the point of view that they sought to capitalize on these changes by paying institutional attention to the cultivation of international public opinion. The states with the resources and motive followed the UN's cue and quickly made public diplomacy a regular means of conducting their international relations. However, peacekeeping was one area in which the UN actually had to catch up with states. It took the Vietnam war to convince the US government of the critical role of control of the media representation of conflict in the outcome of war, and to change lessons learnt into actual policy in conflicts as varied as the 1989–90 invasion of Panama and the 1991 Gulf War. But it took the military and propaganda failures of Somalia, Rwanda and Bosnia to finally convince the UN that it needed to take greater control of the representation of UN peacekeeping by integrating public information into the fabric of peacekeeping operations.

In summary, public information was more important to the fortunes of the UN in 2000 than it was in 1946 at the birth of the organization. The DPI's wider brief – which now included gatekeeper to international civil society and critical technical resource to all new UN peacekeeping missions – was ample evidence of this. How public information ranks as a tool of international relations, compared to others, is a problem that will be discussed in the following chapter.

6
Using the Tool

The last of our questions is perhaps the most difficult to answer. Does the track record of over 50 years prove the utility, and even "success", of the United Nations public information program?

The most straightforward way of answering such a question is to look at the original objectives of the UN public information project and compare these to the evidence more than a half a century later. But this book has already shown that to explain what these original goals were is a challenge unto itself. Therefore, the first part of this chapter will be a critical engagement with this problem, and the second part will be an attempt to answer the question another way: a relative assessment of public information as a tool of international relations compared to others, such as war, conventional diplomacy, sanctions, international law and international organization.

Objectives and results

The 1946 recommendations of the Technical Advisory Committee asserted that the DPI should not be a propaganda agency but that it should "promote to the greatest possible extent an informed understanding of the work and purposes of the United Nations among the peoples of the world". It would also "analyse trends of opinion throughout the world about the activities of the United Nations and the extent to which an informed understanding of the work of the United Nations is being secured".[1] Within six years that basic mandate was amplified to cater to "the special problems and needs" of the "under-developed areas".[2]

Although the mandate of the DPI continued to expand over the years, it also continued to be dogged by institutional ambivalence. U Thant (Secretary-General 1962–71) described it as merely an "international information service"[3] in the latter years of his time in office. But in the 1970s that mere information service was called upon to propagate "universally approved causes and movements"[4] and "future of the world" issues[5] such as industrialization, disarmament, decolonization, environmentalism and the protection of human rights. And from the late 1970s through to the end of the century, the DPI acquired an expanding list of responsibilities given to it by General Assembly mandates. These included counter-propaganda campaigns on South African apartheid and the South African occupation of Namibia (see Chapter 4), running a service to cater to the needs of NGOs (see Chapter 5), starting and running public information programs in collaboration with the Department of Peacekeeping Operations (DPKO) (see Chapter 5), and running special training programs for "Third World" and Palestinian journalists (see Chapter 2).

This expanded plate of responsibilities became even more difficult to understand because the various activities of the UN in the area of public information always lacked coherence, even as they got more numerous. A 1972 report said of the state of co-ordination of public information policy within the UN system that: "such a common policy is almost completely lacking and such coordination is rudimentary".[6] Despite the creation of the Joint United Nations Information Committee (JUNIC) in 1974,[7] a 1981 review of co-ordination of public information activities in the UN system criticized the duplication and waste. For example, in 1978 the UN system had 148 points for distributing public information in 74 cities. This meant that in 25 cities there were between two and 14 information services. The report said that in Geneva alone there were 14, there were 11 in New York, seven in Washington DC and four in Bangkok,[8] and that where co-operation and co-ordination existed it was half-hearted.

Of course, during the UN's first 50 years the organization did consider questions similar to that being asked by this chapter. But the UN was afraid of what it might find out because investigating and reporting on the "impact" of UN public information work is potentially subversive. What if it was discovered that UN public information did win over public opinion in many parts of the world? What if the information from the UN contradicted the official versions and policies of member governments? What if these publics were mobilized by UN information to rise up against their governments demanding such claims as "human rights"? In the case of apartheid in South Africa, it could be argued that such scenarios did occur. A 1972 review of public information policy by the Secretary-General's office noted that for public information policy, "impact" means "results produced in the form of influencing opinion, changing minds or initiating concrete action in given directions".[9] However, it warned that

> ...the United Nations Office of Public Information [the name of the DPI from 1958 to 1978], as the service arm of an intergovernmental organization, must clearly proceed with extreme discernment and caution. On the one hand...the very purpose of such information activity conducted by and on behalf of the United Nations is to promote a wider understanding and support of United Nations aims and activities. In this

context, therefore, the success of United Nations information activity is necessarily to be gauged by the extent to which it in fact is achieving this objective of developing wider understanding and support. "Impact" in this wider sense, the Office of Public Information attempts to ensure by making its output as professionally imaginative and effective as possible within the necessary limitations of objectivity and impartiality. However, the Office has neither the machinery nor the mandate to conduct any field research or opinion surveys on the extent of such an impact, other than through the actual utilization of its information materials and services...[10]

The assertion that the UN did not have the mandate to do public opinion research was actually not true. Paragraph 13 of the 1946 principles explicitly stated that the DPI should "analyse trends of opinion throughout the world" and the extent to which there is an informed understanding of the UN's work. As a 1972 UNITAR report on the public image of the UN noted, it was striking that a 1946 document would make such a stipulation during a time when public opinion research was still in its infancy. According to the report, "no organizational effort of some consequence has been made during all these years to implement paragraph 13 of the basic principles".[11] And, continuing on this theme that the results of UN public opinion research might be subversive, the report went on to say that "[i]t may not be very opportune in the present situation of the United Nations and of the world to stress too much the existence of this provision in the basic principles and this is probably the reason why this paragraph 13 is being so little quoted or referred to nowadays in official documents".[12] Because of these fears a new meaning was given to "impact". It would be "feedback", which was "the degree and extent to which the various information services and activities of the Office of Public Information are being received and utilized by the audiences to which they are directed".[13] This was a much less threatening goal. But, as has been noted already in this book, it is impossible to run a public information program where its target audiences are not clearly defined, and, moreover, where its real objectives are not admitted.

In light of all these contradictions, the results of international public opinion polls on perceptions of the UN (such as the 1999 Gallup Survey that was cited in Kofi Annan's Millennium Report) cannot be read as gauges of the utility or even success of the organization's public information program. They can only be read as such when there is less institutional ambivalence about the DPI and what it ought to be doing.

International public opinion surveys do point to possible problem areas for the UN that would serve to give its public information program more focus. For example, although the UN and international development organizations lobbied for years to get rich countries to devote larger percentages of their gross national product (GNP) to development assistance, public opinion research in these countries often revealed much ignorance about poorer countries and why these regions were poor.

The Live Aid Legacy – a survey of attitudes in the UK by the aid organization Voluntary Service Overseas (VSO) – found a very distorted view of the world:

> 80% of the British public strongly associate the developing world with doom-laden images of famine, disaster and Western aid. Sixteen years on from Live Aid [the 1985 transnational rock concert to raise funds for famine in Africa], these images are still top of mind and maintain a powerful grip on the British psyche.
>
> Stereotypes of deprivation and poverty, together with images of Western aid, can lead to an impression that people in the developing world are helpless victims. 74% of the British public believe that these countries "depend on the money and knowledge of the West to progress."
>
> The danger of stereotypes of this depth and magnitude is the psychological relationship they create between the developed and the developing world, which revolves around an implicit sense of superiority and inferiority.
>
> The "Live Aid Legacy" defines the roles in our relationship with the developing world. We are powerful, benevolent givers; they are grateful receivers. There is no recognition that we in Britain may have something to gain from the relationship.
>
> Researchers remarked on the respondents' confidence in such one-dimensional images. British consumers are not hesitating or seeking reassurance for their views. Unconsciously accumulated images of the developing world have led to a certainty on the part of consumers that they have all the facts.[14]

International development was one of the "future of the world" issues the DPI was to promote, but findings such as these can lead to the conclusion that the UN's public information program made little impact, even in countries with extensive mass-media infrastructure, such as the UK. Conversely, one could argue (on the basis of conjecture) that the ignorance might be worse were it not for UN propaganda!

Similarly, UN-sponsored public opinion surveys of 28 countries during the years 1989 to 1991 revealed that a key variable in determining positive or negative perceptions of the UN was not levels of economic development but levels of involvement in UN programs. However, this meant that the UN got some of its worst ratings in some of the most powerful countries, such as the US, UK, France and Australia. There were also very negative perceptions of the UN in places where the organization was most heavily involved, such as Jordan and South Africa. American sociologist William J. Millard

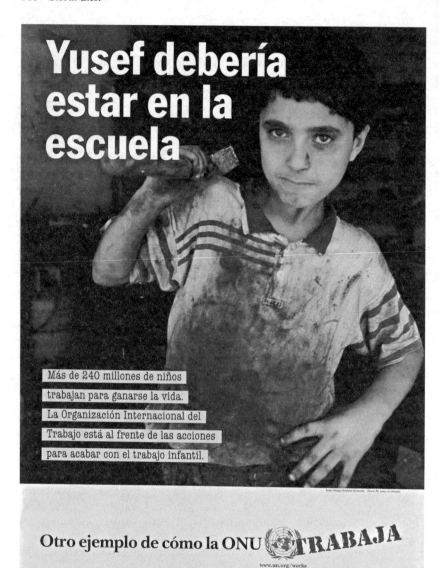

Figure 6.1 *"Yusef should be in school..."* One of the Spanish posters produced as part of the "UN Works" campaign in 2000. "More than 240 million children work to earn a living. The International Labor Organization is leading the fight to end child labor. Another example of how the UN works."

summarized the findings by explaining that:

> Nations in which a predominantly favorable opinion was found (e.g. Scandinavia) are largely dependent on multilateral arrangements for national security, and have been active in providing peacekeeping forces and leadership to the UN Secretariat. Those with predominantly negative appraisals are countries at the receiving end, who perceive their national security to have been damaged by UN action, or are disappointed that in international disputes the UN has not been helpful. There is another category of countries – major English-speaking nations – in which substantial minorities were critical of the UN. In the 1970s and 1980s this was due perhaps to widespread dissemination of negative news reports by major western news agencies, linking Third World demands to the United Nations system. In the United States and the UK available research data show that opinions became more favorable when the United Nations proved to be the key for cooperative international action against Iraq. Extent of knowledge of the UN seems to be a function of the institution's relevance to national concerns. Public opinion within a nation about UN performance appears to depend on the extent to which that institution is perceived to contribute to the well-being of the country, or is thought detrimental.[15]

Despite all these problems that complicate the definition of the objectives of the UN public information program, and, consequently, the ability to evaluate it coherently, the DPI expanded in function for two main reasons. The first was that the trends in international relations that accounted for the initial utility of the DPI in the first place – such as the changed nature of war, internationalism and the increasing relevance of public opinion – continued apace. The second was that public information became more important to the role of the UN in international politics.

Public information as a tool

A second way of answering the opening question is a thematic approach to international public information, examining it within the context of the field of international relations. This approach does not look at UN public information policy and practice in a "reflexive" fashion (as above) but in an "objective" way. Here the term "objective" is used not to denote a lack of bias (which is its common usage) but a way of viewing the record of the DPI in relation to other "tools" used in international politics to extract the same or similar results. It should be noted at the start that this approach is not tied to a particular paradigm in the field. A list of tools is devised and they are assessed in relation to each other according to their definition, their function in international politics and their ecology, especially during the time period covered by this book (roughly 1946 to 2000). This way, a measure of the utility of the UN's public information program is gained by comparing its role and results to the roles and results achieved by other tools. This thematic approach is in the tradition of Martin Wight and Marcel Merle. Wight's approach in *Power Politics*[16] was of a realist paradigmatic bent, while Merle's *The Sociology of International Relations*[17] incisively anticipated much of the innovative thinking on globalization and international civil society that was to appear in the 1990s.

Before this second means of answering the question is tackled, the parameters of the discussion must be clearly defined. The discussion that follows about the relative utility of such tools as diplomacy, sanctions and international law in relation to public information is confined to the consideration of "multilateral governance" alone. International relations contains a variety of actors who are motivated by a plethora of objectives. However, we are concerned here with the utility of the public information program of an actor in the business of multilateral governance – the UN. Multilateralism – "a system of coordinating relations between three or more states in accordance with certain principles of conduct"[18] – means that the UN is a very different actor from states, for example. The UN, and other actors like it, must usually develop policy and practice in a much more deliberate fashion compared to states. They must also appeal to much broader constituencies. States have the luxury of acting solely in their own interests. In contrast, the very identity of multilateral organizations is shaped by the collection of states on whose behalf these bodies are supposed to act. This means that how states use diplomacy, force or international law is markedly different from how the UN, the European Union (EU) or the Organization of American States (OAS) might do so.

The basic premise of this section is that the UN's public information program can be compared to five other tools used by multilateral organizations: international organization, international law, conventional diplomacy, force and sanctions. This short list is by no means exhaustive of the range of strategies used in international relations but it does include the main tools employed by multilateral organizations. If this discussion were about the tools used by states as unitary (or unilateral) actors, the list would be much longer; for example it would include intelligence and covert action, trade and even marriage (a practice more common when kings and queens had more dominion over the planet than was the situation at the close of the twentieth century).

International organization

The UN was the core of the greatest experiment in international relations in the second half of the twentieth century. As noted in Chapter 2, the vision was that the creation of a network of functional international organizations would be the panacea needed to avoid another World War. Functionalism was based on the four key assumptions: (a) the provision of economic and social welfare would diminish the threat of war; (b) all states had a harmony of interest that made them co-operate; (c) "political" and "technical" matters could be separated; and (d) the doctrine of functionalism itself would become even more popular as states saw its benefits and moved to create new international organizations in areas of international activity not yet covered by functional bodies. By 2000 the list of these functional international organizations, the UN Specialized Agencies – the "[a]utonomous organizations working with the United Nations and each other through the co-ordinating machinery of the Economic and Social Council"[19] – had grown to more than 15. But the UN Specialized Agencies did not include all the international organizations that were playing such a critical role in international relations by then that they seemed to provide living proof of the theoretical soundness of functionalism. One such body that was not a formal UN entity but which had become a critical component of the international political infrastructure was the International Committee of the Red Cross, winner of the Nobel Peace Prize on more than one occasion and the leading international relief organization in virtually all tragic conflicts and disasters.

Functional international organizations varied in size and type almost as much as they varied in number during the last 50 years of the century. One basic classification was the distinction between *forum* and *service* entities. The former were those that "provide a framework for member states to carry on many different activities ranging from the exchange of views to the negotiation of binding legal instruments", and also used by states "for the collective legitimation of their policies or for propaganda". The latter were those that "conduct activities themselves; they provide common or individual services or both".[20] The United Nations Educational, Scientific and Cultural Organization (UNESCO) was a classic example of a forum organization, and a good example of a service organization was the International Monetary Fund (IMF), which bailed out member states in financial straits.

When states create and become members of international organizations they participate in a trade-off. For the benefits of membership they give up some of their freedom to act unilaterally. For example, members of the International Telecommunication Union (ITU) (the oldest international organization) must abide by the ITU Convention, which means they must follow specified procedures for the establishment and operation of international broadcasting stations and other telecommunications. In return, some of the benefits they enjoy are order in the international broadcasting system and access to technical expertise for the development of their domestic and international telecommunications. Debate about the nature of this trade-off has been one of the key controversies surrounding the utility of multilateral organizations.

Because of the issue areas in which they operate, some intergovernmental organizations (IGOs) have been able to attract large memberships. By the end of the century, IGOs with memberships in excess of 180 states included the World Bank, the IMF and the Universal Postal Union (UPU). In contrast, organizations with much fewer members included the International Maritime Organization (IMO), because a number of states are landlocked, the United Nations Industrial Development Organization (UNIDO), because not all states have to be as concerned about planned promotion of industrial development, and the International Atomic Energy Agency (IAEA), because not all states have nuclear power. States have joined and participated in IGOs according to their own interests and the configurations of their foreign policies. In some issue areas (especially those that have the organizations with the largest memberships) it has been easy to see the "harmony of interest" that undergirds functionalism and explains the continued saliency of the practice.

However, it has been more difficult to justify some of the functionalist assumptions. For example, the idea that "political" and "technical" issues could be separated begged the question of what is "political" and what is "technical"? This dubious distinction was at the basis of a number of controversies in the 1970s and 1980s over the "politicization" of UN agencies when external conflicts found their way into the organizations' deliberations. For example, some of these agencies became additional fronts in the anti-apartheid struggle when a number of states sought to have racist South Africa excluded from membership. Similarly, supporters of the Palestinians tried to put pressure on Israel through these bodies. Strategies such as these were considered by some to be unfair "politicization" of "technical" bodies, and, the argument went, these organizations should be left alone to conduct their business oblivious to politics. The counter-argument was that the "technical" and the "political" could not be separated: racism or other forms of discrimination that granted privilege to some at the expense of others permeated all forms of social life, determining the character of the supposedly "technical" issues, such as healthcare, access to technology and collective bargaining rights.

In the 1990s, assumptions about how best to achieve global social and economic welfare would also cause serious questions to be raised about the efficacy of functionalism. Neo-liberal doctrine that gained ascendancy following the end of the Cold War said that international free trade would not only be the means to economic prosperity but also to world peace. The World Trade Organization (WTO) was created in 1994 to promote principles and norms to that end. But by the end of the century it had become perhaps the world's most controversial organization. Activists demonstrated and provoked riots in cities around the world where the WTO convened. They argued that policies sanctioned by the WTO made it even harder for poor countries to survive because they were forced to open up their markets to products from rich countries while their own products could not compete on the international market. Instead of a functional international organization promoting global harmony, peace and prosperity, the WTO was viewed by some as a tool of a minority of rich states to perpetuate free-market policies that gave them unfair advantages.

At first it might seem paradoxical to identify international organization as a strategy used by multilateral organizations to conduct their international relations. The UN is, after all, an international organization itself, and it would seem that states and other non-state actors in international politics are the ones who actually use the strategy of creating international organizations to achieve particular ends. But in the context of this discussion about the DPI it is indeed possible to compare international organization (the strategy in international relations) with the strategy of public information. The key promise of functionalism was exactly in the assumption that in time the successful functional international organizations would inspire replication in issue areas not yet covered by functional bodies. The expansion of international organization in the latter half of the twentieth century did seem to prove this point, and the case of the WTO is particularly interesting here.

My 1995 book *International Power and International Communication* applied international regime theory to international communication to argue that trade in cultural products (i.e. books, magazines, phonograms, advertising and movies) was a "non-regime" area where net exporters were engaged in a pitch battle to secure their "economic rights" against net importers who were trying to protect "cultural rights". The existing international intellectual property regime, headed by the World Intellectual Property Organization (WIPO) and its Paris and Berne Conventions, had proved useless in stemming the piracy of cultural products. Meanwhile, states at the receiving end were complaining about the "cultural imperialism" of leading producers of cultural products, especially the US. As the book was being completed the WTO was created with the mission of solving many of the world's trading problems. The WTO would secure compliance to international intellectual property law by linking such compliance to the privileges of participating in the international free trade system and the gains it offered through the Most Favored Nation (MFN) principle. Those charged with permitting the violation of international intellectual property law would be subject to WTO procedures for resolving trade disputes and the possible sanction of losing trading privileges.

At face value, international trade was a classic case of functionalism at work. Although the idea of an IGO to regulate international trade had been proposed as far back as when the UN was set up, it took 50 years and an international trading system that was drastically different to realize the dream. During this period the importance of services and other so-called "non-tangible" items had risen in economic significance but the rules securing trade in these areas had not been developed to protect the economic interests of those with the most to lose from this new and expanding form of international trade. But it was exactly this question of in whose interest the WTO was acting that made it such a controversial topic at the end of the century and the beginning of the next. Although membership in the WTO was optional, it appeared that membership was not in fact an option for the many small, poor states that needed the MFN status to survive. And, although the WTO agreements contained some concessions for poor countries (for example, extra time to comply with some of its provisions) the general tenor of its agreements seemed to favor the richer, more powerful countries.

This was all taking place within the context of a new "neo-liberal" international political economy, characterized by the leading ideology that free-market, capitalist economies, free trade, deregulation and privatization would be the best means of achieving economic development and prosperity. The WTO was yet another front in this ideological wave that was already being led by the World Bank and IMF, the two so-called "Bretton Woods" institutions that had risen to greater prominence and power in the 1980s when their "structural adjustment policies" had to be adopted by several seriously indebted countries in order to get balance of payments support. For those opposed to WTO, World Bank and IMF policies, these functional international bodies in particular did not bring the world any closer to international peace. Instead their policies were blamed for producing greater income inequality in countries that already suffered blinding poverty, giving rich countries greater control over the fortunes of other states and strengthening the role of transnational corporations in running the global economy.

The debates over neo-liberalism suggest an inherent contradiction in the basic assumptions of functionalism: the spill-over effect could occur and more functional bodies could be created despite the apparently false assumption that functional international organizations would produce greater social and economic welfare. Although the majority of the UN specialized agencies emerged in the early post-Second World War years, the WTO was not the only IGO created to cover an un-covered issue area during the 50 years after the founding of the UN. Other examples included the WIPO (1970), the World Tourism Organization (1975) and the Organization for the Prohibition of Chemical Weapons (1997).

As this global network of agencies has expanded, public information has been an important part of the international discourse on international organization. The empirical evidence suggests that the expansion of the public information bureaucracy of the UN system as a whole was due in large part to the growing network of functional international organizations. As has been noted in Chapter 2, 38 of the 53 UN Specialized Agencies, offices and programs surveyed in the mid-1990s had some form of public information component as part of their bureaucracies. Public information has not been a competing tool of the UN's international relations but rather a critical part of how the UN and its related organs construct their identities and represent themselves to global public opinion. Chapter 7 covers this point in further detail.

International law

The increased importance of law and justice in an international context became one of the key features of what has been described as the emergence of "international civil society", a very contested discourse that was analyzed in Chapter 5. The International Court of Justice – the legal arm of the UN – adjudicates cases between states but it has no mechanism for forcing compliance. However, one of the UN's major contributions was as a forum through which a number of significant sources of international law were developed. The most famous of these by the end of the century were the Universal Declaration of Human Rights (1948) and the two international human rights covenants – on social and economic rights, and on civil and political rights. In addition, by 2000, thanks to the UN's leadership on the issue, all regions of the world (except Asia) had some form of regional human rights convention.

Human rights is a good example of how an IGO uses international law. After getting member states to create international law that reflects their basic principles, these bodies can then publicize these sources of law as standards of acceptable conduct. Indeed, whenever a new IGO is created, the realm of international law expands because there is another set of regulations to which actors in the international environment are likely subject.

By the 1990s three international legal trends related to multilateral governance had become evident: (1) the increased incorporation of non-state actors in the development of international law; (2) movement towards the creation of international courts to try criminals said to have committed "crimes against humanity"; and (3) increased pressure to have courts in other countries try persons (especially ex-government functionaries) alleged to have committed crimes in their home states.

The first trend was most poignantly illustrated in what happened at international organizations operating in the issue area of international communication as the so-called "information revolution" continued apace. International communication was distinguished as an issue area by how much the development of law governing communication technologies lagged behind technological development, the most striking case of which was the Internet. However, even before the Internet, new technologies (such as video and phonogram recorders) had made regulation of many communication technologies (such as the rules on piracy) very difficult. International communication was also one issue area where transnational corporations had outpaced governments in their ability to provide many technologies and services.

Matters eventually came to a head in the mid-1990s when the key IGOs changed their regulations to allow transnational corporations either full membership or at least a much greater say in their day-to-day operations and regulatory processes. This was in response to a scenario in which corporations such as Time-Warner and Rupert Murdoch's News Corporation had become more powerful international broadcasters than state-owned entities like the Canadian Broadcasting Corporation (CBC) or the British Broadcasting Corporation (BBC). International courier services (such as Federal Express and United Parcel Service) were providing more superior mail services than those of traditional postal authorities. The consequence was that the ITU and UPU in particular were forced to end the traditional monopolies that states had enjoyed over the international regulatory process.

The second trend had a longer history because it effectively began with the war crimes tribunals following the Second World War. The genocides in Rwanda and Bosnia provided renewed impetus for creating a standing international judicial body with the ability to try criminals and impose sentences. This was necessary not only because of the gravity of the crimes, but also due to the lack, in some cases, of functional state judiciaries to try such criminals in the places where the crimes occurred. An International Criminal Court was finally established under UN auspices in 2002.

The UN's success in developing international human rights law and propagating globally the language of human rights partly accounts for the third trend, the effective convergence of the discourses on international law and transnational civil society. Social movements promoting the causes of victims (from the "disappeared" in Chile to indigenous peoples) stridently called for various personalities to be brought to justice on charges of having committed crimes against them. The former Argentine dictator, Augusto Pinochet, and the former US Secretary of State Henry Kissinger were just two targets. Those who supported an international criminal court also hoped that such a body would make it easier for such charges to be verified and the guilty brought to justice.

Just as in the case of international organization, it is hard to imagine these trends in international law developing without the propaganda support of UN public information. Indeed, the UN's facilitation of networking by NGOs, through the services provided by the DPI and the various international conferences, is one of the ways in which social movements have been emboldened to pursue various legal causes.

Conventional diplomacy

The increased role of public opinion in international politics, and the rise of practices such as UN public information and public diplomacy, have actually helped to more clearly define what is conventional diplomacy. Indeed there would not have been any need to put the "conventional" in the term were it not for the fact that public diplomacy had come to challenge the traditional work of diplomats. Conventional diplomacy is the tool most affected by the growing role of mass media in international relations. The comparison between its part and that of public information in how IGOs conduct their international affairs is very stark. It is the one of the five tools discussed in this chapter that arguably has been made obsolete because of public information and public diplomacy. Conventional diplomats have not only lost power because of these practices that employ international mass media but in some cases have been made redundant.

During the first 50 years of the UN there was a significant change in the idea that a diplomat was essentially an honest man sent abroad to lie for the good of his country. Diplomacy had been an elite affair, a field in which privileged government operatives spoke foreign tongues, guarded government secrets and even engaged in trickery. The League of Nations began the process of change for the practice of conventional diplomacy by requiring that its members engage in open diplomacy and bring their publics more into their confidence. Prior to the Second World War, governments maintained programs for cultivating foreign public opinion only on a temporary and ad hoc basis. However, in the period after the war, state-run public diplomacy programs and the public information initiatives of IGOs became a standard part of the system of international relations.

Although the realm of conventional diplomacy has figured prominently in some accounts of the utility of IGOs – the most well-known being the so-called "good offices" of the UN Secretary-General to help resolve disputes, or the use of IGOs as fora to quietly "back down" from confrontation without losing face – diplomacy as practiced by international organizations is very different from that conducted by states. When states join organizations like the UN they undertake an obligation to represent themselves in the deliberations of those bodies, even if in most cases this representation is not permanently based in the locations where the organizations are headquartered and diplomats are not assigned exclusively to one organization. But, unlike states, international organizations do not have an obligation to have diplomatic representation in all the countries that comprise their membership. States exchange diplomats when they establish diplomatic relations with each other but this practice is less standard between states and IGOs and among IGOs. Indeed, prior to the end of the Cold War there were very few operatives of international organizations that had the international profiles of prominent diplomats who represented states. Those with comparable prominence to personages such as Henry Kissinger, Andrey Gromiko and Chou En-lai would have been only the heads of organizations such as the UN, the World Bank and IMF. The vast majority of those conducting relations on behalf of IGOs were relegated to the relatively faceless status of "international civil servants". This situation was changed somewhat from the 1990s onwards when the UN became more significant in the field of peacekeeping, and those holding the post of "Special Representative" to the various hotspots became the faces and mouthpieces of the UN on these conflicts to those in the regions concerned and to the rest of the world. Some UN diplomats who became famous in such roles included the Japanese Yusushi Akashi (in the former Yugoslavia) and the Algerian Lakhdar Brahimi (who became something of a trusted confidant of Kofi Annan and was given a number of assignments, including heading the comprehensive review of UN peacekeeping operations).

But despite the greater exposure and prestige the conventional diplomat enjoyed in relation to "international civil servants", conventional diplomacy lost ground in the latter half of the twentieth century for three main reasons.

First, traditional diplomats lost more power and influence the more open diplomatic practice became. The more governments felt a need to show that they were not engaging in secret diplomacy the less need there was for the traditional diplomat. This trend continued apace due to the spread of participatory democracy (of various types). The term "participatory" is used here advisedly because it is not meant to suggest that these forms of government are any more "democratic" or just than others. However, the key variable is that governments that say they are participatory have an obligation to *appear* so. IGOs are good illustrations of this idea as they must appear to be operating in the interest of the overall good. Under such conditions, the producer of an international broadcast to be seen and/or heard by millions, or a web page with a similar public reach, is more important (or at least just as important) than a Special Representative or ambassador, no matter how talented the diplomat might be.

The second factor accounting for the decline of conventional diplomacy was graphically illustrated for the first time during the Gulf War when it became clear that international mass media had increased the "velocity" of international relations so much that Cable News Network (CNN) replaced conventional diplomats as the leading player in international diplomacy at the time. The term "CNN effect" was coined to describe a phenomenon that, despite its various definitions, still amounted to a description of international relations where conventional diplomacy was in second place. The "CNN effect" has been defined variously to mean: (1) the practice much used during the Gulf War of governments engaging in "diplomatic ping-pong" by sending messages to each other through news leaks or interviews to CNN instead of via traditional diplomatic channels; (2) the pressure policy-makers feel to respond to world events because of the instantaneous relay of news; (3) the way governments and conventional diplomats can be marginalized from the policy-making process itself by the real-time relay of events as they happen, especially in matters involving mass action by demonstrators or other actors who are essentially playing to the cameras;[21] and (4) the tendency of the international broadcast media, instead of governments and conventional diplomats, to set the agenda for world politics.[22]

The third factor is that the role of ideology in international relations expanded. The public mattered, not only to states as domestic constituencies to bolster their foreign policies, but as another means of spreading influence beyond their borders. The public also mattered to international organizations because the propagation of ideology meant more to these actors in international relations than it did to states. The objectives of the international propaganda programs of states can have a number of objectives. Some of the most prominent include territorial expansion, the promotion of trade and cultural chauvinism. However, none of these goals have featured prominently in the discussion of the UN public information program in this book. The "universally approved causes" and "future of the world" issues for the UN have been in the realm of ideas and idealogy: decolonization, antiracism, environmentalism, human rights and the like. Public diplomacy and public information policies are more suited to this kind of propaganda work than conventional diplomacy.

While the increased role of IGOs and ideological struggle in international relations did not make the conventional diplomat obsolete, these phenomena did change the nature of international politics forever. In some areas of international relations – the negotiated resolution of disputes, for example – propaganda could not displace conventional diplomacy. However, in comparison to conventional diplomacy, propaganda's stock as a tool IGOs used to conduct their international relations rose by leaps and bounds.

Force

As is the case with conventional diplomacy, IGOs and states use force in very different ways. International organizations do not have standing armies as do states. Also, under the post-Second World War peace system they can never declare that they are using force for purposes that are not defensive or aimed at maintaining the collective security of the entire international system or part of it.

At century's end, among IGOs the UN was in a unique position as the only *political* international organization authorized to sanction force. Though the international system included other international organizations that sanctioned force, these were largely regional *security* bodies, such as the Economic Community of West African States Cease-Fire Monitoring Group (ECOMOG) and the North Atlantic Treaty Organization (NATO). Even when the UN sanctioned the use of force it had to follow specific guidelines for endorsing such action, and then the authority for doing so rested with the Security Council. These bureaucratic restrictions and the political constraints of the Cold War meant that in the twentieth century the UN enjoyed a very checkered and undistinguished history where the issue of force was concerned. The so-called "police action" in Korea in the early 1950s was in reality one of the first proxy wars of the Cold War, and the UN effort was essentially an American operation. The war contained North Korea but it did not end tensions or the continued threat of war, and as a result thousands of American troops would remain stationed on the border between the two Koreas for the rest of the century in order to maintain the shaky truce.

The UN was not a significant player in any of the largest interstate wars, for example Vietnam, the Arab-Israeli wars and the Falklands War, of the rest of the Cold War period. However, its profile with regard to the use of force did rise after the Cold War, and this happened in two chief ways. First, the UN was the obvious and available forum for building security coalitions to deal with states deemed to have violated international law and to have posed a threat to international society. In all cases these coalitions were inspired and led by the United States, the only state to enjoy "superpower" status in the post-Cold War world. The most notable cases were the Gulf War in the early 1990s and the so-called "War on Terrorism" that began in Afghanistan a decade later. The second way the UN became a more significant actor was in peacekeeping. However, all major UN-led peacekeeping operations of the 1990s that involved the largest amount of military resources were well-publicized fiascos, mainly due to inadequate firepower, a slowness to act on the part of the Security Council, bureaucratic incompetence and lack of political will.

Although less ambivalence towards the use of force on the part of the UN and the powers that controlled it would have certainly saved thousands of lives in Rwanda and Bosnia, by the 1990s the idea that force was of declining utility in international relations had become a key premise in thinking that aimed to provide grand theory for the field of international relations. For example, as early as the late 1970s theories of "complex interdependence" were based on this assumption.

Three main factors have contributed to the decline in the use of force in international relations. The first is the risk of nuclear annihilation, a risk that became even greater as more states gained access to nuclear weapons technology. Second was that the time period during which wars enjoy popular support became shorter the more civilians became the chief casualties of war and the more media depictions of war became a factor in the discourse on the use of force. Third was that the increased destructive capability of modern conventional weapons meant that defeated states could become burdens on the entire international system because of the toll taken on other states through flows of refugees, the absence of trade and environmental damage.

Measures taken by the UN to integrate public information into its peacekeeping operations were further evidence of how propaganda had become a key dimension of all cases where there is force or the threat of force. The discourse on force in international relations is also the discourse on the ecology of the use of propaganda in international relations. While propaganda could be deployed without the use of force, it increasingly became the case that force could not be deployed without propaganda.

Sanctions

Just as the end of the Cold War gave renewed life to UN peacekeeping, the use of sanctions by the organization became a very popular strategy during the 1990s to bring offending states into line. Under Chapter VII of the UN Charter, the Security Council is empowered to investigate whether there is "any threat to the peace, breach of the peace, or act of aggression", and to determine what action will be taken if its attempts to solve the problem by appealing to the guilty parties fail.

The UN Charter did not use the word "sanctions". "The Security Council may decide what measures not involving the use of armed force are to be employed to give effect to its decisions, and it may call upon the Members of the United Nations to apply such measures," states Article 41. "These may include complete or partial interruption of economic relations and of rail, sea, air, postal, telegraphic, radio, and other means of communication, and the severance of diplomatic relations." In the absence of a comprehensive definition of sanctions, measures such as those described in the second paragraph of Article 41 were considered to be what could be termed sanctions. Sanctions in this sense are penalties imposed on an offending party to bring about some change in action. However, it can be difficult to distinguish between penalties suffered because a party has lost a conflict (for example the wages imposed on Germany after the First World War) and sanctions in the sense described above. This and other reasons account for why sanctions have become a contentious area of international political and legal discourse.[23]

Before the end of the Cold War, the UN imposed sanctions only twice: on Rhodesia (1966–79) and South Africa (1977–94). However, it seemed as though the floodgates had been opened for the imposition of UN sanctions during the 1990s when such penalties were imposed on over a dozen countries: Afghanistan, Angola, Ethiopia, Eritrea, Haiti, Iraq, Liberia, Libya, Rwanda, Sierra Leone, Somalia, Sudan and the former Yugoslavia. The pretexts varied: in the case of Libya it was its failure to extradite suspects wanted for the Lockerbie airline bombing, while in Haiti the sanctions were to punish the military government that had overthrown a civilian government. So ethnic oppression, support of terrorism and the overthrowing of government were the main collective reasons for the use of this tool.

This increased use of sanctions during the 1990s was one of the clearest indications of the higher profile enjoyed by the United Nations after the Cold War. The ability to marshal coalitions in the General Assembly and on the Security Council allowed bold actions to be taken in the name of the organization. And as might be expected, the more popular sanctions became for the UN as a means of conducting its international relations, the more scrutiny was placed on the efficacy of this tool. Apart from the problems of definition identified above, the UN's use of sanctions was problematic for three main reasons.

First, the mechanism by which sanctions were imposed seems unjust and biased in favor of the permanent members of the Security Council. The General Assembly could not impose sanctions, even though it could recommend them. That privilege rested solely with the Security Council, and it could approve only those sanctions with nine affirmative votes and no veto by any of the permanent members (China, France, Russia, the UK and the US). Obviously none of these countries was on the long list of those penalized during the 1990s, and under the existing arrangements this would never happen.

Second, the success of sanctions regimes evoking the change demanded was questionable. In some cases military force still had to be used, and this was certainly true in Serbia. In Iraq, after a decade of UN sanctions there were still complaints that the country was supporting terrorism and making chemical weapons, a situation that put it on the list of countries scheduled for attack in the United States' "War on Terrorism". The use of UN sanctions on Iraq actually seemed to be a case of history repeating itself because it appeared to be a clear illustration of a maxim in international relations that a punitive peace is an unstable peace. Just like Germany after the First World War, Iraq was forced into a situation where it could argue that it had very little to lose from violation of the terms of the Gulf War truce, and because it had remained victimized by sanctions, a no-fly zone and punitive bombings for so long, the UN and the United States had more reason not to trust Iraq when it claimed not to be building chemical weapons nor supporting international terrorism as a means of retaliation.

The Iraq situation also illustrated another problem with the UN's use of sanctions: that innocent civilians often suffered from the various embargos while the guilty governments or ruling individuals suffered little or not at all. In addition, neighboring countries and those with strong economic and social relations with states under sanction stood to suffer as well. This problem seems even more significant when one considers that relatively poor African countries dominated the list of those countries penalized by UN sanctions during the 1990s. Margaret Doxey, an expert on sanctions, has noted that "wider social and economic effects produced in both Iraq and Yugoslavia (Serbia-Montenegro) have included the erosion of the middle-class, the criminalization of society and long term economic damage – all of which bring increased insecurity and instability and undermine goals of economic development for the target and possibly for other states in the region".[24]

The relationship between sanctions and public information as means by which international organizations conduct their international relations is more difficult to define than is the case with the other tools surveyed in this section. In international organization, force and conventional diplomacy, it has been easy to see how public information (or propaganda generally) has played a critical role in their ecologies. Propaganda work has even helped to diminish some traditional functions of conventional diplomacy. But often sanctions are imposed when other means of persuasion, such as conventional diplomacy and propaganda, are spent. Here, sanctions and propaganda strategies, such as public information, are not mutually reinforcing, and this was certainly the case with the UN and Iraq in the lead-up to the Gulf War. However, there are instances where sanctions and propaganda strategies are mutually reinforcing, i.e. where the offending state is itself engaging in propaganda as a means of justifying its illegal behavior. The best example of this was apartheid South Africa, where the UN arms embargo was coupled with an elaborate counter-propaganda program run in large part out of the DPI (see Chapter 4).

A similarity shared by sanctions and public information was that their status as tools used by the UN to conduct its international relations rose during the post-Cold War period. However, the big difference between the two was that sanctions – a tool of punishment – are collectively an *aggressive* strategy, while public information – a tool of ideological maintenance intended to win recognition and consent for the UN and its policies among states and international public opinion – is more often than not a *defensive* strategy. When we compare public information to other tools used by international organizations to conduct their international relations we achieve a more sophisticated way of thinking about the role of public information practice in international politics. While we can talk about specific problems being resolved directly due to force or even sanctions, we cannot make the same claims about public information. Indeed, this is how it is in popular rhetoric about change in international relations: offending parties are said to capitulate under the pressure of overwhelming force, because severe economic sanctions deny them the resources to maintain resistance, or even due to the maneuvers of a particularly skilled diplomat. In contrast, public information and propaganda tactics generally are never mentioned as strategies for change in their own right. Indeed, in the 1990s when it had become obvious that this realm of international affairs could no longer be ignored by the international relations mainstream, it was still given a secondary role in the way it was rhetorically labeled as "soft" power.[25]

The UN's founding bureaucrats envisioned a "supporter" role for public information and it remained that way during the first half-century of the UN's life and beyond. A 1983 report on the DPI, by the Committee for Programme and Co-ordination, explained that:

> This "supporter role" had been a fundamental element in the basic mandate of the Department, as enunciated by the General Assembly in its resolution 13(I) of 13 February 1946, and reaffirmed in its resolution 595(VI) of 4 February 1952. The logic underlying this concept, as outlined in the reappraisal report, was that the resources that could, realistically, be made available to the United Nations for public information would

never be adequate to enable the Organization to bear the primary responsibility, in practical terms, of informing the peoples of the world about
the United Nations and its activities. Thus, other agencies of information,
whether official or private, would have to assume that responsibility.
However, in order to carry out information activities on the aims and
work of the United Nations, national information services depend on the
Department of Public Information, as an *international information service,*
to provide the indispensable infrastructure of necessary raw materials as
well as the basic motivations and stimuli [italics added].[26]

Examples of what the DPI should provide in that role of supporter included:

physical facilities, such as office space, radio and television studios, satellite transmission facilities and lounges, as well as material services, such
as press releases, press briefings, radio news bulletins, live television feeds,
and briefings and documentation for non-governmental organizations.
Raw materials (as distinct from finished products) include not only press
releases but also film footage, audio recordings, videotape, photographs
and newsreel summaries. Two items, although finished products, were
described as basic reference materials constituting an important part of
the supporter services. These are the *Yearbook of the United Nations* and the
UN Chronicle.[27]

The report found that, with the exception of briefings and other services for
NGOs (the number of which accredited to the UN during the 1970s had
rapidly increased), these supporter functions had either not expanded or
had declined by the early 1980s. But while our investigation in this book
does affirm the view that public information cannot be placed on the same
pedestal as force or even sanctions in international relations, and that public information served to reinforce other practices in international politics,
the role of public information in the international relations of the United
Nations actually rose. We can say at the beginning of the twenty-first century that public information still performs a supporter role but that its support is not of the kind envisaged at the founding of the UN. In place of being
merely a bureaucratic handmaiden, disseminating press releases, providing
facilities for journalists covering the UN and the like, the DPI became the
ideological back-up for the UN's work throughout the world, portraying
to the millions its message that the UN is something worthwhile. This
argument is based on the related proposition that the arena of international
politics evolved from being more a power play of armies and force to
a power play of ideology. Chapter 7 will look at perspectives from critical
postmodern theorists regarding this argument, but to end this chapter
I need to explain in more detail here the idea that "superstructure" (the
realm of ideas, images and meanings) has increased in importance in the
way international relations is conducted.

"The minds of men"

At the turn of the twenty-first century the transnational superstructure is to states, international organizations and other actors what the high seas were to the naval powers of old. The only difference between these two arenas of conflict is that the possibilities of participation in the latter are greater for many more actors than was the case with the former. Today's players are not just states with access to the sea – the UK, Spain, France, Portugal and the like – but also the UN, Australia, the Catholic Church and even Amnesty International.

"Superstructure" was selected for lack of a better term, and it is necessary to make very clear very quickly the way it is being used. It is most often associated with the primitive Marxist formulation of how ideology works in capitalist societies – the so-called base/superstructure metaphor, in which the dominant ideas in such social systems are said to be almost mechanically predetermined by those in control of the economic base. The conceptualization was expressed in essence in the famous paragraph from Marx and Engels' *The German Ideology*.[28] However, the twentieth century saw much theoretical innovation and debate in this area of social theory – for example Antonio Gramsci's theory of hegemony, the structuralism of Claude Lévi-Strauss and Ferdinand de Saussure, the structuration of Anthony Giddens, poststructuralism of Michel Foucault and Jacques Derrida, and the postmodernism of Jean Baudrillard and Fredric Jameson. More recently the label "public sphere" has been employed to describe this intellectual realm to which the vulgar Marxists referred but which has been theorized in a more sophisticated way by later thinkers.

John Keane defines a public sphere as "a particular type of spatial relationship between two or more people, usually connected by a certain means of communication (television, radio, satellite, fax, telephone, email, etc.), in which non-violent controversies erupt, for a brief or more extended period of time, concerning the power relations operating within their given milieu of interaction and/or within the wider milieux of social and political structures within which the disputants are situated".[29] Keane then goes on to distinguish between three types of public sphere: *micro-public spheres* (at the sub-state level), *meso-public spheres* (at the nation-state level), and *macro-public spheres* (involving millions or billions of people "enmeshed in disputes at the supranational and global levels of power"). Keane's idea of the macro-public sphere is what most closely approximates the idea of the international superstructure being discussed here. However, Keane's project is confined to the theorizing of the relationship between mass media and society. The idea of an international superstructure here includes but is not limited to the mass media. It also includes that area of international politics where ideas about "world order" are proposed, promoted, debated and imposed at various junctures in world history.

These ideas are present in mass media discourse (especially as global as this has become in the era of globalization of media technology and firms), but the superstructure of international society is also the terrain in which the international public diplomacy of states, IGO public information, the symbolic meaning of who gets a Nobel Prize, and even the pastiche of international sports events operate. It is the arena where all actors in international society say who they are, how they want to be understood, what ideologies and myths should have precedence and what version of international society they want to see. And while the old Marxist notion of superstructure was rightly criticized for failing to adequately account for the agency of actors within it, this conception says that the members of international society actually do have agency, even though some are more capable than others.

The United Nations is critical to the understanding of this international superstructure because its founders effectively declared that there should be such a global arena of ideas when they created the UN system after the Second World War. The implements they crafted to ensure that it would be a superstructure according to their own terms were the DPI and UNESCO. It has already been explained in this book that a prominent part of this vision was universality. But the creation of UNESCO was evidence that the UN's founders intended that the new world would not be confined to the overtly political. As the organization's name suggested, just about every facet of human life would be covered: education, science, culture, communication. The UNESCO Constitution of 1945 declared that:

> ... since wars begin in the minds of men, it is in the minds of men that the defences of peace must be constructed;
> ... That a peace based exclusively upon the political and economic arrangements of governments would not be a peace which could secure the unanimous, lasting and sincere support of the peoples of the world, and that the peace must therefore be founded, if it is not to fail, upon the intellectual and moral solidarity of mankind.

The UN was actually the first systematic project to create peace and a new international system by trying to attend to the various concerns of human life in one place. Other international organizations before it, in the spirit of internationalism, had shown that they understood how international interaction in such fields as sport, journalism or business could present an alternative vision of world society, but the UN was the first to attempt conflation of all these areas of activity.

That superstructure – which the creators of UNESCO clearly understood was important – rose in significance in the latter 50 years of the twentieth century but was a radically different plain from that which the founders of UNESCO and the UN might have envisaged. It differed not only in scope but also in character. Instead of a structured realm where universality according to a Eurocentric modernist vision prevailed, it had become an unruly pastiche where the Pope was competing for the attention of teenagers distracted by advertising for Pokemon and Coca-Cola, where a videotape of Osama Bin Laden shared broadcast time with a trailer for the latest Hollywood action adventure that its makers claimed to be "just entertainment," and where a sports celebrity is a spokesman about the plight of AIDS not because of her expertise in the field but because of her fame.

The depiction of such an apparently disorderly world, where image often supersedes substance, and surprise is more common than the routine, is the stock in trade of postmodern theorists. In the context of international relations this distinction between the modern and the postmodern is even more stark than it is in discussions of so-called domestic society. The creators of the DPI and UNESCO wanted a modern world where new ideas would be injected into the way international relations were conducted via a global system dominated by states. But within 50 years what they got was in fact a postmodern world. In such a world it is often unclear whether or not states are the most influential entities, and while the project of universality did score some gains (such as making "human rights" a fixture in the language of international politics), phenomena such as the remarkable survival of Cuban communism, the Gulf War and the World Trade Center attacks were evidence that alternative visions of what the human condition should be would not only survive but sometimes triumph in the face of seemingly overwhelming force.

One of the best illustrations of postmodern international relations is the international spectacle. Although spectacles were a feature of politics as far back as ancient times they did not become a routine and regular part of political life until the twentieth century.[30] Spectacles are elaborate crowd events staged to propagandize the thousands who participate directly and the millions more who might participate indirectly as audiences for these events that are broadcast via mass media. Actors in postmodern international relations invest heavily in the staging of international spectacles for a variety of reasons but many of these involve the realm of ideas, myth, symbolism, emotion and reputation. For example, competition to stage regional and international sporting events to be broadcast to international audiences is stiff, with states investing much money in order to not only win the right to be host but also to provide the needed infrastructure (such as stadiums and housing).

In the language of postmodern critical theory, spectacles are more *simulation* than *representation* because they say and do more than what they seem to overtly represent. For example, in soccer the 1998 World Cup – staged in France and won by a multiracial French team – is of utility as a spectacle to French nationalists and the French government (all concerned about their *image*) not for what it *produced* (i.e. evidence that France could successfully host such a large event, and a French victory) but for what it *meant* symbolically and mythically. In the sociopolitical context of the time, it simulated the best of France – a multiracial democracy where Arabs, blacks and whites could co-operate for the common good to successfully stage a complex world-class event. This contradicted the messages sent by news media coverage of France in the lead-up to the 1998 World Cup: public-sector strikes, police harassment and even murder of ethnic minorities, popular support for racist right-wing parties, extensive public opposition and debate over African immigration to France.

The *Chicago Tribune* got the message in an editorial on the French victory and spectacle some days after the final:

> It was enough to make a bigot cry.
>
> Last weekend's sports news, that is. Elsewhere in the realm of human affairs, it was reality as usual: Protestants marching against Catholics in Northern Ireland, Serbs besieging ethnic Albanians in Kosovo, Hutu and Tutsi going at it in Rwanda.
>
> But in sports, things were different. Someone named Zinedine Zidane, the son of an Algerian construction worker, headed in two goals and sparked France to its first-ever World Cup soccer championship. The losing country, Brazil, always had been known for multiracialism. But France? This is the place where Jean-Marie Le Pen and his anti-immigrant National Front party want to send all the dark-skinned – Algerians, other Africans, Turks – back where they came from.
>
> Too bad they'd have to deport half of France's championship team ...[31]

The editorial also talked about other events in golf, baseball and basketball (where players of multiple races and nationalities were excelling) as being "the new reality" of sports and life. From the perspective of critical theory it was a shallow version of social life and international relations, but critical theorists do not populate the streets, or even the editorial boards, of popular newspapers. So, for a moment at least, France was a land where racial harmony triumphed over bigotry, and Brazil (one of the most institutionally racist countries) was "known for multiracialism". This could all be summed up in the words of a jazz/pop medley by Bobby McFerrin – "Don't worry. Be happy".

The 2000 Summer Olympics was another simulation. The host, Australia, used the event to say through spectacle that it should mean something completely different from that which some media accounts and personal experience with Australia and Australians might suggest. The opening ceremony, broadcast with such fanfare to millions around the world, featured images and symbols of racial harmony. The aboriginal sprinter Cathy Freeman played a critical role in this pageant. At the 1994 Commonwealth Games in Victoria, Canada, where she had won two gold medals and one silver, Freeman had made a political statement and sparked controversy by taking a victory lap draped in the aboriginal flag. But in Sydney six years later she was chosen to light the Olympic flame at the opening ceremony. And, after she won the gold in the 400 meters, millions around the world saw her loyally singing the Australian national anthem at her presentation ceremony. In one fell swoop her history of protest and the reality of racist aboriginal oppression seemed to be gone – at least at the level of the popular and superficial. "For once an Aborigine – she's from MacKay in Queensland – was on the front pages for all the right reasons," one journalist commented. "And the heroine worship and adulation showed that Australians are now far more concerned about national triumph than the colour of the victor's skin".[32] The Australia of the Olympic Games was a different Australia from the Australia journalist John Pilger wrote about just months earlier. In Pilger's Australia the aboriginal child mortality rate was three times that of white children, the life expectancy of aboriginal people was 25 years shorter than that of whites, aboriginal children were still being blinded by trachoma (a disease of poverty that even poorer Sri Lanka had defeated), and it was an Australia with the shameful history of genocide, which included "nigger hunts" (lynchings) of aboriginals and a systematic program of "breeding out the colour" by taking tens of thousands of mixed race children from their parents between the 1920s and 1960s in an attempt to exterminate aboriginal culture.[33]

The commodification of sport (especially global spectacles such as the World Cup and the Olympics) has attracted much scholarly attention because the numbers are easy to find and read. Media scholar Michael R. Real reported that in 1960 money from television accounted for one of every US$400 of the cost of hosting the Summer Olympics, but by 1984 it paid for one of every two dollars.[34] The American TV network NBC paid $705 million for the rights to broadcast the 2000 Summer Olympic Games and it sold $900 million in advertising on the Olympics broadcasts.[35]

However, the ideological uses of these events have been less easy to grasp and theorize. John Sugden and Alan Tomlinson make the connection between the propaganda projects of the League of Nations and the UN, and the seemingly contradictory ideological uses of transnational sports spectacles, in particular the World Cup that is run by the Federation Internationale de Football Association (FIFA):

> The missions of more formally politically constituted international organizations, such as the League of Nations between the two world wars and the United Nations since, have been undone by the pervasive persistence of forms of nationalism. One of FIFA's main problems has been balancing its global ideals with the fact that international football per se tends to stimulate and promote parochial forms of nationalism. Sport in general and football in particular have proven to be significant theaters for the expression of national identity, and in its mobilized form,

nationalism...We do not routinely spend time wondering of worrying about what nation we belong to, unless there is a perceived threat to that identity, such as in times of war (international or civil). It is during such times of jingoistic political rhetoric, emblematic mass rallies, and national flag waving that meanwhile passive notions of national identity become mobilized as nationalism.[36]

It would therefore be very short-sighted to attempt a theorization of UN propaganda as though it existed in a modernist vacuum, disconnected from the other representations and simulations that tug at the emotional strings of world publics. Real notes that even though sport accounts for between 1 and 2 per cent of the GNP of the United States, "its symbolic or expressive importance is far greater than that for many because it provides a language or interpretive structure that at once reflects, explains, and interprets social life".[37] In writing on the transnational political and emotional significance of FIFA and the World Cup, Sugden and Tomlinson explain that in football "the newly independent countries of Latin America discovered a vehicle through which to express national self-determination, first within the subcontinent and eventually on a world stage".[38]

Sport is mentioned here merely to provide an example of just one of multiple sites of discourse in the international superstructure. Just as sport has utility in identity formation and is therefore very significant in the study of international politics, so too do labor (the "world of work"), popular music, technology or even the family. The DPI must be contextualized as part of this unruly ideological mix. It is a far cry from the vision of the late 1940s. And the persistence of international conflict – especially the shedding of blood over religion, ethnicity and ideology – is evidence enough to show that more intellectual capital needs to be invested into understanding this dimension of international affairs to better articulate its political relevance.

7
UN Ideological Work and International Change

Early in George Orwell's *Homage to Catalonia* is a passage that expresses Orwell's fascination with a brand of unsophisticated propaganda used by those fighting alongside him to defend the Spanish Republican government. Although the Spanish Civil War (1936–39) was yet another manifestation of how the post-First World War order and the League of Nations had failed, Orwell's observation – in 1937 – was a profound insight into the thinking that would eventually guide the United Nations' approach to propaganda. The illiteracy in Spain in the late 1930s and the complicated nature of the international politics of the war made the Spanish Civil War a fascinating arena of propaganda practice. The various combatants produced numerous propaganda posters and these have become compelling historical artifacts in the ecology of propaganda as an instrument of conflict.[1] But the propaganda Orwell was reflecting on was as basic as shouting out statements calculated to sap the enemy's morale – to convert him rather than kill him. Wrote Orwell:

> On the Government side, in the party militias, the shouting of propaganda to undermine the enemy morale had been developed into a regular technique. In every suitable position, usually machine-gunners, were told off for shouting-duty and provided with megaphones. Generally they shouted a set-piece, full of revolutionary sentiments which explained to the Fascist soldiers that they were merely the hirelings of international capitalism, that they were fighting against their own class, etc., etc., and urged them to come over to our side. This was repeated over and over by relays of men; sometimes it continued almost the whole night. There is very little doubt that it had its effect; everyone agreed that the trickle of Fascist deserters was partly caused by it. If one comes to think of it, when some poor devil of a sentry – very likely a Socialist or Anarchist trade union member who has been conscripted against his will – is freezing

at his post, the slogan "Don't fight against your own class!" ringing again and again through the darkness is bound to make an impression on him. It might make just the difference between deserting and not deserting. Of course such a proceeding does not fit into the English conception of war. I admit I was amazed and scandalized when I first saw it done. The idea of trying to convert your enemy instead of shooting him![2]

When Franco claimed victory and declared the Spanish Civil War ended in 1939, the most vicious propaganda of the Second World War was yet to come. But the UN's vision was that "bad propaganda" (the type that incited hatred and war) would be outlawed, and that it would lead the world in spreading "good propaganda". Instead of killing the people with whom we disagreed we would make sure they shared the same values.

Because this idea has been central to the UN's propaganda project it is the most appropriate way to begin this final chapter, which seeks to pull together the various points made throughout the book into a coherent whole and to contextualize them.

Questions answered

The UN's record concerning propaganda was a contradictory one. Although various resolutions decried the practice as dangerous to world peace, the UN never operated on a principle of absolute intolerance of propaganda. The real policy was to devise a type of propaganda that would promote the principles of the UN Charter and the various causes championed by the UN over time. In some cases this project was marvelously successful. Perhaps the best example of this was the UN's promotion of human rights. The propagation of human rights was the most effective part of the UN's work with respect to human rights, which became part of the "common sense" of international relations to such an extent that it is now hard to imagine a world without the concept.

Bureaucratic ineptitude

However, the UN's inability to be honest about the fact that it ran a propaganda program compromised the program's very utility. For example, this meant that it could not carry out public opinion studies to gauge the effectiveness of its propaganda in actually influencing international public opinion. And because the DPI was not officially a propaganda or public relations organization it was not in a position to engage in the developments in social science research that would have helped it to refine considerably its strategic mission. Indeed, the DPI was stuck in time with a "two-step" model of mass communication that was based on faulty assumptions about the process and restricted the reach of the UN's message, despite the organization's contradictory use of popular mass-media technologies. In addition, this ambivalent attitude towards its propaganda work left the UN vulnerable to charges of duplicity.

Ambivalence towards the UN's propaganda program originated in a failure to recognize it for what it was, but this is not the only explanation. What the bureaucratic history presented in this book has shown is that the first 50 years of the DPI was marked by continued concern and institutional reviews related to three problems: concern over waste of resources and mismanagement; the search for a clear definition of target audiences; and uncertainty regarding the role of public information in international relations. In other words, the DPI suffered a serious identity crisis and continued to be preoccupied with this issue.

These examples of bureaucratic ineptitude did not mean that the UN was always static in its public information policy. One area that evolved considerably was the way it conducted its relations with NGOs. By the late 1990s, NGOs were viewed as critical to the UN's attempts to gain relevance and legitimacy in international politics because they were considered the soul of "transnational civil society", a highly contested term but a useful rhetorical construct for the UN at the time. The change with regards to NGOs meant that instead of regarding them as mere vehicles for "spreading information about the United Nations" (according to the 1946 Technical Advisory Committee), the DPI saw them as "spurring the United Nations system and other intergovernmental structures towards greater transparency and accountability".[3]

Image problem

But it must be pointed out that the UN's image problems at the end of the century may not have been better even had its propaganda or public relations been any more decisive, as the empirical evidence covered in this book shows that the UN's prominent public relations debacles all originated in deeper political crises. Flashy public relations ultimately cannot shore-up an organization in need of serious reform. At the kernel of the Waldheim and 1990s peacekeeping scandals was the inability of the UN to reform the Security Council and become a more representative world body. Until a Secretary-General can make his or her name by becoming the first to instigate this most important and fundamental transformation, the UN will continue to be a source of ridicule in some circles, as the body dedicated to tolerance and world peace that ironically had an ex-Nazi at its helm for a decade, and as the organization that was impotent to prevent two of the worst cases of genocide (in Rwanda and Bosnia) the world has ever seen even though it had a contingent of peacekeepers on the ground at the time.

The UN's image problems can also be explained by looking at what happened to the organization during its first 50 years. Decolonization and the changed demographics of membership that it brought led some to think that the UN had become captive to the so-called "Third World", and hostile to the interests of the minority of North American and European states that underwrote most of its expenses. Similarly, it has also been noted in the book that the initial high expectations for the UN were naïve, and that the disappointment that followed in the succeeding years should not have come as a surprise.

However, in considering the UN's image problems it is important to note the differential decline in the organization's reputation. The stark drop in the UN's standing was more characteristic of public opinion in the rich countries (especially the United States). In the early 1960s it was an organization considered valuable enough by certain sectors of the American intelligentsia that they invested millions of dollars and donated their talents to propagandize on its behalf. The Xerox-sponsored Telsun project (see Chapter 3) was the most clear example of this. However, by the 1990s the once-impotent UN that needed US support to survive had become a power-crazy villain in American films, a sinister entity bent on world domination. In tune with this representation, opinion polls and actual US policy were no longer as supportive of the organization.

Increased relevance

Ironically, as ambivalence towards the DPI continued, the importance of the department to the UN's work increased rather than declined. The need for a Department of Public Information had been questioned throughout the history of the UN, but by the turn of the century all the evidence showed that the UN could not hope to effectively function in the new world of international politics without careful attention to what one writer had labeled its "signifying mission". The DPI increased in importance for three main reasons.

The most obvious of these was that the effort to create a New World Information Order (NWICO) – a controversy that led the US, UK and Singapore to withdraw from UNESCO in the early 1980s – was effectively transferred from UNESCO to the DPI. At the behest of the General Assembly's Information Committee the DPI was asked to conduct activities to realize a NWICO that were previously the sole domain of UNESCO but which that organization could no longer perform. So, for example, by century's end the DPI was involved in the training of journalists from developing nation-states, an activity that really should have been the responsibility of UNESCO.

The second reason was the need for the UN to run counter-propaganda campaigns in various national and regional conflicts. The case given special attention in this book is apartheid South Africa. In time, the DPI's involvement in such regional and civil wars would be expanded to UN peacekeeping operations that were established in their aftermath.

Third, the DPI became a more significant actor because the very nature of international politics had evolved. The preponderance of international mass media, the phenomena of international spectacles, the Internet and the rise of public diplomacy at the expense of conventional diplomacy were just some of the factors that made international politics as much a power play of symbols and images as it was of bombs and bullets. The DPI was the part of the UN formally designated the portal of entry into this new world of politics.

New politics

Of necessity, this investigation of the DPI has covered a fascinating array of themes that at first glance seem unrelated to each other. However, this very diverse mix is what characterizes the new international relations of the twenty-first century. So the story of the DPI, especially in the 1990s, is also an illustration of how the political fortunes of a matter as serious as genocide might be linked to matters as seemingly trivial as Hollywood movies, the political fancies of celebrities and the Olympic Games.

The book's attention to representation of the UN in Hollywood film and the UN's courting of celebrities should not be seen as a departure into triviality but a serious attempt to understand the full dimension of world politics at the turn of the twentieth century. With a topic such as the DPI it is hard to see where pop culture ends and politics begins. Early warning of how international politics would change came at the beginning of the 1980s when an ex-actor was elected United States President. Bob Geldof – a rock star – became more famous for his work on famine than for his music. Ted Turner and Bill Gates used money made from entertainment and media to underwrite UN health programs. And Latin American *telenovela* stars arguably have more prestige and emotional appeal than Presidents of their countries, which is why political bodies – such as the United Nations Children's Fund (UNICEF) – enlist them to attract attention.

The symbols of international pop culture became the language of mass-mediated international relations. So the mass communication of governments, NGOs and other actors in international politics is more about the manipulation of symbols than it is about the manipulation of words. To illustrate this we can look at how states plagued by racial oppression and conflict began to use ethnic minorities as part of a symbolic language to suggest national harmony and inclusion. Australia's use of Cathy Freeman at the 2000 Olympics (discussed in Chapter 6) was a case in point. However, this form of communication runs the risk of reducing profound issues to the level of the banal and cynical. Does the inclusion of non-white faces in the Cabinet of a US President, because it symbolizes ethnic inclusion and is therefore good foreign policy, mean a significant change in government policy (especially policies towards the ethnic sectors of the population from which the non-whites come, or towards parts of the world populated by people who look like them)? And did the pageant of racial harmony at the 2000 Sydney Olympics change anything for oppressed Australian aboriginals?

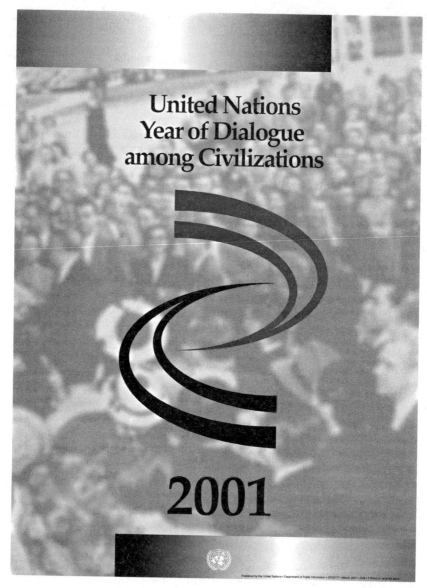

Figure 7.1 Poster published by the DPI to promote the United Nations Year of Dialogue among Civilizations.

This attention to symbolism in international politics is key to contextualizing and ultimately theorizing the role of public information at the UN and other institutions in the field of multilateral governance. When the decision was made at the turn of the century to upgrade the role of public information in UN peacekeeping operations, this was further evidence of awareness on the part of the UN that it needed to cultivate its symbolic role. To talk about actions and events related to the UN's work without explaining this symbolism is to miss an important way of understanding the organization. Over the years, writers on the UN have mentioned this function of the UN in international politics. Conor Cruise O'Brien remarked that, in creating the UN, the allies "showed themselves conscious, as the pre-war democracies had not been, of the importance of symbolic action, ritual and ceremonial ... "[4] Journalist Bernard Nossiter remarked that the UN's blue-helmeted peacekeepers "provide symbolic barriers between Cypriot Greeks and Turks, Indians and Pakistanis, Israelis and Syrians".[5] William Over described the UN as "a symbolic theatre where human rights are researched and analyzed, taught, broadcast and monitored".[6] And François Debrix (see below) said the UN "does not have to approximate a (collective) reality that may never be", but that instead it was "the sign of something else: the will of sovereign states to find a common resolve and cooperate only on certain issues".[7] However, there has been little in the way of comprehensive theoretical work on this subject.

The theoretical context

This book is an empirical study of an obscure and often misunderstood part of the United Nations bureaucracy, and the task left for the remaining pages is to compare and contrast the evidence presented in the book to the thinking in fields relevant to this topic. The discussion of theory here is meant as a way of helping the reader organize in his or her mind what might be regarded as a large and intimidating volume of information. It is also a way of bringing reflexivity to the book. But it is not a way of setting out an alternate new theory; those thinkers whose stock-in-trade it is to develop theory can do that for themselves and others, perhaps using the empirical evidence supplied here.

The DPI and its work can be explained in relation to conceptual thought from two areas of scholarly investigation: public relations and international relations.

Public information as public relations

One of the main arguments of this book is that for 50 years the United Nations maintained a propaganda program while denying that what it did was propaganda, and for that reason the suggestion here that what the DPI does is essentially public relations is likely to raise some eyebrows at the UN.

Public relations professionals are also likely to be displeased that the discussion here treats public relations and propaganda as basically the same thing. However, the public relations press has been in no doubt about the DPI's public relations identity, and this is why, over the years, it has written so much about the organization. Articles have pointed out how quick DPI officials have been to deny the public relations aspect to their work, an attitude similar to that of Ingrid Lehmann discussed in Chapter 1. For example, soon after the controversy over the TV series "Amerika" in the mid-1980s, an article in *Public Relations Journal* quoted one DPI official as saying: "We don't have a PR department here – it's not in the mandate of the General Assembly". Another was quoted, in the same article, as explaining that the term "public relations" was not used at the DPI, and that: "We don't try to manipulate public opinion".[8] In early 2001, *Public Relations Strategist* published an interview with the Indian novelist and career UN civil servant Shashi Tharoor, who succeeded Kensaku Hogen at the helm of the DPI at the beginning of the century. Tharoor said his challenge was "promoting concern for the poor and the victimized in the media of the rich and the tranquil".[9] He also talked about the striking similarity between the strategies the UN had put in place and those advocated by public relations practitioners, especially the move to make the UN more open to reporters.

My contention here is that the distinctions often made between public relations, advertising, marketing and even public information are often artificial. These distinctions might make sense to professionals in these fields, who crave separate identities and professional particularity, but in the context of this research on the political uses and consequences of formal persuasion programs the demarcations are often useless. Cases to illustrate this point can actually be found in the United States where the fields above were developed during the twentieth century. The American advertising industry created the Advertising Council in 1941 as a means of improving the public image of advertising. By producing advertising in the public interest it was hoped that the Advertising Council would show a skeptical public how advertising was not merely shady manipulation but actually a practice that benefited society.[10] Over the years the body became famous for a number of "public service" campaigns, such as war mobilization, promoting blood donation, preventing forest fires and stemming illegal drug use. The fact that public relations firms have been hired to conduct similar campaigns on behalf of firms and municipalities, and that there seems to be little difference between this kind of work and what the UN calls "public information", illustrates the point that advertising, public relations and public information techniques are used to produce (in the eyes of a political scientist) basically the same results. Ironically, by the late 1990s the UN had teamed up with the International Public Relations Association (IPRA) to run an international award contest for the best public relations campaigns "with a social purpose". The three finalists in 1999 were on the themes of child prostitution, national pride and public awareness of health.[11]

It is also my hope that if a reader has reached this far in the book, by now he or she will be aware of how the term "propaganda" is used in this work. Instead of a blanket dismissal of "propaganda" as a label to describe all organized persuasive communication as negative, the history of the UN's approach to, and use of, propaganda suggests many more dimensions. Indeed, by the 1990s a number of scholarly writers in the field of public relations were beginning empirical and theoretical studies of the links between public relations and international activities that are often dismissed as propaganda, such as Cutlip's study of the history of public relations firms working on the behalf of governments,[12] and Signitzer and Coombs' exploration of the "conceptual convergences" between public relations and public diplomacy.[13]

Before turning to the specific discussion of public relations theory, we must first look at the ecology of research on propaganda that is the context within which it can also be placed.

Formal propaganda research had gone out of vogue in the United States in the years since the end of the Second World War. When Harold Lasswell's seminal dissertation *Propaganda Technique in the World War* was published in 1927, and for several years after, propaganda was a sexy topic. During both World Wars, and during the conflicts in between, governments had set up ad hoc propaganda bureaus that were promptly disbanded when the conflicts ended. Lasswell himself was Director of War Communications Research at the US Library of Congress from 1939 to 1945. However, propaganda as a technique of conducting foreign policy and international relations became institutionalized during the years after the Second World War to the extent that many propaganda institutions are now not even recognized as such.[14] The list of these bodies include the Alliance Française, British Council, United States Information Agency, Japan Foundation, British Broadcasting Corporation (BBC) and the Goethe Institut.

However, this is not to say that certain subsidiary bodies, such as Radio Marti, are so unabashedly propagandistic that their specific role in international politics is unclear. Allied to this development in policy and practice is the fact that the relatively new field of cultural studies has made the early work of Lasswell, Paul Lazarsfeld and Kurt Lewin seem rather rudimentary. So Leah R. Vande Berg's 1999 survey of 30 years of "critical media studies" research could cover the terrain of sub-categories such as "mythic studies", "hegemony studies" and "audience-oriented critical media studies" without ever once speaking about research into something called "propaganda".[15] It is now clear, with the benefit of hindsight, that what sustained Lasswell's generation was the initial fascination with propaganda, spurred as it was by such developments as the new science of psychology and the changed nature of war.[16]

In time, this generation of research in the United States was superseded by a whole range of cultural studies of *messages, audiences, myths, meanings, values, norms* and *ideologies*. In such an intellectual environment where it is now taken for granted by both reactionaries and progressives that culture is a contested terrain, why study propaganda? Indeed, it would seem that to think in terms of propaganda would be to think about mass communication in a shallow, two-dimensional way – the "normal" or regular that is not propagandistic, and the propagandistic that is assumed to be something abnormal.

Seen through this lens, the type of propaganda research that looks at formal persuasion campaigns offers nothing exciting, and the more intellectually stimulating work has come from those exploring the obscure but important political uses of education, religion and pop culture to unearth the texture of power relationships in society. This explains the great popularity and influence of various French, German and British schools of "critical theory" that would influence all dimensions of social science in the 50 years following the Second World War. However, the names of these writers and their personalities are often more recognizable than the significance of their ideas; a partial list would include Michel Foucault, Roland Barthes, Jügen Habermas, Jean Baudrillard, Stuart Hall, Raymond Williams and Theodor Adorno. In the very last pages of this chapter the point will be made that the rise of critical theory has had an impact on the formal study of international relations, thus enabling the investigation of "low politics" of this book to be taken more seriously in the field than it may have been previously.

But as a pathway to explaining how critical theory has contributed to the metatheory in international relations that inspires a work such as this one, we must explain here how public information is conceptualized as a professional practice.

Grunig and Hunt have argued that public relations programs are of four varieties: (1) the press agency model; (2) the public information model; (3) the two-way asymmetrical model; and (4) the two-way symmetrical model.[17] This typology has proven to be very popular as a means of contextualizing and explaining the character of mass persuasion.[18] The models follow a line of continuum from the least sophisticated – the press agency model – to the most sophisticated – the two-way symmetrical model. The sophistication of a public relations program is based on a number of factors, including: (a) how much it is based on research; (b) how symmetrical it is (i.e. how much it is based on a mutual exchange between the target and the entity sponsoring the program); and (c) how much it assumes that the organization sponsoring the public relations program will change as a result of the exchange. The press agency model simply seeks to get favorable publicity, and it can do this through the dissemination of misleading information. The public information model is also a simple search for favorable publicity, though more elaborate. According to Grunig: "With the public information model, an organization uses so-called journalists-in-residence – public relations practitioners who act as though they are journalists – to disseminate relatively objective information through the mass media and controlled media such as newsletters, brochures and direct mail".[19]

Grunig dismisses these first two types of public relations as being particularly unsophisticated because they are asymmetrical and do not attempt to change the behavior of the organization but try to achieve a favorable image for the organization through hype or simply spreading favorable information. In contrast, the two-way asymmetrical model "uses social science research to identify attitudes and to develop messages that appeal to those attitudes that persuade publics to behave as the organization wants".[20] Grunig cites as an example of this the famous campaign run in the United States by Hill and Knowlton in the lead up to the Gulf War. The firm used alleged Iraqi atrocities as the prominent theme of its campaign because survey research of the American public that it had sponsored found that such information would move Americans to accept US military intervention to free Kuwait. However, an even more sophisticated model is the two-way symmetrical model as this is based not only on research but also assumes that the sponsoring organization will change as a result of the feedback from the campaign.

This typology from the literature of public relations is helpful in contextualizing the public information program of the United Nations because it provides a set of criteria on which to assess UN public information policy and practice. How sophisticated is the UN program? How much does it rely on research? Is the objective of the program symmetry, which Grunig says should be the goal of the most sophisticated public relations campaigns?

This does not mean that placing the UN's public information program within a public relations typology labels it as an inherently sinister and evil activity. Indeed, Grunig argues that sophisticated public relations is a management practice employed by all savvy organizations because it "contributes to the planning process by communicating and building relationships with publics that support the mission of the organization, or that can constructively divert it from its mission".[21] Seen through the lens of public relations, "public diplomacy consists essentially of the application of public relations to strategic relationships of organizations with international publics".[22] The benefit of analyzing public diplomacy and public information practice by public relations standards is not only that it injects intellectual honesty into the discussion but that the ethical standards of public relations can also be used to evaluate such campaigns. Indeed, the public relations literature has begun to do this.[23] This literature questions whether it is ethical for firms to take on government clients that are corrupt, questions the ethics of falsehood in public relations practice, and even the basic fairness of asymmetrical models. Another way it enhances analysis of UN public information policy and practice is that it has been more sophisticated empirically and theoretically on the question of who are, or should be, target audiences – a serious deficiency of the DPI during its first 50 years.

Based on Grunig's typology and the empirical research done for this book, it is very clear that the UN's public information program after 50 years did not follow a sophisticated public relations model. Ironically, it can be best described as conforming to the "public information" model. This is so due to a combination of factors, and the argument here is that UN public information required more sophistication in order to avoid the continuation of what has been to this point in UN history a serious waste of resources. The program is asymmetrical; it is not grounded on research and there is no assumption embedded in UN public information practice that feedback to the public information program will actually change the UN. The converse of this scenario concerning target audiences would be a situation in which the UN boldly declared a public relations strategy, providing it with the foundation to use concepts and techniques from public relations, for example the situational theory of publics and the notion of "active" and "passive" publics.[24] This type of work is a project for the twenty-first century for those interested in improving the UN's propaganda program.

Public information as international relations

"World order" appears in the subtitle of this book as a result of my belief that all work in international relations is about world order. This is because international relations is the study of peace and war in the international system, and all paradigms and theories in the field are based on ideas about the relationship, or ordering, of international actors. One of the patron saints of the so-called "English School" of international relations, Hedley Bull, described world order as a pattern of activity that maintains the primary goals of international society. But the English School came up against others with very different visions of what international order was like, and who saw the international system not as resembling an international society, anarchical (as Bull argued) or otherwise, but as a Weberian ideal type, more often than not about what should be than what is – more about possibility.

So the large number and variety of visions of world order are a characteristic feature of international relations literature, and range from dependency theory to the New International Economic Order, from Woodrow Wilson's "Fourteen Points" to the Atlantic Charter, and from George Bush's new world order in the wake of the Gulf War to the UN Charter. And these visions are often proclaimed after some grave international crisis, when the tenets of one order have been found wanting and there is a need to suggest something new and improved.

From this perspective, the DPI and its work were part of the project to impose the vision of world order of the UN Charter on the international system. The idea was to propagandize order in the hope that some day this vision would become so ingrained that it would be as natural as the air we breathe, and that some day the various dimensions of that vision, such as the UN's version of human rights, the peaceful resolution of disputes, and sovereignty, would be the common sense of international politics.

This conceptual approach to the topic of this book helps explain why when there is any discussion of the UN's success or failure there is often a de facto reference to the achievements or shortcomings of its propaganda work. Of course the term "propaganda" is never used, but reference is made to the realm of ideas that are part of the superstructure of the new world order the UN was created to maintain. If one takes George Bush's new world order of 1990 seriously, then we can say that the UN survived three grand projects of world order in the twentieth century: the few years after its founding and before the Cold War; the Cold War, when it was essentially marginalized; and the post-Cold War period when it was "re-discovered" and there was plenty of evidence that it was given a new role, particularly as international peacekeeper. Throughout all these transformations, the UN's propaganda has essentially remained committed to promoting the high-minded ideals proposed for the organization in 1946. The picture painted is of a line of continuum that starts at the founding of the organization and has progressed, with set-backs here and there, to the present, a struggle to fix the ideas of the UN Charter as the dominant principles running international politics. So when UN officials talk about success over the broad sweep of the organization's history they talk about how some of these ideas ceased to be exotic and became commonplace. Similarly, there is a suggestion of defeat in the realm of propaganda when there is an account of failure. To illustrate this point we can juxtapose two quotes.

In his Millennium Report of 2000, Secretary-General Kofi Annan explained that the achievement of the UN in its first 50 years was in the "force of the values" the organization represented, values that established and sustained "global norms":

> The importance of principles and norms is easily underestimated; but in the decades since the United Nations was created, the spreading acceptance of new norms has profoundly affected the lives of many millions of people. War was once a normal instrument of statecraft; it is now universally proscribed, except in very specific circumstances. Democracy, once challenged by authoritarianism in various guises, has not only prevailed in much of the world, but is now generally seen as the most legitimate and desirable form of government. The protection of fundamental human rights, once considered the province of sovereign states alone, is now a universal concern transcending both governments and borders.[25]

We can contrast Annan's optimism with that of Dame Margaret Anstee, a UN Under Secretary-General from 1987 to 1993, and UN Special Representative to Angola from 1992 to 1993. This is not the vision of order depicted by Annan, but one of chaos, disorder and confusion caused by an inability to control and predict the flow of ideas:

> In many respects, the UN is made a scapegoat for more general ills. The
> world is in turmoil at the end of the century, and no one, and no gov-
> ernment, quite knows what to do about it. We are faced with drastic and
> difficult transitions. There is the vertiginous technological transforma-
> tion, overshadowing and outpacing the development of ideas. There is
> the communications and information revolution, which is outdating
> existing political systems and institutions, giving the media ever-increasing
> influence on policy-making. Parliaments have lost the battle to fax
> machines, computers and the information superhighway. The Internet
> can purvey anything across the globe, from pornography to instructions
> on how to make bombs.[26]

Both Annan and Anstee seem to share a common view of world order. It is
a place where ideas can take hold and impose a discipline that would
otherwise not exist. Their attitudes also suggest that actors in international
relations (especially political entities such as governments and the UN) try
to impose this control through ideas. The communication revolution is seen
as taking away this means of control because more actors have a say in
deciding what should be the important ideas. More ideas mean more alternatives. More options mean less power for those who before were able to
represent their preferences as the only alternatives available. Of course, not
all is lost, and this is why there was a sense of optimism in Annan's
Millennium Report. In his view, some ideas did take hold.

The approach to the study of international relations presented in this
book is therefore one that places more emphasis on the realm of international communication as a means of understanding world order. Instead of
a focus on military force it explores intellectual force. Instead of emphasiz-
ing what an organization does, it looks at what the organization says about
what it does.

A related study of the UN has been that by Debrix who argued that we
should employ postmodernist techniques not only to understand the UN's
rhetoric but also how the realist paradigm in international relations prepares
us for reading the UN. The realist paradigm cannot exist without the
discursive-rhetorical construction of anarchy and order, Debrix argues. A less
dogmatic, postmodern reading of Hobbes might reveal Hobbes to be less a
theorist of world anarchy than realists like to characterize him in order to
justify the assumptions of the paradigm. But if the post-Cold War world is
viewed as a dangerous place that is hard to control, this has implications for
how one views the place of the UN within it. According to Debrix:

> It is not a question of materially re-creating the UN as a Leviathan, as a
> world government capable of using force, coercion, and discipline to

impose order. Rather, it is a matter of forming a rhetoric, a new discursive platform, that will make possible the belief (or the promise) that the UN can indeed fulfill the mandate of a Leviathan in international politics, even if it does not possess the physical capacities that were necessary to the original Leviathan to centralize fear.[27]

The approaches of this book and that of Debrix to the study of international phenomena are by no means new lenses through which to view international politics, even though the specific topics they have selected for scrutiny in this way are innovative. Elsewhere I have noted that writers from the poorer, non-white world have had a long history of engaging with the role of intellectual force in international relations; the list is as diverse as Indira Gandhi, Ngugi wa Thiong'o, Steve Biko, Michael Manley, Frantz Fanon and Kwame Nkrumah. Indeed, the formal international propaganda works of various religions, imperialisms and colonialisms were the forerunners and inspirations for the more secular, ecumenical political work of the post-Second World War period. It was the desire to break free from what some have called "mental slavery" that inspired the NWICO at UNESCO, a movement that had significant repercussions for the DPI, as this book has argued. This writing from the South is no less doctrinaire than the works of such people as Henry Kissinger and George Kennan, and as such it should be included in the body of literature on the field of international relations just as these Americans have been. However, the so-called "Third Debate" of the 1990s and the turn of the century – which now puts culture, communication and ideology squarely on the plate of international relations – often ignores the work of these writers from outside North America and Europe who have written about these issues for so long, and an indication of the blatant myopia and prejudice in the field can be gleaned from Martin Griffiths' *Fifty Key Thinkers in International Relations*, published in 1999.[28] Despite the apparent token presence of Francis Fukuyama, serious thinking in international relations is depicted as a basically white, North American and Western European domain. Just as the subject matter of international relations is in urgent need of reform, the view of who qualifies to produce the important ideas within it needs also to change.

In the late 1980s and throughout the 1990s, some of those who led the effort to transform international relations were aware that the field would be of little intellectual and explanatory utility if it did not widen its methodological and epistemological base. Therefore the Third Debate is about a rethinking of the rationalist approaches to the field, shared by both neo-liberal and neo-realists, and the proposition that international relations can be of greater utility if it integrates approaches inspired by critical theory, such as postmodernism and constructivism. The first two debates – realism versus idealism, and behavioralism versus qualitative methods (such as historical reconstruction) – were "old hat" by the end of the century. The field could not predict the collapse of the Soviet Union, and it was not the place to look for some of the earliest and most sophisticated theories on globalization. The shortcomings of international relations began with the conceptualization of globalization itself. As late as 1993, one American IR textbook identified "globalism" as one of the three main bodies of theory in international relations (the other two being realism and pluralism).[29] But this view of the global is confined to Marxist theories of international relations, such as those of Lenin,[30] Immanuel Wallerstein,[31] and the dependency school.[32] Some Marxist theorists provided a valuable critique of international capitalism, the role of class relations across state boundaries, and systems of domination and inequality. But they were still as preoccupied with the state as much as were the realists and pluralists. However, the sociological and anthropological conception of the global was more refined than a mere engagement with the global expansion of capitalism and its outgrowths of imperialism and neo-colonialism. Indeed, the Marxist critique of global capitalism does not necessarily involve a critique of Western modernity. A number of Marxists, beginning with Marx himself, actually embrace this modernity, as is evidenced by their very paternalistic attitudes to "subject" – or formally subject – peoples.

Too often IR writers stopped at declaring that the communication and transportation revolutions would create "interdependence".[33] They did not go that step further to theorize the meaning of these changes in relation to values and norms that undergird the international order. In contrast, anthropologists and sociologists led the way in producing more refined theory of what globalization actually meant to an understanding of world order.[34] For example, one sociological view of globalization was that it was about a sharing of symbolic meaning at the global level. Shared symbols are at the core of the concept of culture, therefore globalization involved a profound cultural shift, a change that can be called an "intensification of global consciousness".[35] So one striking characteristic of the condition of globalization was that the most critical issues of the era were articulated in terms of globalism. The problem of AIDS was not just a disease afflicting one region but was articulated by those with access to, and control of, influential public discourse as "the world AIDS crisis", and a popular environmentalist slogan was "Think Globally, Act Locally". The UN promoted this kind of thinking in its "world conferences" on problems as diverse as gender equality, human rights and racism. Similarly, for Arjun Appadurai globalization was the appearance of "diasporic public spheres", where primordial affiliations to race, religion, kinship and other markers of identity are being globalized with the help of modern communication capabilities and migration.[36] Many of the realists, pluralists and Marxists assumed that there was some rationality and order in world politics, but Appadurai disputed this. His view of globalization was of five "scapes": ethnoscapes; mediascapes; technoscapes; financescapes; and ideoscapes. Their forms were more fluid than fixed.[37]

The profound changes spawned by the communication and transportation revolutions required more than mere fine-tuning of theories of inter-state relations. For example, we get a more refined understanding of how such phenomena as ethnic conflict, human rights lobbying and migration work by looking at what is happening to culture (as a consequence of these revolutions) at the local, national and global levels. The traditional prism, and prison, of traditional IR theory did not supply such a framework for relating the local, national and global. International relations remained hopelessly moribund in its theorizing of international processes and change, despite the pioneering work of Karl Deutsch[38] and Wallerstein.[39]

The traditional shortcomings of international relations make it easy to understand why the increased incorporation of critical theory techniques in the field came as a breath of fresh air. This has been so despite the often confusing use of terms. For example, Kubálková, Onuf and Kowert note that: "The structuralism of anthropologist Claude Lévi-Strauss has little to do with the structural Marxism of Louis Althusser and even less to do with the structural realism of IR's Kenneth Waltz".[40] However, the constructivism that acquired its share of disciples in international relations during the 1990s owes its very existence to the various innovations and debates between Marxism, the various brands of structuralism,[41] the structuration of Anthony Giddens,[42] post-structuralism and postmodernism.

Although constructivism and postmodernism have been given separate spaces in the classification of schools in international relations,[43] they generally share approaches to the study of the field that are collectively quite different from the old prisons of neo-realism and neo-liberalism. These include:

- the eschewing of rationalist paradigms to explain international relations;
- the willingness to employ literary and psychoanalytic concepts (such as discourse theory and deconstruction) as qualitative methods;
- the boldness to connect the seemingly unimportant and disconnected in the investigation of international relations;
- a reluctance to propose grand theory, and, conversely, a willingness to explore how discursive formations discipline and restrict ideas; and
- the courage to be reflexive about the whole project of knowledge creation in the field.

All this means that in the brave new world of international relations at the beginning of the twenty-first century, interdisciplinary research and more open minds should craft a more dynamic, interesting field. Some constructivists, such as Onuf – concerned that they might be depicted the same way as some postmodernists – have denied that they are inspired by "emancipatory" politics; and the great skepticism of postmodernism does raise concern that postmodernism can justify reactionary attitudes. But the previous discussion about the relationship between UN public information practice and public relations theory should make clear here that this work is by no means an elaborate justification for abandonment and doing nothing.

This book has shown that the DPI and UNESCO were created to help mold an international "superstructure", but that this superstructure became a drastically different entity from what it was intended to be in 1946. The symbolic representation and meaning of the UN at the end of the twentieth century was a mere part of an international pageant where international governmental organizations, states and other actors in international relations used mass media in very different ways from the practices of 50 years previously. Although this analysis of the DPI eschews the creation of a grand theory of "public information in international relations", or something similar, it does argue that a refined understanding of international politics begins with the boldness to explore the interconnections between the bureaucracies of formal political institutions (e.g. the UN and its DPI) and entities seemingly quite unrelated, such as the soccer World Cup, the Pope, the International Olympic Committee's host-city selection process, charity work by celebrities, global satellite TV, language programs by the Instituto Cervantes, and even the Miss World beauty pageant. Such a panoply of themes, and the exploration of the political significance of connections between them in one work, have not traditionally been on the plate of the formal study of international relations but they must be placed there as urgently as possible.

Appendix I

(League of Nations) International Convention Concerning the Use of Broadcasting in the Cause of Peace September 23, 1936

Official texts in French and in English. This Convention was registered with the Secretariat, in accordance with its Article II, on April 2nd, 1938, the date of its entry into force.

ALBANIA, THE ARGENTINE REPUBLIC, AUSTRIA, BELGIUM, THE UNITED STATES OF BRAZIL, THE UNITED KINGDOM OF GREAT BRITAIN AND NORTHERN IRELAND, CHILE, COLOMBIA, DENMARK, THE DOMINICAN REPUBLIC, EGYPT, SPAIN, ESTONIA, FRANCE, GREECE, INDIA, LITHUANIA, LUXEMBURG, THE UNITED STATES OF MEXICO, NORWAY, NEW ZEALAND, THE NETHERLANDS, ROUMANIA, SWITZERLAND, CZECHOSLOVAKIA, TURKEY, THE UNION OF SOVIET SOCIALIST REPUBLICS and URUGUAY.

Having recognised the need for preventing, by means of rules established by common agreement, broadcasting from being used in a manner prejudicial to good international understanding;

Prompted, moreover, by the desire to utilise, by the application of these rules, the possibilities offered by this medium of intercommunication for promoting better mutual understanding between peoples:

---

1 Ratifications:

INDIA .... August 11th, 1937
GREAT BRITAIN AND NORTHERN IRELAND........ August 18th, 1937
DENMARK................................. October 11th, 1937
NEW ZEALAND............................. January 27th, 1938
LUXEMBURG............................... February 8th, 1938
BRAZIL.................................. February 11th, 1938
FRANCE.................................. March 8th, 1938
NORWAY.................................. May 5th, 1938
EGYPT................................... July 29th, 1938
ESTONIA................................. August 18th, 1938

Accessions:

AUSTRALIA (including the territories of
Papua and Norfolk Island and the Mandated
Territories of New Guinea and Nauru) .... June 25th, 1937
BURMA .... October 13th, 1937
SOUTHERN RHODESIA .... November 1st, 1937
UNION OF SOUTH AFRICA (including the Mandated
Territory of South West Africa)................. February 1st, 1938
IRELAND .... May 25th, 1938

SWEDEN . . . . June 22nd, 1938
EL SALVADOR . . . . August 18th, 1938
GUATEMALA. . . . . November 18th, 1938
FINLAND. . . . . November 29th, 1938

Have decided to include a Convention for this purpose, and have appointed as their Plenipotentiaries:

ALBANIA: M. Thomas LUARASSI, Secretary of the Permanent Delegation to the League of Nations.

ARGENTINE REPUBLIC: M. Carlos A. PARDO, Commercial Advised to the Legation at Berne.

AUSTRIA: His Excellency, Dr. Marcus LEITMAIER, Envoy Extraordinary and Minister Plenipotentiary.

BELGIUM: M. Maurice BOURQUIN, Professor at the University of Geneva.

THE UNITED STATES OF BRAZIL: M. Elyseu MONTARROYOS, Delegate to the International Institute of the Intellectual Co-operation.

UNITED KINGDOM OF GREAT BRITAIN AND NORTHERN IRELAND: Viscount CRANBORNE, M.P., Under-Secretary of State for Foreign Affairs; Mr. Fredrick William PHILLIPS, Director of Telecommunications, General Post Office; Mr. Henry George Gordon WELCH, Principal, General Post Office.

CHILE: M. Enrique GAJARDO V., Head of the Permanent Office to the League of Nations.

COLOMBIA: His Excellency Dr. Gabriel TURBAY, Permanent Delegate to the League of Nations, Envoy Extraordinary and Minister Plenipotentiary; His Excellency Dr. Carlos LOZANO Y LOZANO, Envoy Extraordinary and Minister Plenipotentiary to the President of the Spanish Republic.

DENMARK: M. Holger Oluf Quistgaard BECH, First Secretary of the Permanent Delegation to the League of Nations.

THE DOMINICAN REPUBLIC: M. Charles ACKERMANN, Consul-General at Geneva.

EGYPT: M. Abd-el-Fattah ASSAL, Acting Charge d'Affairs at Berne.

SPAIN: M. Jose RIVAS Y. GONZALEZ, Head of the Radio-Communications Sections of the Ministry of Communications; M. Manuel MARQUEZ MIRA, Professor at the Official School of Telecommunications.

ESTONIA: M. Johannes KODAR, Permanent Delegate a.i. to the League of Nations.

FRANCE: M. Marcel PELLENC, Director-General of Broadcasting of the Ministry of Posts, Telegraphs and Telephones; M. Yves CHATAIGNEAU, Chief of Section at the Ministry of Foreign Affairs.

GREECE: His Excellency M. Raoul BIBICA-ROSETTI, Permanent Delegate to the League of Nations, Minister Plenipotentiary.

INDIA: Sir Denys DE SAUMAREZ BRAY, K.C.S.I., K.C.I.E., C.B.E.

LITHUANIA: M. Juozas URBSYS, Minister Plenipotentiary, Political Director in the Ministry of Foreign Affairs.

LUXEMBURG: His Excellency M. Emile REUTER, Honorary Minister of State, President of the Chamber of Deputies.

UNITED STATES OF MEXICO: His Excellency M. Narciso BASSOLS, Ambassador, Envoy Extraordinary and Minister Plenipotentiary accredited to the Court of St. James; His Excellency M. Primo VILLA MICHEL, Permanent Delegate to the League of Nations, Envoy Extraordinary and Minister Plenipotentiary.

NORWAY: M. Einar MASENG, Permanent Delegate to the League of Nations.

NEW ZEALAND: Mr. William Joseph JORDAN, High Commissioner in London; Sir Christopher James PARR, G.C.M.G.

THE NETHERLANDS: His Excellency Ridder C. VAN RAPPARD, Permanent Representative to the League of Nations, Envoy Extraordinary and Minister Plenipotentiary to the Swiss Federal Council.

ROUMANIA: M. Tudor A. TANASESCO, Engineer, attached to the Ministry of Communications, Lecturer at the Bucharest Polytechnic School.

SWITZERLAND: M. Camille GORGE, Counsellor of Legation, Chief of the League of Nations Section at the Federal Political Department;

M. Jakob BUSER, Chief of Division at the General Directorate of Posts and Telegraphs.

CZECHOSLOVAKIA: His Excellency M. Rudolf KUNZL-JIZERSKY, Permanent Delegate to the League of Nations, Envoy Extraordinary and Minister Plenipotentiary to the Swiss Federal Council.

TURKEY: His Excellence M. Necmeddin SADAK, Permanent Delegate to the League of Nations, Minister Plenipotentiary.

UNION OF SOVIET SOCIALIST REPUBLICS: M. Edouard HOERSCHELMANN, Secretary-General of the People's Commissariat for Foreign Affairs.

URUGUAY: His Excellency M. Victor BENAVIDES, Engineer, Envoy Extraordinary and Minister Plenipotentiary to the Swiss Federal Council.

Who, having communicated their full powers, found in good and due form, have agreed upon the following provisions:

Article 1

The High Contracting Parties mutually undertake to prohibit and, if occasion arises, to stop without delay the broadcasting within their respective territories of any transmission which to the detriment of good international understanding is of such a character as to incite the population of any territory to acts incompatible with the internal order or the security of a territory of a High Contracting Party.

Article 2

The High Contracting Parties mutually undertake to ensure that transmissions from stations within their respective territories shall not constitute an incitement either to war against another High Contracting Party or to acts likely to lead thereto.

Article 3

The High Contracting Parties mutually undertake to prohibit and, if occasion arises, to stop without delay within their respective territories any transmission likely to harm good international understanding by statements the incorrectness of which is or ought to be known to the persons responsible for the broadcast.

They further mutually undertake to ensure that any transmission likely to harm good international understanding by incorrect statements shall be rectified at the earliest possible moment by the most effective means, even if the incorrectness has become apparent only after the broadcast has taken place.

Article 4

The High Contracting Parties mutually undertake to ensure, especially in time of crisis, that stations within their respective territories shall broadcast information concerning international relations the accuracy of which shall have been verified – and that by all means within their power – by the persons responsible for broadcasting the information.

Article 5

Each of the High Contracting parties undertakes to place at the disposal of the other High Contracting Parties, should they so request, any information that, in his opinion, is of such a character to facilitate the broadcasting, by the various broadcasting services, of items calculated to promote a better knowledge of the civilisation and the conditions of life of his own country as well as of the essential features of the development of his relations with the other peoples and of his contribution to the organisation of peace.

Article 6

In order to give full effect to the obligations assumed under the preceding Articles, the High Contracting Parties mutually undertake to issue, for the guidance of governmental broadcasting services, appropriate instructions and regulations, and to secure their application by these services.

With the same end in view, the High Contracting Parties mutually undertake to include appropriate clauses for the guidance of any autonomous broadcasting organisations, either in the constitutive charter of a national institution, or in the conditions imposed upon a concessionary company, or in the rules applicable to other private concerns, and to take the necessary measures to ensure the application of these clauses.

Article 7

Should a dispute arise between the High Contracting Parties regarding the interpretation or application of the present Convention for which it has been found impossible to arrive at a satisfactory settlement through the diplomatic channel, it shall be settled in conformity with the provisions in force between the Parties concerning the settlement of international disputes.

In the absence of such provisions between the Parties to the dispute, the said Parties shall submit it to arbitration or to judicial settlement. Failing agreement concerning the choice of another tribunal, they shall submit the dispute, at the request of one of them, to the Permanent Court of International Justice, provided they are all Parties to the Protocol of December 16th, 1920, regarding the Statute of the Court; or, if they are not all Parties to the above Protocol, they shall submit the dispute to an arbitral tribunal, constituted in conformity with the Hague Convention of October 18th, 1907, for the Pacific Settlement of International Disputes.

Before having recourse to the procedures specified in paragraphs 1 and 2 above, the High Contracting Parties may, by common consent, appeal to the good offices of the International Committee on Intellectual Co-operation, which would be in a position to constitute a special committee for this purpose.

Article 8

The present Convention, of which the French and English texts are both authentic, shall bear this day's date, and shall be open for signature until May 1st, 1937, on behalf of any Member of the League of Nations, or any non-member State represented at the Conference which drew up the present Convention, or any non-member State to which the Council of the League of Nations shall have communicated a copy of the said Convention for that purpose.

Article 9

The present Convention shall be ratified. The instruments of ratification shall be sent to the Secretary-General of the League of Nations, who shall notify the deposit thereof to all the Members of the League and the non-member States referred to in the preceding Article.

Article 10

After May 1st, 1937, any Member of the League of Nations and any non-member State referred to in Article 8 may accede to the present Convention.

The notifications of accession shall be sent to the Secretary-General of the League of Nations, who shall notify the deposit thereof to all the Members of the League and to all the non-member States referred to in the aforesaid Article.

Article 11

The present Convention shall be registered by the Secretary-General of the League of Nations, in conformity with the provisions of Article 18 of the Covenant, sixty days after the receipt by him of the sixth ratification or accession.

The Convention shall enter into force on the day of such registration.

Article 12

Every ratification or accession effected after the entry into force of the Convention shall take effect sixty days after the receipt thereof by the Secretary-General of the League of Nations.

Article 13

The present Convention may be denounced by a notification addressed to the Secretary-General of the League of Nations. Such notification shall take effect one year after its receipt.

The Secretary-General shall notify the receipt of any such denunciation to all Members of the League and to the non-member States referred to in Article 8.

If, as the result of denunciations, the number of High Contracting Parties should fall below six, the present Convention shall cease to apply.

Article 14

Any High Contracting Party may, on signing, ratifying or acceding to the present Convention, or at any subsequent date, by a written document addressed to the Secretary-General of the League of Nations, declare that the present Convention shall apply to all or any of his colonies, protectorates, overseas territories, or territories placed under his suzerainty or mandate. The present Convention shall apply to the territory or territories specified in the declaration sixty days after its receipt. Failing such a declaration, the Convention shall not apply to any such territory.

Any High Contracting Party may at any subsequent date, by a notification to the Secretary-General of the League of Nations, declare that the present Convention shall cease to apply to any or all of his colonies, protectorates, overseas territories, or territories placed under his suzerainty or mandate. The Convention shall cease to apply to the territory or territories specified in the notification one year after its receipt.

The Secretary-General shall communicate to all Members of the League and to the non-member States referred to in Article 8 all declarations received under the present Article.

Article 15

A request for the revision of the present Convention may be made at any time by any High Contracting Party in the form of a notification addressed to the Secretary-General of the League of Nations. Such notification shall be communicated by the Secretary-General to the other High Contracting Parties. Should not less than one-third of them associate themselves with such request, the High Contracting Parties agree to meet with a view to the revision of the Convention.

In that event, it shall be for the Secretary-General of the League of Nations to propose to the Council or Assembly of the League of Nations the convening of a revision conference.

Chile: Enrique J. GAJARDO V
Colombia: As referendum; Gabriel TURBAY; Carlos LOZANO Y LOZANO
Denmark: Holger BECH
Dominican Republic: Ch. ACKERMANN
Egypt: F. ASSAL
Spain: Sous reserve de la declaration inseree dans le proces-verbal de la seance de cloture de la Conference. Jose RIVAS Y GONZALEZ; Manuel MARQUEZ MIRA
Estonia: J. KODAR
France: M. PELLENC; Yves CHATAIGNEAU
Greece: Ad referendum; Raoul BIBICA-ROSETTI
Union of Soviet Socialist Republics: Sous reserve des declarations inserees dans le proces-verbal de la seance de cloture de la Conference[1]. Ed. HOERSCHELMANN
Uruguay: V. BENAVIDES

Footnotes

1. Under reservation of the declaration mentioned in the procès-verbal of the final meeting of the Conference.
   This declaration is worded as follows:

   The Spanish Delegation declares that its Government reserves the right to put a stop by all possible means to propaganda liable adversely to affect internal order in Spain and involving a breach of the Convention, in the event of the procedure proposed by the Convention not permitting of immediate steps to put a stop to such breach.

1. Under reservation of the declarations mentioned in the procès-verbal of the final meeting of the Conference.
   These declarations are worded as follows:

   The Delegation of the Union of the Soviet Socialist Republics declares that, pending the conclusion of the procedure contemplated in Article 7 of the Convention, it considers that the right to apply reciprocal measures to a country carrying out improper transmissions against it, in so far as such a right exists under the general rules of international law and with the Conventions in force, is in no way affected by the Convention.

The Delegation of the Union of Soviet Socialist Republics declares that its Government, while prepared to apply the principles of the Convention on a basis of reciprocity to all the Contracting States, is nevertheless of opinion that certain of the provisions of the Convention presuppose the existence of diplomatic relations between the Contracting Parties, particularly in connection with the verification of information and the forms of procedure proposed for the settlement of disputes. Accordingly, the Government of the Union of Soviet Socialist Republics is of opinion that, in order to avoid the occurrence of differences or misunderstandings between the States Parties to the Convention which do not maintain diplomatic relations with one another, the Convention should be regarded as not creating formal obligations between such States.

SOURCE: League of Nations–Treaty Series
   Treaties and International Engagements registered with the Secretariat of
   the League of Nations.
   Volume: CLXXXV, 1938
   Nos. 4270–4300 and Annex XLV

Appendix II

United Nations General Assembly Resolution 13(I), Annex I,
Recommendations of the Technical Advisory Committee on
Information Concerning the Policies, Functions and
Organization of the Department of Public Information
February 13, 1946
A/RES/13(I)

The United Nations cannot achieve the purposes for which it has been created unless the peoples of the world are fully informed of its aims and activities.

Therefore the Technical Advisory Committee on Information makes the following recommendations:

1. A Department of Public Information should be established under an Assistant Secretary-General.
2. The activities of the Department of Public Information should be so organized and directed as to promote to the greatest possible extent an informed understanding of the work and purposes of the United Nations among the peoples of the world. To this end the Department should primarily assist and rely upon the co-operation of the established governmental and non-governmental agencies of information to provide the public with information about the United Nations. The Department of Public Information should not engage in "propaganda". It should on its own initiative engage in positive informational activities that will supplement the services of existing agencies of information to the extent that these are insufficient to realize the purpose set forth above.
3. The United Nations should establish as a general policy that the press and other existing agencies of information be given the fullest possible direct access to the activities and official documentation of the Organization. The rules of procedure of the various organs of the United Nations should be applied with this end in view.
4. Subject to the general authority of the principal organs of the United Nations, responsibility for the formulation and execution of information policy should be vested in the Secretary-General and under him in the Assistant Secretary-General in charge of the Department of Public Information.
5. When negotiating an agreement with a specialized agency the Economic and Social Council should be requested to take into consideration the matter of co-ordinated information services and of a common information policy, and to consult with the Secretary-General concerning each individual agreement.
6. In order to ensure that peoples in all parts of the world receive as full information as possible about the United Nations, the Department of Public Information should consider the establishment of branch offices at the earliest practicable date.
7. The functions of the Department of Public Information appear to fall naturally into the following categories: press, publications, radio, films, graphics and exhibitions, public liaison and reference.

8. The Department should provide all the services for the daily, weekly and periodical press, both at the Headquarters of the United Nations and through its branch offices, that may be required to ensure that the press is supplied with full information about the activities of the United Nations.

9. The Department should prepare and publish pamphlets and other publications on the aims and activities of the United Nations, within the limits of the criteria set forth in recommendation 2.

10. The Department should actively assist and encourage the use of radio broadcasting for the dissemination of information about the United Nations. To this end it should, in the first instance, work in close co-operation with radio broadcasting organizations of the Members. The United Nations should also have its own radio broadcasting station or stations with the necessary wavelengths, both for communication with Members and with branch offices, and for the origination of United Nations programmes. The station might also be used as a centre for national broadcasting systems which desire to co-operate in the international field. The scope of the radio broadcasting activities of the United Nations should be determined after consultation with national radio broadcasting organizations.

11. In addition to assisting the newsreel and photographic press agencies, the Department of Public Information should also promote and where necessary participate in the production and non-commercial distribution of documentary films, film strips, posters and other graphic exhibits on the work of the United Nations.

12. The Department and its branch offices should actively assist and encourage national information services, educational institutions and other governmental and non-governmental organizations of all kinds interested in spreading information about the United Nations. For this and other purposes it should operate a fully equipped reference service, brief or supply lectures, and make available its publications, documentary films, film strips, posters and other exhibits for use by these agencies and organizations.

13. The Department and its branch offices should also be equipped to analyse trends of opinion throughout the world about the activities of the United Nations and the extent to which an informed understanding of the work of the United Nations is being secured.

14. Consideration should be given to the setting up of an Advisory Committee to meet periodically at the seat of the United Nations to discuss and forward to the Secretary-General observations regarding the information policy and programme of the United Nations. This Advisory Committee would be composed of experts appointed on the basis of broad geographical representation, personal qualifications and experience. They would be representative of the various media of information of the Members, and would be in a position to reflect to the Secretary-General the needs and desires of the general public of the Members in the matter of public information about the aims and activities of the United Nations.

15. In order that the Advisory Committee may be as widely representative as possible and receive the maximum support from the information organizations of all Members, the Secretary-General might, in consultation with the Governments of the Members, communicate with the representative officers of the leading organizations of the press, radio, film and other media and government information services of the Members on the establishment of such an Advisory Committee.

16. If it is found possible to set up an Advisory Committee, then at a later stage consideration should be given to establishing similarly composed national or regional advisory committees working in touch with the branches of the Department of Public Information.

Appendix III

United Nations General Assembly Resolution 110(II),
Measures To Be Taken Against Propaganda and the
Inciters of a New War
November 3, 1947
A/RES/110(II)

Whereas in the Charter of the United Nations the people express their determination to save succeeding generations from the scourge of war, which twice in our lifetime has brought untold sorrow to mankind, and to practice tolerance and live together in peace with one another as good neighbors, and

Whereas the Charter also calls for the promotion of universal respect for, and observance of, fundamental freedoms which include freedom of expression, all Members having pledged themselves in Article 56 to take joint and separate action for such observance of fundamental freedoms,

The General Assembly

1. Condemns all forms of propaganda, in whatsoever country conducted, which is either designed or likely to provoke or encourage any threat to the peace, breach of the peace, or act of aggression;
2. Requests the Government of each Member to take appropriate steps within its constitutional limits:
   (a) To promote, by all means of publicity and propaganda available to them, friendly relations among nations based upon the Purposes and Principles of the Charter;
   (b) To encourage the dissemination of all information designed to give expression to the undoubted desire of all peoples for peace;
3. Directs that this resolution be communicated to the forthcoming Conference on Freedom of Information.

Appendix IV

Final Act, UN Conference on Freedom of Information, Annex C
April 22, 1948

CHAPTER I: General Principles

Resolution No. 1 [Fundamental Principles]

WHEREAS Freedom of Information is a fundamental right of the people, and is the touchstone of all the freedoms to which the United Nations is dedicated, without which world peace cannot well be preserved; and

Freedom of information carries the right to gather, transmit, and disseminate news anywhere and everywhere without fetters; and

Freedom of information depends for its validity upon the availability to the people of a diversity of sources of news and of opinion; and

Freedom of information further depends upon the willingness of the press and other agencies of information to employ the privileges derived from the people without abuse, and to accept and comply with the obligations to seek the facts without prejudice and to spread knowledge without malicious intent; and

Freedom of information further depends upon the effective enforcement of recognized responsibilities,

The United Nations Conference on Freedom of Information

Resolves, therefore,

1. That everyone shall have the right to freedom of thought and expression: this shall include freedom to hold opinions without interference; and to seek, receive and impart information and ideas by any means and regardless of frontiers;
2. That the right of news personnel to have the widest possible access to the sources of information, to travel unhampered in pursuit thereof, and to transmit copy without unreasonable or discriminatory limitations, should be guaranteed by action on the national and international plane;
3. That the exercise of these rights should be limited only by recognition of and respect for the rights of others, and the protection afforded by law to the freedom, welfare, and security of all;
4. That in order to prevent abuses of freedom of information, governments in so far as they are able should support measures which will help to improve the quality of information and to make a diversity of news and opinion available to the people;
5. That it is the moral obligation of the press and other agencies of information to seek the truth and report the facts, thereby contributing to the solution of the world's problems through the free interchange of information bearing on them, promoting respect for human rights and fundamental freedoms without discrimination, fostering understanding and co-operation between peoples, and helping maintain international peace and security;
6. That this moral obligation, under the spur of public opinion, can be advanced through organizations and associations of journalists and through individual news personnel;

7. That encouragement should be given to the establishment and to the functioning within the territory of a State of one or more non-official organizations of persons employed in the collection and dissemination of information to the public, and that such organization or organizations should encourage the fulfillment *inter alia* of the following obligations by all individuals or organizations engaged in the collection and dissemination of information;

   (a) To report facts without prejudice and in their proper context and to make comments without malicious intent;

   (b) To facilitate the solution of the economic, social and humanitarian problems of the world as a whole through the free interchange of information bearing on such problems;

   (c) To help promote respect for human rights and fundamental freedoms without discrimination;

   (d) To help maintain international peace and security;

   (e) To counteract the spreading of intentionally false or distorted reports which promote hatred or prejudice against States, persons or groups of different race, language, religion or philosophical conviction;

8. That observance of the obligations of the press and other agencies of information, except those of a recognized legal nature, can also be effectively advanced by the people served by these instrumentalities, provided that news and opinion reach them through a diversity of sources and that the people have adequate means of obtaining and promoting a better performance from the press and other agencies of information.

Resolution No. 2 [Propaganda Inciting War and False Reporting]

WHEREAS the peoples of the world have embodied in the United Nations their determination to protect mankind from the scourge of war and to prevent the recurrence of aggression from Nazi, Fascist, or any other source;

WHEREAS the attainment of a just and lasting peace depends in great degree upon the free flow of true and honest information to all peoples and upon the spirit of responsibility with which all personnel of the press and other agencies of information seek the truth and report the facts;

and WHEREAS, by inaccurate reports, by defective or distorted presentation and deliberate or malicious misinterpretation of facts in various parts of the world, peoples have been misled and their mutual understanding has been seriously endangered;

The United Nations Conference on Freedom of Information

Endorses the resolutions of the second General Assembly on propaganda which is either designed or likely to provoke or encourage any threat to the peace, breach of the peace, or act of aggression, and on the spreading of false and distorted reports;

Declares that all such propaganda and such reports:

   (a) are contrary to the purposes of the United Nations as defined in the Charter;

   (b) constitute a problem of the first importance calling for urgent corrective action on the national and international planes;

Condemns solemnly all propaganda either designed or likely to provoke or encourage any threat to the peace, breach of the peace, or act of aggression, and all distortion and falsification of news through whatever channels, private or governmental, since such activities can only promote misunderstanding and mistrust between the peoples of the world and thereby endanger the lasting peace with which the United Nations is consecrated to maintain;

Appeals vigorously to the personnel of the press and other agencies of information of all the countries of the world, and to those responsible for their activities, to serve the aims of friendship, understanding and peace by accomplishing their tasks in a spirit of accuracy, fairness and responsibility;

Expresses its profound conviction that only organs of information in all countries of the world that are free to seek and to disseminate the truth, and thus to carry out their responsibility to the people, can greatly contribute to the counteracting of Nazi, Fascist or any other propaganda of aggression or of racial, national and religious discrimination and to the prevention of recurrence of Nazi, Fascist, or any other aggression;

And therefore *recommends* that all countries take within their respective territories the measures which they consider necessary to give effect to this Resolution.

Resolution No. 3 *[Propaganda Inciting to War and False Reporting]*

WHEREAS the first Committee of the United Nations Conference on Freedom of Information on 9 April 1948 unanimously adopted a Resolution declaring that all propaganda designed or likely to provoke or encourage any threat to the peace, or act of aggression, and also the spreading of false and distorted reports likely to injure friendly relations between States, constitute a problem of the first importance calling for urgent corrective action on the national and international planes, and

WHEREAS in the said Resolution the first Committee expressed its profound conviction that only organs of information in all countries of the world which are free to seek and to disseminate the truth and thus to carry out their responsibility to the people, can greatly contribute to the counteracting of Nazi, Fascist, or any other propaganda of aggression or of racial, national and religious discrimination and to the prevention of recurrence of Nazi, Fascist, or any other aggression, and

WHEREAS, the said Resolution having been adopted by this Conference, it is desirable that all appropriate steps should be taken to implement this Resolution,

The United Nations Conference on Freedom of Information

Transmits the said Resolution to the Economic and Social Council, and

Recommends that appropriate national bodies should supplement the work of information agencies and associations of journalists and of others engaged in the collection, publication and dissemination of news, in ensuring the impartial presentation of news and opinion;

Recommends that the United Nations should give consideration to means by which they may be able to assist in implementing the Resolution; and further

Recommends that the Sub-Commission on Freedom of Information and of the Press in carrying out the functions which may be assigned to it in accordance with the recommendations of the Conference should consider appropriate means by which measures taken to give effect to the Resolution may be co-ordinated.

Resolution No. 4 *[Racial and National Hatred]*

CONSIDERING that there are in some countries media of information which disseminate racial and national hatred,

The United Nations Conference on Freedom of Information

Recommends that the governments of such countries should:

(a) Encourage the widest possible dissemination of free information through a diversity of sources as the best safeguard against the creation of racial and national hatred and prejudice;

(b) Encourage in consultation with organizations of journalists, suitable and effective non-legislative measures against the dissemination of such hatred and prejudice; and

(c) Take, within their constitutional limits, appropriate measures to encourage the dissemination of information promoting friendly relations between races and nations based upon the purposes and principles of the United Nations Charter.

CHAPTER II: Measures To Facilitate the Gathering and International Transmission of Information

Resolution No. 5 *[Facilitating Movement of Correspondents]*

The United Nations Conference on Freedom of Information
  Resolves that:

1. Governments should encourage the freest possible movement of foreign correspondents in the performance of their functions; and that
2. Governments should expedite in a manner consistent with their respective laws and procedures the administrative measures necessary for the entry, residence, movement and travel of foreign correspondents, together with their professional equipment, and should impose no special, discriminatory or unusual restrictions on such ingress or egress, or upon the transit through or residence in their territories of such correspondents.

Resolution No. 6 *[Identification of Foreign Correspondents]*

CONSIDERING that a clear definition of which news personnel are to be regarded as professional foreign correspondents of newspapers, news agencies, periodicals, broadcasting enterprises and newsreel enterprises has not been established; and

  CONSIDERING that the various recommendations adopted by this Conference are of particular importance in securing free and unhampered working conditions for foreign correspondents; and

  CONSIDERING that the establishment of adequate means of identifying the professional foreign correspondents will facilitate for governments the realisation of their commitments for furthering the free flow of information;

  The United Nations Conference on Freedom of Information
  Recommends to the Economic and Social Council that the Sub-Commission on Freedom of Information and of the Press be requested to:

(1) Study the possibility of obtaining a clear and practically applicable definition of such news personnel as are to be given the status of professional foreign correspondents;

(2) Consider whether such measures should be taken with a view to providing foreign correspondents with appropriate documents of identification as to their professional capacity;

(3) Consider additional administrative and technical facilities might be granted to foreign correspondents holding such documents of identification;

(4) Conduct this work in close collaboration with international and national professional organizations of the press, radio and newsreel, especially by drawing upon the experience of news personnel actively engaged in the gathering and transmission of news; and

(5) Consider whether the task of handling any practical measures to be taken could be entirely or partially entrusted to a permanent organisation collaborating with professional bodies of the press, radio and newsreel, or to such professional bodies.

Resolution No. 7 *[Expulsion of Foreign Correspondents]*

The United Nations Conference on Freedom of Information while recognizing that all foreign news personnel must conform to the laws in force in the countries in which they are operating,

Declares that no such person legally admitted to a foreign territory should be expelled on account of any lawful exercise by him of his right to seek, receive and impart information or opinion.

Resolution No. 8 *[Access to News]*

The United Nations Conference on Freedom of Information

Resolves

That Governments should permit and encourage the widest possible access to news, official and non-official, for all foreign correspondents on the same basis as national correspondents;

And further resolves

That Governments should make no discrimination between foreign correspondents as regards to access to news provided for in the above paragraph.

Resolution No. 9 *[Access to U.N. Meetings]*

CONSIDERING that the United Nations, in accordance with the aims and purposes of its Charter, should be prepared to grant all the necessary facilities for enabling media of information to function with full freedom and responsibility in following the course of its work and that of the Conferences called by it and its specialized agencies

The United Nations Conference on the Freedom of Information

Recommends that the United Nations General Assembly adopt a resolution urging that accredited news personnel of all countries should have free access

(a) to countries where meetings of the United Nations or its specialized agencies or any Conferences convened by them take place, in accordance with the terms and conditions of agreements made by the United Nations or its specialized agencies with the governments of such countries; and

(b) to all sources of information connected with such meetings except in cases where, in accordance with the Rules of Procedure, meetings are held in private.

Resolution No. 10 *[Racial Discrimination]*

CONSIDERING that one of the purposes and principles of the United Nations as enunciated in the United Nations Charter is the encouragement of respect for human rights and for the fundamental freedoms for all without distinction as to race;

BELIEVING that any racial discrimination is incompatible with freedom of information and that the latter can be facilitated by the unconditional application of the principle of racial equality; and

CONSIDERING that it is imperative that access to all sources of information and to public utilities should be available to foreign correspondents, within the framework of existing laws and regulations without distinction as to race;

The United Nations Conference on Freedom of Information

Declares that in order to ensure the application of this principle, it is essential that governments and public utilities should not deny to foreign correspondents on racial grounds:

(a) access to any sources of information within the framework of existing laws and regulations;

(b) access to press conferences, legislative bodies, public meetings and demonstrations, theatres, concerts, exhibitions, public lectures, and educational institutions, etc.;

(c) access to communication facilities;

(d) access to means of transport; and

(e) access to facilities relative to accommodation and supplies.

Resolution No. 11 [Discriminatory Taxes]

The United Nations Conference on Freedom of Information

Invites governments to conclude bilateral or multilateral agreements with a view to eliminating unreasonable or discriminatory taxes affecting the operations of foreign information agencies and news personnel, being guided, in particular, by the results of the work of the Fiscal Commission of the Economic and Social Council concerning double taxation.

Resolution No. 12 [Censorship]

The United Nations Conference on Freedom of Information

Resolves

That governments should permit egress from their territory of all news material of foreign correspondents and foreign information agencies, whether of information or opinion, and whether visual or auditory, without censorship, editing or delay; provided that governments may make and enforce regulations relating directly to the maintenance of national military security; and

That such regulations should, however, be communicated to foreign correspondents and should apply equally to all foreign correspondents and foreign information agencies.

Further resolves

That if the requirements of national military security should compel governments, in peace-time, to establish censorship for a certain period of time, they should:

(1) establish in advance such categories of information or photographs for the use of a newspaper, news agency, broadcasting station or newsreel enterprise in another country, as are subject to previous inspection and publish the directives of the censor announcing forbidden matters;

(2) carry out censorship as far as possible in the presence of the journalists; and

(3) where censorship in the presence of the person concerned has not been possible:

(a) fix the time-limit allowed the censors for the return of the copy or photograph;

(b) require the return of copy submitted for censorship direct to the reporters or news agencies so that journalists may know at once what has been censored in their text and what use they may make of the censored information;

(c) base the charge on the number of words composing a telegram after censorship; and

(d) return the total telegraph charges for telegrams submitted for censorship, the transmission of which has been delayed more than six hours.

Resolution No. 13 [Censorship]

STRONGLY CONVINCED that Freedom of Information should be assured to everyone,

HOLDING that any form of censorship constitutes a curtailment of this freedom,

CONSIDERING that censorship deprives the information which it passes of its credibility and often gives information from unspecified sources an unwarranted value;
The United Nations Conference on Freedom of Information
Solemnly condemns the use in peace-time of censorship which restricts or controls freedom of information, and
Invites governments to take the necessary steps to promote its progressive abolition;
And considers that
Nothing in this resolution shall, however, prevent governments from maintaining regulation of newsreels provided their release may only be prohibited on grounds of public morality.

Resolution No. 14 [Teleprinter Lines]

The United Nations Conference on Freedom of Information
Recommends to the Economic and Social Council for suggestion to the *International Telecommunication Union* that where teleprinter lines have been installed on long-term lease between two or more news agencies, not only may the agencies bound by contract exchange news over these lines, but correspondents of the affiliated agencies may also use them without extra charge for transmitting news to the news agencies for which they work.

Resolution No. 15 [Access to Transmission Facilities]

The United Nations Conference on Freedom of Information
Resolves that foreign correspondents should have access to all facilities generally and publicly used for the international transmission of news material and should be enabled to transmit news material from one country to another on the same basis and at the same rates applicable to all users of such facilities for similar purposes.

Resolution No. 16 [Restrictions on Importations]

BELIEVING that the widest possible publication, circulation, movement and interchange of news, newspapers, news periodicals, newsreels, and other media of a distinct news character are a necessary part of freedom of information, and
RECOGNIZING that governments should, to the extent of their abilities and within the limits of their currency positions, facilitate the securing of raw materials and equipment needed for the development of their domestic information agencies and organizations,
The United Nations Conference on the Freedom of Information
Recommends that, as hard currencies and foreign exchange become increasingly available and more free, governments should encourage and, as far as possible, facilitate the necessary action which will ease quantitative, exchange and tariff restrictions on the importation of news, news publications and productions, and raw materials and equipment therefore, and
Further recommends that the governments of countries which possess hard currencies encourage by appropriate steps the above-mentioned action.

Resolution No. 17 [Newsreels]

CONSIDERING that it is advisable to adopt measures relating to the free reception and exhibition of newsreels,
The United Nations Conference on Freedom of Information
Recommends that all States should take steps to foster the interchange of newsreels in proportion to each nation's productive capacity, and should at the same time study

the disparities in the development of the production enterprises in the different countries and deal with the problem of the development of national enterprises by means of provisional measures; and

Further recommends that monopolistic practices, in all their forms, open or concealed, in relation to the showing of such films, be eliminated, in order to avoid any kind of restriction, exclusion or privilege.

Resolution No. 18 [Entry of News Material]

The United Nations Conference on Freedom of Information

CONSIDERS that governments should permit all news material of foreign correspondents and foreign information agencies to enter their territories and reach information agencies operating therein on the same conditions as are accorded to any other foreign information agencies.

Resolution No. 19 [Protection of Under-developed Information Agencies]

WITH A VIEW to encourage wider and freer flow of information through the development of national news agencies in countries where such agencies are under-developed,

The United States Conference on Freedom of Information

Recommends that any foreign news agency operating within the territory of a country where national news agencies are under-developed, while it should enjoy full freedom as regards the international transmission of news, should refrain from releasing, at the locality of its operation, news concerning the country's domestic affairs, and further refrain from transmitting such news to any other locality in that country for publication, except by mutual agreement with the national news agencies or with local newspapers.

Resolution No. 20 [Encouragement of Under-developed Information Agencies]

The United States Conference on Freedom of Information

WHILE AFFIRMING its conviction

THAT effective news agencies are a natural outgrowth of the vigour and co-operation of the organs of publication which they serve, and

THAT the dependence of news agencies on those organs themselves is an important factor in ensuring the objectivity of the information which they supply,

Is however of opinion that in countries where national news agencies are not sufficiently developed provisional measures may appropriately be taken by governments to encourage their development as independent news agencies, and is further of opinion that at no time should the development of foreign news agencies by unfair or abnormal means be allowed to prejudice the normal development of national agencies.

Resolution No. 21 [Improved Coverage]

CONSIDERING that the increase in the amount of information should apply without exception and in equal measure to all countries with a view to obtaining an ever-wider and more accurate knowledge of their problems, achievements and contributions to international co-operation and world peace; and

CONSIDERING that this aim has not been fully realised in the case of all nations, about some of which information is scanty and in many cases distorted or biased, and that as a result there is too often ignorance as to the true character of their civilisations and their importance in material progress, intellectual achievements and contribution to social justice, the defence of freedom and world harmony;

The United Nations Conference on Freedom of Information

Recommends that press enterprises and agencies for the publication and dissemination of news be encouraged to establish an efficient information service dealing with all countries, and especially with their achievements and concern for human progress, for their own political, economic and social independence and for the closest friendship and harmony among peoples; and

Further recommends that stress be laid on the desirability of all governments making permanently available to such enterprises and agencies all information material likely to contribute to the above aim, and to the elucidation or rectification of news and comments which tend to hamper or prevent its realisation.

Resolution No. 22 *[Facilities for Transmission and Dissemination]*

The United Nations Conference on Freedom of Information

CONSIDERING the desirability for the full realization of freedom of information in all countries,

Resolves that all countries should co-operate in the procurement and advancement of the facilities for the transmission and dissemination of information.

Resolution No. 23 *[Telecommunication Services]*

The United Nations Conference on Freedom of Information

TAKES NOTE of the Secretariat Document on International Communications and the Freedom of Information (E/CONF.6/29), and

Recommends that, in view of the highly technical nature of the matter, the Economic and Social Council refer it to the International Telecommunications Union for its consideration.

Resolution No. 24 *[Governmental Information Services]*

The United Nations Conference on Freedom of Information

HAVING GIVEN CONSIDERATION to the problems involved in the establishment of governmental and semi-governmental information services in order to make information available in countries other than their own,

Requests the Economic and Social Council to refer consideration of this matter to the Sub-Commission on Freedom of Information and of the Press, and to draw its attention to the views expressed at this Conference and to the proposal of the United Kingdom delegation on the subject.

CHAPTER III: Measures Concerning the Free Publication and Reception of Information

Resolution No. 25 *[Non-Discrimination in Providing Facilities]*

CONSIDERING that governments should put no obstacles in the way of persons and groups wishing to express themselves through the means of mass-communication,

The United Nations Conference on Freedom of Information

Recommends that all governments should, to the extent that they make available materials and facilities for the mass media, undertake not to discriminate on political or personal grounds or on the basis of race, nationality, sex, language or religion, or against minorities.

Resolution No. 26 [Libel]

The United Nations Conference on Freedom of Information

CONSIDERING that, in view of the diversity of the laws or libel in force in different countries, and the diversity of legal systems and conditions with reference to which laws are made, this Conference is not in a position to make a close study of such laws for the purpose of recommending specific improvements; and

RECOGNIZING that all branches of law must be kept in accord with public opinion and that this is especially true of laws relating to the liberty of discussion,

Recommends that States should from time to time review their laws of libel, taking into consideration the general conclusions of this Conference, in order to remove anomalies, and to secure to all persons the maximum freedom of expression compatible with the maintenance of order and with due regard to the rights of others; and

CONSIDERING it necessary to determine the fundamental principles in this matter which may serve as a uniform basis for the laws of the various countries,

Further recommends:

(1) that the Economic and Social Council invite a Committee of Jurists or an International organization (such as the International Association of Criminal Law) to:
   (a) study the laws of libel of the various countries in order to note their defects and anomalies; and
   (b) formulate a body of fundamental rules and principles regarding libel, taking into account the role played by the press in a democratic State; and
(2) that the Economic and Social Council draw the attention of the various Governments to this body of rules with a view to their being taken into consideration in the formulation of national laws of libel.

Resolution No. 27 [Discrimination and Monopoly]

The United Nations Conference on Freedom of Information

RECOGNIZING that there is a diversity in different countries in the ownership and control of media of information and that freedom can flourish under widely different systems;

Recommends that governments should undertake to put no obstacles in the way of persons or groups wishing to express themselves through the means of mass communication, and should ensure insofar as they are able that persons do not suffer discrimination in the use of the media on political or personal grounds or on the basis of race, sex, language or religion, and

Further recommends the investigation of each country in its own way of public and private monopoly, in ownership and control of the media of information, where such monopoly exists.

Resolution No. 28 [Freedom to Listen]

The United Nations Conference on Freedom of Information

CONSIDERING that the free interchange of information and opinions promotes the welfare of all nations and is indispensable to the peace of the world,

Recommends that governments grant the right to all nationals of their States to possess and operate radio receiving sets covering all the bands used for domestic and international broadcasts, free from intimidation or pressure and subject only to the accepted rules governing licensing and copyright.

Resolution No. 29 [Cheaper Radio Sets]

CONSIDERING that in many countries the price of radio receiving sets is unduly high; and

CONSIDERING that one of the aims of the Conference is to recommend means to increase the amount of domestic and international information available to all peoples;

The United Nations Conference on Freedom of Information

Recommends to the Economic and Social Council that a study be made of all appropriate measures so that the general public can obtain radio receiving sets at low prices.

Resolution No. 31 [Multiple-Address Newscasts]

WHEREAS one of the means of expanding interchange of information is by the reception of press transmissions by radio addressed to multiple destinations, and

WHEREAS thirty-seven nations now permit private reception of multiple-address newscasts;

The United Nations Conference on Freedom of Information

TAKES NOTE of the practice of private reception of multiple-address newscasts, and

Suggests to the Economic and Social Council that the problem be referred for further study to the International Telecommunication Union or any other competent body.

Resolution No. 32 [Technical Needs]

The United Nations Conference on Freedom of Information

HAVING CONSIDERED the investigations of UNESCO into the technical needs of war-devastated countries,

1. *Expresses* the hope that UNESCO will proceed with the utmost speed to carry out the programmes it has prepared in this connection;
2. *Notes* with satisfaction that UNESCO is taking expeditious steps for ascertaining the requirements of other countries, whose detailed wants have not been investigated so far but which are handicapped, on account of material inadequacies, in making satisfactory arrangements for the provision of domestic and international information;
3. *Recommends* that the Economic and Social Council instruct its regional economic commissions and request the competent specialised agencies to assist UNESCO in its task of reducing the inequalities in information facilities caused by the devastations due to war, or other handicaps, and
4. *Further recommends* that very early arrangements may be made by UNESCO, with the help of other specialised agencies concerned in the matter, for dealing with the requirements of these countries.

Resolution No. 33 [Newsprint]

TAKING COGNISANCE of the conclusions regarding newsprint reached by UNESCO as the outcome of its enquiry carried out in 1947 in twelve war-devastated countries of Europe and the Far East, and one of the decision of UNESCO to continue its enquiry in 1948 in other parts of the world,

The United Nations Conference on Freedom of Information

DRAWS the attention of the Economic and Social Council to the harm and dangers which inadequate production of newsprint, and unequal distribution thereof, have on the exercise of freedom of information;

Recommends that the Economic and Social Council consider as soon as possible, in the light of the enquiries carried out by the Council and by UNESCO, practical measures to remedy the situation; and

Recommends that governments give their support to the UNESCO plan for aid to war-devastated countries; and

Invites UNESCO to extend such aid to other countries suffering from an acute shortage of newsprint.

Resolution No. 34 [International Press Institute]

The United Nations Conference on Freedom of Information
    TAKING NOTE of the proposal submitted directly by UNESCO to establish under the auspices of that agency and International Institute of Press and Information, and
    CONSIDERING that such an Institute could be conducive to the improvement of quality of information.

Requests the Economic and Social Council to invite governments and professional organisations, national and international, to examine together the possibility of implementing this proposal and, if it is found to be practical, to co-operate in carrying it out.

Resolution No. 35 [Schools of Journalism]

The United Nations Conference on Freedom of Information
    DESIRING to improve the quality of information,
    Recommends

(1) That the curricula of schools of journalism, governmental and private, include
    (a) intensive study of the history and culture of other peoples as a background for correct interpretation of international news and events;
    (b) inculcation in future journalists of a keen sense of the moral and social responsibility of the profession, stressing the undesirability of commercialism, sensationalism and racial and religious intolerance; and
    (c) training in the habit of objectivity, accuracy and comprehensiveness in reporting and writing;
(2) That journalistic organizations exchange views concerning the desirable qualifications, technical requirements, and the working conditions of foreign correspondents;
(3) That systems of awards be established for news personnel for conspicuous service in upholding high journalistic ideals and for excellence in writing, especially in the field of international news and its interpretation, and in promoting the ideals of the United Nations, thereby strengthening friendship between peoples.

Resolution No. 36 [International Code of Honour]

CONSIDERING that the task of drafting and enforcing an international code of honour for journalists and other information personnel requires as a principal condition the discussion in advance by the professional organizations active in this field; and
    CONSIDERING also that any such code of honour should be sufficiently wide to include all media of information and to cover the activities of all information enterprises, including the activities of journalists, editors, managers, directors and publishers of such enterprises,

The United Nations Conference on Freedom of Information,
Recommends:

1. That the question of drafting an international code of honour and of the possibility of establishing an international court of honour be referred to the Sub-Commission on Freedom of Information and of the Press;
2. That the Sub-Commission should also examine in this connection the Draft Convention concerning and International Court of Honour proposed by the Delegations of Colombia and Peru, which the Conference has taken note of without pronouncing an opinion on its substance, and any other Draft Conventions on the subject referred to in paragraph 1 which may be proposed;
3. That national and international professional organizations be invited to contribute such material as they may consider to be of value to the Sub-Commission in its deliberations; and
4. That the Sub-Commission be requested to present the results of its investigations to the Economic and Social Council for consideration by any international conference of journalists, editors, managers, directors and publishers which may be convened by the United Nations to consider these specific matters.

Resolution No. 37 [Security for News Personnel]

The United Nations Conference on Freedom of Information

CONSIDERING the desirability of encouraging the adoption of measures guaranteeing the independence of news personnel and consequently the freedom of information; and

CONSIDERING that to attain this end all those who derive their main livelihood from the practice of the profession should be assured freedom from want in their old age, or in the case of disability, sickness or unemployment, or for their families in the event of death,

Recommends:

That the Economic and Social Council invite governments to include in their legislation a system of social security guaranteeing apart from the rights conferred on news personnel by their contracts of unemployment,

(a) payment (pension or lump sum) during their old age and in the event of disability;
(b) compensation for a certain period in the event of unemployment or sickness including an adequate notice of discharge; and
(c) payment (pension or lump sum) to the widow and dependent children; and

Further recommends that social benefits be financed by contributions made on the one hand by employers and on the other by news personnel themselves, and, possibly, by contributions from the State.

Resolution No. 38 [Security for News Personnel]

CONSIDERING

That the problem of freedom of information, in relation to the reception and transmission of true and objective news, is intimately bound up with the economic conditions under which professional news personnel work,

The United Nations Conference on Freedom of Information

Recommends that in all states Members of the United Nations and Non-Member States the advisability be considered of assuring, by free negotiation between employers and employees, or, where necessary, by law, the protection of news personnel whose main source of livelihood is the gathering and dissemination of news or opinion, whether they work for daily newspapers, news periodicals, news agencies, or news departments of broadcasting or motion picture organizations; and

Further recommends that such provisions should cover the following points without exclusion of other benefits:

1. The initial emoluments of the professional journalist;
2. Automatic system of increase in salaries for seniority, taking into account previous experience;
3. Stability of employment and compensation in case of wrongful dismissal;
4. Superannnuation and retirement;
5. Payment of salaries during vacations;
6. System of compensation for accidents at work and occupational diseases; and
7. Settlement of professional disputes.

CHAPTER IV: Continuing Machinery to Promote the Free Flow of Information

Resolution No. 39

CONSIDERING

That the work of the various Committees has shown the need to set up continuing international machinery to carry out the work undertaken by the Conference of Freedom of Information and, in particular, to study the problems involved in the application of the resolutions adopted by this Conference and the implementation of the draft conventions recommended by it,

CONSIDERING

That it is expedient, in order to avoid the multiplication of specialized agencies, to entrust this task to the Sub-Commission on Freedom of Information and of the Press,

The United Nations Conference on Freedom of Information

Resolves

1. That the economic and Social Council be requested to continue the Sub-Commission on Freedom of Information and of the Press for a period of three years;
2. That the Sub-Commission's terms of reference include the consideration of issues and problems involved in the dissemination of information by newspapers and news periodicals, radio broadcasts and newsreels;
3. That, to carry out these terms of reference, the Sub-Commission may:
   (a) Study and report to the Economic and Social Council on:
      (1) Political, economic and other barriers to the free flow of information;
      (2) The extent to which freedom of information is accorded to the various peoples of the world;
      (3) The adequacy of the news available to them;
      (4) The development of high standards of professional conduct;
      (5) The persistent dissemination of information which is false, distorted or otherwise injurious to the principles of the Charter of the United Nations;
      (6) The operation of any inter-governmental agreements in the field of freedom of information;
   (b) Receive for its own information communications from any legally constituted national or international press, information, broadcasting or newsreel enterprise or association relating to the item enumerated in paragraph 3(a) above with a view to assisting it in the formulation of general principles and proposals in the field of freedom of information;

    (c) Discharge with the approval of the General Assembly and the Economic and Social Council such other functions as may be entrusted to it by inter-governmental agreements on information; and

    (d) Initiate studies and make recommendations to the Economic and Social Council concerning:

        (1) The promotion of a wider degree of freedom of information and the reduction or elimination of obstacles thereto;

        (2) The promotion of the dissemination of true information to counteract Nazi, Fascist or any other propaganda of aggression or of racial, national and religious discrimination;

        (3) The conclusion or improvement of inter-governmental agreements in the field of freedom of information; and

        (4) Measures to facilitate the work of foreign news personnel.

4. That the General Assembly be requested to make adequate funds available for the work of the Sub-Commission and in particular, funds for providing the Sub-Commission with the full-time expert staff, within the Secretariat of the United Nations, necessary for the discharge of its important functions.

CHAPTER V: Miscellaneous

Resolution No. 40 [Day of Friendship and Mutual Understanding]

HAVING CONSIDERED the proposal of the International Organization of Journalists regarding a Day of Friendship and Mutual Understanding in the Press,

    The United Nations Conference on Freedom of Information

    Requests the Economic and Social Council to refer the proposal of the International Organization of Journalists to the Sub-Commission on Freedom of Information and of the Press for consideration and such action as may be considered desirable.

Resolution No. 41 [Lev Sychrava]

The Conference requests the Secretary-General of the United Nations to convey to Dr. Lev Sychrava its appreciation of his memorandum on The Principles of Free Exchange of Information (Document E/CN.4/SUB.1/50) and the regret of the Conference that he could not be present at its meetings.

CHAPTER VI: Possible Modes of Action by Means of Which the Recommendations of the Conference Can Best Be Put Into Effect

Resolution No. 42

The United Nations Conference on Freedom of Information

    Resolves that some of the recommendations of the Conference can best be put into effect in the form of Conventions.

Resolution No. 43

The United Nations Conference on Freedom of Information

    Resolves:

1. That all documents passed by the Conference, Resolutions or Draft Conventions, be referred to the Economic and Social Council for study at its next session;

2. That all governments invited to this Conference be requested to forward to the Secretary-General of the United Nations before 5 July 1948 their comments on the Draft Conventions proposed by the Conference and proposals for other Draft Conventions based on the recommendations of this Conference;

3. That the Economic and Social Council be requested to examine at its Seventh Session the Draft Conventions referred to it by the Conference in the light of such comments and other proposed Draft Conventions as provided in paragraph 2, and to submit to the General Assembly at its Third Session Draft Conventions which may thereafter be opened at that session for signature or accession by those States entitled and willing to become parties thereto, and remain open subsequently for additional accessions.

Appendix V

Report of Sub-Committee 8 of the Fifth Committee on Public Information, Annex, Basic Principles Underlying the Public Information Activities of the United Nations January 28, 1952 A/C.5/L.172

The United Nations cannot achieve the purposes for which it has been created unless the peoples of the world are informed of its aims and activities.

The basic policy of the United Nations, in the field of public information, is, therefore, to promote to the greatest possible extent, within its budgetary limitations, an informed understanding of the work and purposes of the Organization among the peoples of the world. To this end, the Department of Public Information should primarily assist and rely upon the services of existing official and private agencies of information, educational institutions and non-governmental organizations. It should not engage in "propaganda"; it should undertake, on its own initiative, positive informational activities that will supplement the services of existing agencies. In so doing it should pay particular attention to the special problems and needs of those areas where, in relation to other areas of information media are less fully developed, with a view to ensuring the most effective use of the facilities and resources available. The principles to be applied in implementing the basic policy are set forth hereunder:

1. Subject to the general authority of the principal organs of the United Nations[,] responsibility for the formulation and execution of information policy should be vested in the Secretary-General and under him in the Assistant Secretary-General in charge of the Department of Public Information.
2. In order to ensure that peoples in all parts of the world receive as full information as possible about the United Nations, the Department of Public Information should establish and maintain a system of Information Centres on an adequate regional and/or linguistic basis with due regard to actual varying needs.
3. The Department of Public Information should provide services in the following main fields: press, publications, radio, television, films, graphics and exhibitions, public liaison and reference.
4. The Department should plan the public information work of the United Nations according to prevailing regional, language and other requirements. In the use of media and methods, due regard should be paid to their relative importance which may vary in different parts of the world and from time to time.
5. The Department should actively assist and encourage the use of radio broadcasting for the dissemination of information about the United Nations. To this end it should, in the first instance, work in close co-operation with the radio broadcasting organizations of Member States. The United Nations should also have at its disposal, for the origination of United Nations programmes, broadcasting facilities under its own control and capable of reaching all Member States, as approved in principle by the General Assembly.

6. The Department should provide at the Headquarters of the United Nations and through its Information Centres and directly to other areas, such services as may be necessary to ensure that the daily, weekly and periodical press is supplied with full information about the activities of the United Nations.

7. The Department should prepare and publish, and encourage the outside preparation and publication of, pamphlets and other literature on the aims and activities of the United Nations.

8. In addition to assisting the newsreel and photographic press agencies, the Department of Public Information should also promote and where necessary participate in the production and distribution of documentary films, film strips, posters and other graphic exhibits on the work of the United Nations.

9. The Department should maintain a reference and inquiry service, brief and arrange lecturers, and make available appropriate materials for use by national information services, educational institutions and other governmental and non-governmental organizations.

10. Free distribution of materials is necessary in the public information activities of the United Nations. The Department should, however, as demands increase and whenever it is desirable and possible, actively encourage the sale of its materials. Where appropriate, it should seek to finance production by means of revenue-producing and self-liquidating projects.

11. In the interests of efficiency and economy there should be co-ordination of information policy between and, wherever practicable, common information services for the United Nations and the specialized agencies.

12. The press and other agencies of information should be given the fullest possible direct access to the activities and official documentation of the organization wherever organs and agencies of the United Nations are at work. The rules of procedure of the various organs and subsidiary bodies of the United Nations should be applied with this end in view.

In furtherance of the above principles the Department of Public Information should keep under continuous review the extent to which an informed understanding of the Organization's aims and activities is being created by existing information media and by its own services.

The General Assembly, on the recommendation of the Secretary-General, or on its own initiative, should consider from time to time the desirability of establishing an *ad hoc* committee to report on the manner in which the information policy and programme of the United Nations is being implemented.

Appendix VI

Principles Governing the Use by States of Artificial Earth Satellites for International Direct Television Broadcasting
December 10, 1982
A/RES/37/92

The General Assembly,

Recalling its resolution 2916(XXVII) of 9 November 1972, in which it stressed the necessity of elaborating principles governing the use by States of artificial earth satellites for international direct television broadcasting, and mindful of the importance of concluding an international agreement or agreements,

Recalling further its resolutions 3182(XXVIII) of 18 December 1973, 3234(XXIX) of 12 November 1974, 3388(XXX) of 18 November 1975, 31/8 of 8 November 1976, 32/196 of 20 December 1977, 33/16 of 10 November 1978, 34/66 of 5 December 1979 and 35/14 of 3 November 1980, and its resolution 36/35 of 18 November 1981 in which it decided to consider at its thirty-seventh session the adoption of a draft set of principles governing the use by States of artificial earth satellites for international direct television broadcasting,

Noting with appreciation the efforts made in the Committee on the Peaceful Uses of Outer Space and its Legal Sub-Committee to comply with the directives issued in the above-mentioned resolutions,

Considering that several experiments of direct broadcasting by satellite have been carried out and that a number of direct broadcasting satellite systems are operational in some countries and may be commercialized in the very near future,

Taking into consideration that the operation of international direct broadcasting satellites will have significant international political, economic, social and cultural implications,

Believing that the establishment of principles for international direct television broadcasting will contribute to the strengthening of international co-operation in this field and further the purposes and principles of the Charter of the United Nations,

Adopts the Principles Governing the Use by States of Artificial Earth Satellites for International Direct Television Broadcasting set forth in the annex to the present resolution.

Annex
Principles Governing the Use by States of Artificial Earth Satellites for International Direct Television Broadcasting

A. *Purposes and objectives*

1. Activities in the field of international direct television broadcasting by satellite should be carried out in a manner compatible with the sovereign rights of States, including the principle of non-intervention, as well as with the right of everyone to seek, receive and impart information and ideas as enshrined in the relevant United Nations instruments.

2. Such activities should promote the free dissemination and mutual exchange of information and knowledge in cultural and scientific fields, assist in educational, social and economic development, particularly in the developing countries, enhance the qualities of life of all peoples and provide recreation with due respect to the political and cultural integrity of States.

3. These activities should accordingly be carried out in a manner compatible with the development of mutual understanding and the strengthening of friendly relations and co-operation among all States and peoples in the interest of maintaining international peace and security.

B. Applicability of international law

4. Activities in the field of international direct television broadcasting by satellite should be conducted in accordance with international law, including the Charter of the United Nations, the Treaty on Principles Governing the Activities of States in the Exploration and Use of Outer Space, including the Moon and Other Celestial Bodies, of 27 January 1967, the relevant provisions of the International Telecommunication Convention and its Radio Regulations and of international instruments relating to friendly relations and co-operation among States and to human rights.

C. Rights and benefits

5. Every State has an equal right to conduct activities in the field of international direct television broadcasting by satellite and to authorize such activities by persons and entities under its jurisdiction. All States and peoples are entitled to and should enjoy the benefits from such activities. Access to the technology in this field should be available to all States without discrimination on terms mutually agreed by all concerned.

D. International co-operation

6. Activities in the field of international direct television broadcasting by satellite should be based upon and encourage international co-operation. Such co-operation should be the subject of appropriate arrangements. Special consideration should be given to the needs of the developing countries in the use of international direct television broadcasting by satellite for the purpose of accelerating their national development.

E. Peaceful settlement of disputes

7. Any international dispute that may arise from activities covered by these principles should be settled through established procedures for the peaceful settlement of disputes agreed upon by the parties to the dispute in accordance with the provisions of the Charter of the United Nations.

F. State responsibility

8. States should bear international responsibility for activities in the field of international direct television broadcasting by satellite carried out by them or under their jurisdiction and for the conformity of any such activities with the principles set forth in this document.

9. When international direct television broadcasting by satellite is carried out by an international intergovernmental organization, the responsibility referred to in

paragraph 8 above should be borne both by that organization and by the States participating in it.

G. *Duty and right to consult*

10. Any broadcasting or receiving State within an international direct television broadcasting satellite service established between them requested to do so by any other broadcasting or receiving State within the same service should promptly enter into consultations with the requesting State regarding its activities in the field of international direct television broadcasting by satellite, without prejudice to other consultations which these States may undertake with any other State on that subject.

H. *Copyright and neighbouring rights*

11. Without prejudice to the relevant provisions of international law, States should co-operate on a bilateral and multilateral basis for protection of copyright and neigh-bouring rights by means of appropriate agreements between the interested States or the competent legal entities acting under their jurisdiction. In such co-operation they should give special consideration to the interests of developing countries in the use of direct television broadcasting for the purpose of accelerating their national development.

I. *Notification to the United Nations*

12. In order to promote international co-operation in the peaceful exploration and use of outer space, States conducting or authorizing activities in the field of international direct television broadcasting by satellite should inform the Secretary-General of the United Nations, to the greatest extent possible, of the nature of such activities. On receiving this information, the Secretary-General should disseminate it immediately and effectively to the relevant specialized agencies, as well as to the public and the international scientific community.

J. *Consultations and agreements between States*

13. A State which intends to establish or authorize the establishment of an international direct television broadcasting satellite service shall without delay notify the proposed receiving State or States of such intention and shall promptly enter into consultation with any of those States which so requests.

14. An international direct television broadcasting satellite service shall only be established after the conditions set forth in paragraph 13 above have been met and on the basis of agreements and/or arrangements in conformity with the relevant instruments of the International Telecommunication Union and in accordance with these principles.

15. With respect to the unavoidable overspill of the radiation of the satellite signal, the relevant instruments of the International Telecommunication Union shall be exclusively applicable.

Appendix VII

Boilerplates of Movies and TV Shows Discussed in Chapter 3

Movies

The Glory Brigade
- 1953
- Directed by Robert D. Webb
- Leading cast members: Victor Mature, Alexander Scourby, Lee Marvin, Richard Egan, Nick Dennis, Roy Roberts, Alvy Moore, Russell Evans and Henry Kulky
- During the Korean War, an American platoon must overcome cultural differences when assigned to escort a group of Greek soldiers behind Communist lines
- War drama

A Global Affair
- 1964
- Directed by Jack Arnold
- Leading cast members: Bob Hope, Michelle Mercier, Robert Sterling, Lilo Pulver, Elga Anderson and Yvonne DeCarlo
- Female representatives of several nations demand custody of a baby abandoned at the United Nations building
- Comedy

Gidget Grows Up
- 1969
- Directed by James Sheldon
- Leading cast members: Karen Valentine, Edward Mulhare, Paul Petersen, Nina Foch, Paul Lynde, Warner Anderson and Bob Cummings
- Gidget decides to make a difference in the world by becoming a youth worker at the United Nations where she falls in love with an Australian diplomat
- Comedy/romance

Operation Condor
- 1990
- Directed by Frankie Chan and Jackie Chan
- Leading cast members: Jackie Chan, Carol Cheng, Eva Cobo and Shôko Ikeda
- A secret agent is hired to find gold that was allegedly left in the Sahara Desert by Nazis during the Second World War
- Action/comedy

Welcome To Sarajevo
- 1997
- Directed by Michael Winterbottom
- Based on the book *Natasha's Story* by Michael Nicholson
- Leading cast members: Stephen Dillane, Woody Harrelson, Marisa Tomei, Emira Nusevic, Kerry Fox, Goran Visnjic, James Nesbitt, Emily Lloyd, Igor Dzambazov,

Gordana Gadzic, Juliet Aubrey, Drazen Sivak, Vesna Orel, Davor Janjic and Vladimir Jokanovic
- Journalists working in Sarajevo during the Bosnian conflict discover an orphanage near the frontline and become emotionally involved
- War drama

Austin Powers: International Man of Mystery
- 1997
- Directed by Jay Roach
- Leading cast members: Mike Myers, Elizabeth Hurley, Michael York, Mimi Rogers, Robert Wagner, Seth Green, Fabiana Udenio, Mindy Sterling, Paul Dillon, Charles Napier, Will Ferrell, Joann Richter, Anastasia Sakelaris, Afifi Alaouie and Monet Mazur
- British secret agent Austin Powers works to save the world from Dr. Evil's destructive scheme
- Comedy

The Art Of War
- 2000
- Directed by Christian Duguay
- Leading cast members: Wesley Snipes, Anne Archer, Maury Chaykin, Marie Matiko, Cary-Hiroyuki Tagawa, Michael Biehn, Donald Sutherland, Liliana Komorowska, James Hong, Paul Hopkins, Glen Chin, Ron Winston Yuan, Bonnie Mak, Uni Park and Erin Selby
- A covert agent works to find terrorists who have threatened the United Nations
- Action/drama

TV Shows

"Those In Favor"
- 1952
- Directed by Norman Felton
- From a play by Christopher Mayhew
- Leading cast members: Raymond Massey, Herbert Berghof, Robert Emhardt, Kurt Katch, Stuart McIntosh, Martin Brandt, Guy Sorel, Will Hussung and Francois Grimard; hosted by Robert Montgomery
- Follows a United Nations meeting in Paris and the relationship between the US and Soviet delegates during the Cold War
- TV drama, part of a weekly series

"Carol For Another Christmas"
- 1964
- Directed by Joseph L. Makiewicz, a Telsun Foundation, Inc. production
- Loosely based on Dickens' *A Christmas Carol*
- Leading cast members: Sterling Hayden, Ben Gazzara, Peter Sellers, Eva Marie Saint, Steve Lawrence, Pat Hingle, Robert Shaw, James Shigeta, Barbara Ann Teer, Percy Rodriguez, Britt Ekland and Gordon Spencer
- A bitter industrial tycoon, who resents American involvement in international affairs, is visited by three ghosts
- TV drama

"Amerika"

- 1987
- Directed by Donald Wrye
- Leading cast members: Kris Kristofferson, Kelly Proctor, Keram Malicki-Sánchez, Jason Wild, Graham Beckel, Richard Blackburn II, Lara Flynn Boyle, Ivan Dixon, Mariel Hemingway, Wendy Hughes, Christine Lahti, Armin Mueller-Stahl, Sam Neill, Cindy Pickett, Raynor Scheine, Robert Urich and Vlasta Vrana
- America is taken over by the Soviet Union and citizens are forced into slave-labor camps
- TV drama

Notes

1 Propaganda for Peace?

1. "8 Assistant Secretaries General Of UN Have Varied Backgrounds", *The New York Times*, 11 April 1946.
2. "Secretariat – Public Information", *United Nations Weekly Bulletin*, vol. 1, 23 September 1946, p. 19; "8 Assistant Secretaries General of UN Have Varied Backgrounds", *The New York Times*, 11 April 1946, p. 4, column 4.
3. Benjamin Cohen, "Voice of UN – The Department of Public Information", *United Nations World*, March 1947, p. 55.
4. Ibid., pp. 54–57.
5. See United Nations document A/54/21, *Committee on Information, Report on the Twenty-First Session (3–14 May 1999), Supplement No. 21, Annex, "Statement by the Under-Secretary-General for Communications and Public Information at the Opening of the Twenty-First Session of the Committee on Information"*, 7 June 1999; United Nations document A/54/21/Add.1, *Report of the Committee on Information on the Resumed Twenty-First Session (1–5 November 1999), Supplement No. 21A, Annex, "Statement by the Under-Secretary-General for Communications and Public Information at the Opening of the Resumed Twenty-First Session of the Committee on Information"*, 9 November 1999.
6. Ingrid A. Lehmann, *Peacekeeping and Public Information: Caught in the Crossfire* (London: Frank Cass, 1999), p. 4.
7. Ibid.
8. United Nations document A/RES/13(I), ANNEX I.
9. The first electronic televising of moving objects was by the Scot, John L. Baird, in 1926, according to the *Encyclopedia Britannica*. Baird is also credited with being the first to demonstrate color television in 1928, but using a mechanical process. The British Broadcasting Corporation (BBC) began a television service in 1936. However, it was not until the 1950s that the first regular color television broadcasting in the world was started. During the first 30 years of this new communication medium, its use was very much limited to a minority of richer countries of the world, such as Japan, the US and Europe. However, in 1961 David Sarnoff, the Chairman of the Radio Corporation of America (RCA), one of the pioneers of the medium in the US, predicted that by the early 1970s television stations would be "in virtually every nation on earth". See Robert L. Hilliard and Michael C. Keith, *Global Broadcasting Systems* (Boston, MA: Focal Press, 1996), p. 2.
10. See Alexander Szalai with Margaret Croke and Associates, *The United Nations and the News Media* (New York: United Nations Institute for Training and Research (UNITAR), 1972), pp. 97–98.
11. United Nations document A/54/6/Rev.1, *Proposed Programme Budget for the Biennium 2000–2001, Vol. 1 (Foreword and Introduction), GA: Official Records, 54th Session, Supplement No. 6*, 19 July 1999.
12. See Lynette Finch, "Psychological propaganda: The war of ideas on ideas during the first half of the twentieth century", *Armed Forces and Society*, vol. 26, no. 3, pp. 367–86.

13. Excerpt from *Compton's Interactive Encyclopedia*. Copyright © 1994, 1995 Compton's NewMedia, Inc.
14. Ibid.
15. "Women and Children First", *Man*, April 1939, p. 10, quoted in Finch, op. cit., p. 5 of downloaded database version.
16. Ken Millen-Penn, "Democratic Control, Public Opinion, and League Diplomacy", *World Affairs*, vol. 157, spring 1995, p. 10 of downloaded database version.
17. Finch, op. cit., p. 6 of downloaded database version.
18. E. H. Carr, *The Twenty Years' Crisis* (London: MacMillan Press, 1939), p. 134.
19. Hans Speier, "The future of psychological warfare", *Public Opinion Quarterly*, vol. 12, 1948, pp. 5–18.
20. Finch, op. cit., p. 12 of downloaded database version.
21. Garth S. Jowett and Victoria O'Donnell, *Propaganda and Persuasion* (3rd edn) (Thousand Oaks, CA: Sage, 1999), p. 6.
22. Ibid., p. 12.
23. Ibid., p. 13.
24. Ibid., p. 15.
25. See Benedict Anderson, *Imagined Communities: Reflections on the Origin and Spread of Nationalism* (London: Verso, 1983).
26. See Laura Hein and Mark Seldon (eds), *Censoring History: Citizenship and Memory in Japan, Germany, and the United States* (Armonk, New York: M. E. Sharpe, 2000).
27. Quoted in Millen-Penn, op. cit., p. 5 of downloaded database version.
28. Millen-Penn, op. cit., p. 1 of downloaded database version.
29. Hans Morgenthau, *Politics Among Nations* (5th edn) (New York: Knopf, 1973).
30. Ibid., p. 331.
31. Ibid., pp. 332–33.
32. Morgenthau explained that:

   Diplomacy owes its rise in part to the absence of speedy communications in a period when the governments of the new territorial states maintained continuous political relations with each other. Diplomacy owes its decline in part to the development of speedy and regular communications in the form of the airplane, the radio, the telegraph, the Teletype, the long-distance telephone.

   Ibid., pp. 525–26.
33. "Psychology", Microsoft® Encarta® 98 Encyclopedia. © 1993–97 Microsoft Corporation.
34. Ibid.
35. Harold D. Lasswell (1927) *Propaganda Technique in World War I* (Cambridge, MA: MIT Press, 1971), p. 9.
36. Karin Dovring, *English As Lingua Franca: Double Talk in Global Persuasion* (Westport, CT: Praeger, 1997), p. 69.
37. J. M. Mitchell, *International Cultural Relations* (London: Allen & Unwin, 1986), p. 81.
38. Szalai, op. cit., p. 98.
39. Excerpt from *Compton's Interactive Encyclopedia*. Copyright © 1994, 1995 Compton's NewMedia, Inc.
40. "Public Opinion", Microsoft® Encarta® 98 Encyclopedia. © 1993–97 Microsoft Corporation. All rights reserved.
41. Quoted in Millen-Penn, op. cit., p. 1 of downloaded database version.
42. Ibid., n. 2.

43. See Mark D. Alleyne, "Education for peace: the UN and new ideas for the 'information age'", *Media Development*, no. 4, 2000, pp. 12–14.
44. Finch, op. cit., p. 3 of downloaded database version.
45. Akira Iriye, *Cultural Internationalism and World Order* (Baltimore, MD: Johns Hopkins University Press, 1997), p. 3.
46. Ibid., p. 13.
47. Ibid., pp. 40 and 43.
48. Gerard Herberichs, "On theories of public opinion and international organization", *Public Opinion Quarterly*, vol. 30, no. 4, winter 1966–67, p. 632.
49. Mitchell, op. cit., p. 81.
50. Ibid., p. 81.
51. Ibid., p. 23.
52. Ibid.
53. Ibid., p. 29.
54. Ibid., pp. 51–7.
55. Colin Cherry, *World Communication: Threat or Promise?* (New York: John Wiley, 1971), p. 116.
56. Mitchell, op. cit., p. 34.
57. Ibid., p. 39.
58. Ibid., p. 40.
59. Ibid., p. 50.
60. Central Office of Information, *Summary of the Report of the Independent Committee of Enquiry into the Overseas Information Services (the Drogheda Committee)* (London: Her Majesty's Stationery Office, April, 1954), p. 41.
61. Ibid.
62. UK Foreign Office, "Memorandum, Foreign Cultural Propaganda and the Threat to British Interests Abroad", FO P 823/160/150 (London: Public Record Office, 1937), quoted in Mitchell, op. cit., pp. 32–3.
63. Central Office of Information, op. cit., p. 8.
64. Ibid., p. 5.
65. Central Office of Information, *Britain 1988: An Official Handbook* (London: Her Majesty's Stationery Office, 1988), pp. 72 and 427.
66. William Preston Jr., Edward S. Herman and Herbert I. Schiller, *Hope and Folly: The United States and UNESCO 1945–1985* (Minneapolis: University of Minnesota Press, 1989), p. 31
67. Ibid.
68. Mitchell, op. cit., pp. 51–57.
69. Central Office of Information (1954), op. cit., p. 11.
70. Mitchell, op. cit., pp. 51–57.
71. Cherry, op. cit., pp. 111–12.
72. Mitchell, op. cit., pp. 51–57.
73. Mitchell, op. cit., p. 70.
74. See Kuldip R. Rampal and W. Clifton Adams, "Credibility of the Asian news broadcasts of the Voice of America and the British Broadcasting Corporation", *Gazette*, vol. 46, no. 2, September 1990, pp. 93–111.
75. Nelson described this practice after the Cold War by noting that:

    The broadcasters are increasing their reach by what the Americans call "placement" and the British "rebroadcasting". This involves broadcasting locally, using a variety of techniques, instead of depending only on short-wave transmission.

The one hour daily of VOA Armenian service is broadcast simultaneously on Radio Yerevan. An hour of the Ukrainian service is rebroadcast on almost the entire Ukrainian network. The BBC transmits by satellite two current affairs programmes of half an hour each of the Russian service each weekend, which are relayed on Radio Russia. They also relay a twenty minute feature programme once a week. RL likes to get entire programme schedules rebroadcast, says Gene Pell, President of RFE/RL. For example, the Ukrainian service is rebroadcast for six hours a day on six transmitters.

Michael Nelson, "Why the 'Big Three' must still broadcast across the old Iron Curtain", *Intermedia*, vol. 20, no. 6, November–December 1992, p. 5.

76. World Service TV was started in 1991. By 1993 it was a 24-hour news and information service disseminated by separate feeds tailored to the interests of its regional partners. For example, by early 1993 it was estimated to reach at least nine million homes in Asia via the Star TV satellite package delivered on AsiaSat1. Jeff Hazell, World Service TV's director of sales and distribution, said at the time that the mission of World Service TV was "to be fully global by the end of 1993 using various joint venture partners". Meredith Amdur, "BBC World Service TV looks west", *Broadcasting & Cable*, 19 April 1993, pp. 35–36.
77. "Europe freed, radio signs off?" *The Economist*, 27 February 1993, p. 57.
78. See Nelson, op cit.
79. William A. Hachten, *The World News Prism* (Ames, Iowa: Iowa State University Press, 1987), p. 92.
80. Michael Kunczik, *Images of Nations and International Public Relations* (Bonn: Friedrich-Ebert-Stiftung, 1990), p. 187.
81. Ibid., pp. 21, 118, 123 and 128.
82. Benjamin Cohen, "Of the People, By the People, For the People", in the United Nations, *Peace on Earth* (New York: Hermitage House, 1949), p. 134.
83. Ibid.
84. Conor Cruise O'Brien and Feliks Topolski, *The United Nations Sacred Drama* (New York: Simon and Schuster, 1968), p. 18.
85. Ibid., pp. 9–10.
86. François Debrix, *Re-Envisioning Peacekeeping: The United Nations and the Mobilization of Ideology* (Minneapolis: University of Minnesota Press, 1999), pp. 1–59.
87. Ibid., p. 18.
88. Hernane Tavares de Sá, *The Play Within The Play: The Inside Story of the UN* (New York: Alfred A. Knopf, 1966).
89. See Mark D. Alleyne, *International Power and International Communication* (London: St. Antony's/Macmillan Press – now Palgrave Macmillan, 1995), and Mark D. Alleyne, *News Revolution: Political and Economic Decisions About Global Information* (New York: St. Martin's Press – now Palgrave Macmillan, 1997).

2 Global Information Machine

1. Hoxie R. Gordon, "The United Nations at 50 Years", *Presidential Studies Quarterly*, vol. 25, no. 4, Fall 1995, p. 3 of downloaded database version.
2. See John Corry, "A formula for genocide", *American Spectator*, vol. 31, no. 9, September 1998, pp. 22–27.

3. See Young Whan Kihl, "A Study of Functionalism In International Organization", PhD dissertation, New York University, October 1963.

4. David Mitrany, *A Working Peace System: An Argument for the Functional Development of International Organization* (London: Royal Institute of International Affairs, 1943), pp. 29–30, quoted in Young Whan Kihl, op. cit., p. 29.

5. New Zealand Ministry of Foreign Affairs and Trade, *United Nations Handbook 1999* (Wellington, New Zealand: New Zealand Ministry of Foreign Affairs and Trade, 1999), p. 75.

6. See Richard N. Swift, "The United Nations and its public", *International Organization*, vol. 14, no. 1, winter 1960, pp. 60–91; and Leon Gordenker, "Policy-making and Secretariat influence in the UN General Assembly: The case of public information", *The American Political Science Review*, vol. 54, June 1960, pp. 359–73.

7. United Nations Department of Public Information, *A Guide to Information at the United Nations* (New York: DPI, 1995).

8. See New Zealand Ministry of Foreign Affairs and Trade, op. cit., pp. 337–39.

9. United Nations document A/54/6/Rev.1, *Proposed Programme Budget for the Biennium 2000–2001, Volume III, Expenditure sections 16 to 33 and income sections 1 to 3.*

10. United Nations document ST/SGB/1999/10, *Organization of the Department of Public Information*, 30 June 1999.

11. See United Nations document ST/SGB/Organization, Section DPI/Rev.2, *Functions and Organization of the Department of Public Information*, 14 June 1996.

12. See United Nations document A/AC.198/2000/5, *United Nations Information Centers in 1999: Allocation of Resources from the Regular Budget of the United Nations*, 15 February 2000.

13. United Nations document A/54/6/Rev.1, op. cit.

14. United Nations document ST/SGB/1999/10, op. cit., p. 7.

15. Ibid., p. 3.

16. Interview with Mr. Shashi Tharoor, Acting Under Secretary-General for Communications and Public Information, UN Headquarters, New York City, 11 June 2001.

17. United Nations document A/3928, *Report of the Expert Committee on United Nations Public Information*, 20 September 1958, p. 77.

18. United Nations document A/AC.51/1983/7, *In-Depth Evaluation of the Work of the Department of Public Information: Report of the Secretary-General*, 18 April 1983, p. 19.

19. United Nations document E/AC.51/80Add.2, *Programme Evaluation for the Biennium 1974–1975, Public Information: Report of the Secretary-General*, 23 March 1977, p. 10.

20. General Assembly resolution A/RES/34/182, *Questions Relating to Information*, 18 December 1979.

21. United Nations document A/56/21, *Committee on Information: Report on the Twenty-Third Session (30 April–11 May 2001)*, 1 June 2001, p. 8.

22. Ibid.

23. United Nations document A/55/21, *Committee on Information, Report on the Twenty-Second Session (1–2 May 2000)*, 10 June 2000, p. 13.

24. UN DPI Press Release (No. PI/1245), "World Freedom Day Observed at Headquarters With Panel discussion on 'Reporting the News in a Dangerous World'", 3 May 2000.

25. See Mark D. Alleyne, *News Revolution: Political and Economic Decisions About Global Information* (New York: St Martin's Press – now Palgrave Macmillan, 1997).

26. Ibid., p. 54.

27. United Nations document A/C.5/1320/Rev.1, *Budget Estimates for the Financial Year 1972 – Review and Reappraisal of United Nations Information Policies and Activities: Report of the Secretary-General*, 15 June 1971, p. 3.

28. United Nations document JIU/REP/81/2, *Co-ordination in the Field of Public Information Activities Among the Members of the United Nations System* (Prepared by Sreten Ilic, Joint Inspection Unit), February 1981, p. 4.

29. Ibid., p. 1.

30. United Nations document A/C.5/L.172, *Report of Sub-Committee 8 of the Fifth Committee on Public Information*, 28 January 1952, paragraph 12.

31. Ibid., paragraph 6.

32. UN General Assembly Resolution 1177(XII), 26 November 1957.

33. United Nations document A/3928, *Report of the Expert Committee on United Nations Public Information*, 20 September 1958, p. 81.

34. Ibid., Annex I, p. 7.

35. United Nations document JIU/REP/81/2, op. cit., p. 24.

36. Ibid., pp. 8–10.

37. Ibid., p. 12.

38. Ibid., p. 11.

39. Ibid., p. 13.

40. United Nations document E/AC.51/1986/10, *Triennial Review of the Implementation of the Recommendations Made by the Committee for Programme and Co-ordination at its Twenty-Third Session on the Work of the Department of Public Information: Report of the Secretary-General*, 21 April 1986, p. 25.

41. Ibid., p. 19.

42. United Nations document E/AC.51/1999/L.6/Add.40, *Draft Report. Addendum. Programme Questions: Evaluation (4(c)). Triennial Review of the Implementation of the Recommendations Made by the Committee for Programme Coordination at its Thirty-Sixth Session on the Evaluation of the Department of Public Information*, 24 June 1999, p. 1.

43. United Nations document E/AC.5/1999/4, *Report of the Office of Internal Oversight Services on the Triennial Review of the Implementation of the Recommendations Made by the Committee for Programme and Coordination at its Thirty-Sixth Session on the Evaluation of the Department of Public Information. Note by the Secretary-General*, 30 March 1999, p. 6.

44. Ibid., p. 9.

45. United Nations document A/3928, op. cit., p. 82.

46. Ibid., p. 84.

47. Ibid., p. 87.

48. See Elihu Katz, "The two-step flow of communication: An up-to-date report on an hypothesis", *Public Opinion Quarterly*, vol. 21, 1957, pp. 61–78.

49. Alexander Szalai with Margaret Croke and Associates, *The United Nations and the News Media: A Survey of Public Information on the United Nations in the World Press, Radio, and Television* (New York: UNITAR, 1972), p. 1.

50. Ibid., p. 97.

51. United Nations document E/AC.51/1986/10, *Triennial Review of the Implementation of the Recommendations Made by the Committee for Programme and Co-ordination at its Twenty-Third Session on the Work of the Department of Public Information: Report of the Secretary-General*, 21 April 1986, p. 8.

52. Ibid., p. 9.
53. United Nations document A/7201/Add.1, paragraph 166, quoted in United Nations document A/C.5/1320/Rev.1, *Budget Estimates for the Financial Year 1972 – Review and Reappraisal of United Nations Information Policies and Activities: Report of the Secretary-General*, 15 June 1971, p. 13.
54. United Nations document A/C.5/1320/Rev.1, op. cit., p. 11.
55. Ibid., p. 14.
56. United Nations document E/AC.51/84, *Public Information Activities in the United Nations System: Report of the Administrative Committee on Co-ordination*, 29 April 1977, p. 4.
57. Ibid., p. 5.
58. United Nations document E/AC.51/80Add.2, *Programme Evaluation for the Biennium 1974–1975, Public Information: Report of the Secretary-General*, 23 March 1977, p. 3.
59. Ibid., p. 14.
60. Ibid., p. 28.
61. Ibid., Annex, p. 1.
62. Ibid., p. 20.
63. See United Nations document A/AC.198/53, *Proposals for Developing Systematic Evaluation Procedures for Activities of the Department of Public Information*, 12 April 1982, pp. 2–3.
64. See United Nations document A/AC.51/1983/7, op. cit., paragraph 92, p. 24.
65. United Nations document A/51/829, *Strengthening of the United Nations System*, letter of the Secretary-General to the President of the General Assembly, 17 March 1997.
66. The Task Force was chaired by Mark Malloch Brown, Vice-President, External Affairs/United Nations Affairs, the World Bank, and included Peter Arnett, Foreign Correspondent, CNN; Joan Ganz Cooney, Chairman of the Executive Committee of the Children's Television Workshop; Radghida Dergham, Senior Diplomatic Correspondent, *Al-Hayat*, President of the United Nations Correspondents Association; Djibril Diallo, Director of Public Affairs, United Nations Development Programme (UNDP); Hironobu Shibuya, President of Pacific Basin Partners, Inc.; Ambassador Juan Somavia, Permanent Representative of Chile to the United Nations; Lelei Lelaulu, Office of the Executive Coordinator for United Nations Reform, Editor of *Secretariat News*, who was Secretary of the Task Force; and M. Salim Lome, Chief of Publications, DPI, who was the Task Force's Rapporteur.
67. Task Force on the Reorientation of United Nations Public Information Activities, *Global Vision, Local Voice: A Strategic Communications Programme for the United Nations* (New York: The United Nations, 1997), p. iii.
68. Ibid., p. 10.
69. J. M. Mitchell, *International Cultural Relations* (London: Allen & Unwin, 1986), p. 81.
70. See, for example, Laura K. Murphy, "China's psychological warfare", *Military Review*, vol. 79, no. 56, September–October 1999, pp. 13–23; Neil Munro, "Infowar: AK-47s, lies and videotape", *Association for Computing Machinery – Communications of the ACM*, vol. 42, no. 7, July 1999, pp. 19–23; Barbara Slavin, "Syria's president eager for Golan Heights deal", *USA Today*, 9 July 1999, p. A8.
71. United Nations document A/55/6/Rev.1, *Medium-Term Plan for the Period 2002–2005*, 23 January 2001, p. 194.
72. Ibid.

73. Ibid., p. 196.
74. Ibid., p. 194.
75. United Nations document A/AC.198/2001/9, *Activities of the Joint United Nations Information Committee in 2000 – Report of the Secretary-General*, 1 March 2001, p. 2.
76. Ibid.
77. United Nations document A/54/2000, *We The Peoples: The Role of the United Nations in the Twenty-First Century – Report of the Secretary-General*, 27 March 2000, p. 7.
78. Ibid., pp. 9–11.
79. Ibid., p. 52.
80. Leon Gordenker, "United Nations use of mass communications in Korea, 1950–1951", *International Organization*, vol. 8, no. 3, August, 1954, p. 344.
81. Gordenker, "Policy-making and Secretariat influence in the UN General Assembly: The case of public information", op. cit., p. 371.
82. Ibid., pp. 361–62.
83. "Sec-Gen Announces Membership of Task Force on Reorientation of UN Public Information Activities," *M2 Presswire*, 24 April 1997. Complete text relayed by Lexis-Nexis Academic, load date 23 May 1997.
84. "UNO Aides Appointed," *The New York Times*, 5 March 1946, p. 5.
85. Trevor Rowe, "Canadian UN Official Defends Her Role in Row Over Contracts", *The Toronto Star*, 5 November 1987, p. A3. Complete text relayed by Lexis-Nexis Academic, load date 13 May 1999.
86. Gordenker, "Policy-making and Secretariat influence in the UN General Assembly: The case of public information", op. cit.
87. Tsutomu Wada, "Japanese Lament How Few of Them Hold Top U.N. Jobs; Latest Appointee Tapped to Head Public Relations Team", *The Nikkei Weekly*, 16 February 1998, p. 1. Complete text relayed by Lexis-Nexis Academic.
88. Ibid.
89. Ibid.
90. "Kobayashi Named Chief of Protocol," *Jiji Press Ticker Service*, 20 April 2001. Complete text relayed by Lexis-Nexis Academic.
91. "United Nations; Paying for Puffs, and Then Puffing," *The Economist*, 6 June 1981, p. 56 (US edition, p. 46). Complete text relayed by Lexis-Nexis Academic Universe.
92. United Nations Press Release ORG/982; PI/384, "DPI Launches Oral History of United Nations", 17 September 1982.
93. Hernane Tavares de Sá, *The Play Within the Play: The Inside Story of the UN* (New York: Alfred A. Knopf, 1966), pp. 95–97.
94. Ibid., p. 83.
95. Ibid., p. 115.
96. Ibid., p. 118.
97. Ibid., p. 124.
98. Ibid., p. 37.
99. Ibid., p. 121.
100. Rowe, op. cit.
101. See United Nations Press Release SG/A/366; BIC/2219; PI/558, "Secretary-General Appoints Therese Paquet-Sevigny Under-Secretary-General for Public Information", 26 November 1986; and "Canadian Woman to Get Top U.N. Job", *The Toronto Star*, 26 November 1986, p. A4.

102. "'Feeling of Resistance'," *World Press Review*, vol. 35, no. 7, July 1988, p. 45.
103. Christopher S. Wren, "Era Waning, Holbroke Takes Stock", *The New York Times*, 14 January 2001 (Late Edition, East Coast), section 1, p. 10.

3 Polishing the Tarnished Image

1. Peter Maas, *Love Thy Neighbor: A Story of War* (New York: Alfred A. Knopf, 1996), p. 172.
2. United Nations document SG/SM/1394, UN Press Release, *Address of Secretary-General to News Media Seminar Sponsored by Stanley Foundation*, 3 December 1970, quoted in Alexander Szalai with Margaret Croke and Associates, *The United Nations and the News Media: A Survey of Public Information on the United Nations in the World Press, Radio, and Television* (New York: UNITAR, 1972), pp. 93–94.
3. Bernard D. Nossiter, "UN Gave $432,000 to the Foreign Press to Publish Its Views", *The New York Times*, 28 May 1981, Section A, p. 1.
4. General Assembly resolution A/RES/3201(S-VI), *Declaration on the Establishment of a New International Economic Order*, paragraph 4, sec. (s), 1 May 1974. (This declaration was adopted by the General Assembly at its 6th special session, 2229th plenary meeting, 1 May 1974.)
5. "Dubious Economies; Uniprop", (Editorial) *The New York Times*, 5 June 1981, Section A, p. 26.
6. United Nations document A/42/21, *Report of the Committee on Information*, 1 January 1987.
7. William A. Landskron (ed.), *Annual Review of United Nations Affairs 1982* (Dobbs Ferry, NY: Oceana Publications, 1983), p. 335.
8. Ibid., pp. 337–38.
9. *Facts on File*, vol. 46, no. 2366, 28 March 1986, p. 213.
10. *Facts on File*, vol. 46, no. 2371, 2 May 1986, p. 320.
11. *Facts on File*, vol. 46, no. 2366, 13 June 1986, p. 434.
12. *Facts on File*, vol. 47, no. 2423, 1 May 1987, p. 314. See also Neil M. Sher, *Kurt Waldheim and Nazi Wartime Atrocities: The Uncensored Justice Department Report* (Collingdale, PA: DIANE Publishing Company, 1994).
13. *Facts on File*, vol. 48, no. 2464, 12 February 1988, p. 88. See also William Templer, *Waldheim Report: International Commission of Historians* (Copenhagen: Museum Tusculanum, 1993).
14. See Pearl Marshall, "Waldheim 'Inquiry' Will Make TV History", *Los Angeles Times*, 28 May 1988, p. 2.
15. "Waldheim apologises for misleading Israelis about past", UPI report, 11 May 1990.
16. The novelist Shirley Hazzard (an ex-employee of the UN) wrote extensively on the organization's failures and the Waldheim deception. In the 1970s she first voiced misgivings about the UN in book form in her *Defeat of an Ideal*. Her skepticism about Waldheim was voiced in a 1980 article for the American magazine *The New Republic*. In 1989 she published two long articles on the UN in *The New Yorker*, which were the basis of a 1990 book, *Countenance of Truth: The United Nations and the Waldheim Case* (New York: Viking).
17. Shirley Hazzard, "Breaking Faith – I", *The New Yorker*, 25 September 1989, p. 90.
18. Shirley Hazzard, "Breaking Faith – II", *The New Yorker*, 2 October 1989, p. 81.
19. Quoted in Shirley Hazzard, "Breaking Faith – I", op. cit., p. 92.

20. Robert Edwin Herzstein, "Waldheim: The Missing Years" (Letter to the Editor, Book Review Desk), *The New York Times*, 8 May 1988, Section 7, p. 44.
21. Shirley Hazzard, "Breaking Faith – I", op. cit., p. 66.
22. Ibid., p. 74.
23. See "Waldheim Before the Fall", *The New York Times*, 1 May 1988, Section 7, p. 42 (Letter to the Editor, Book Review Desk, by Brian Urquhart, and response by Shirley Hazzard).
24. Mark Feeney, "Kurt Waldheim and the UN's Low Estate", *The Boston Globe*, 8 April 1990, p. B40.
25. Bernard D. Nossiter, "The Sins of the UN", *The Washington Post Book World*, 8 April 1990, p. X7.
26. United Nations document A/54/2000, *We The Peoples: The Role of the United Nations in the Twenty-First Century – Report of the Secretary-General*, 27 March 2000, p. 36, paragraph 223.
27. See United Nations document S/1999/1257, *Report of the Independent Inquiry into the Actions of the United Nations During the 1994 Genocide in Rwanda*, 15 December 1999; and United Nations document A/54/549, *Report of the Secretary-General Pursuant to General Assembly Resolution 53/35: The Fall of Srebrenica*, 15 November 1999.
28. The Norwegian Nobel Committee, "The Nobel Peace Prize 2001", press release, Oslo, 12 October 2001.
29. Quoted in United Nations document S/1999/1257, op. cit.
30. "United Nations Operation in Somalia II", complete text downloaded from the United Nations website, 21 March 2002, *http://www.un.org/Depts/dpko/dpko/co_mission/unosom2.htm*.
31. United Nations document S/1994/653, *Report of the Commission of Inquiry Established Pursuant to Security Council Resolution 885 (1993) to Investigate Armed Attacks on UNOSOM II Personnel Which Led to Casualties Among Them*, 24 February 1994, quoted in United Nations document S/1999/1257, op. cit.
32. United Nations document S/1999/1257, op. cit.
33. United Nations document A/54/549, op. cit., p. 109.
34. Ibid.
35. International Commission on the Balkans, *Unfinished Peace* (Washington, DC: Carnegie Endowment for International Peace, 1996), p. 69.
36. United Nations document A/55/305-S/2000/809, *Report of the Panel on United Nations Peace Operations*, 21 August 2000.
37. International Commission on the Balkans, op. cit., p. 68.
38. UNESCO, *World Culture Report 2000: Cultural Diversity, Conflict and Pluralism* (Paris: UNESCO, 2000), Table 4, pp. 304–07.
39. Ibid., Graph 6, p. 88.
40. Ibid., Table 3, pp. 300–03.
41. Jayantha Dhanapala, "Communicating the Disarmament Message," speech at the Centre for International Communication, Macquarie University, Sydney, Australia, 30 August 2001.
42. Petronella Wyatt, "Honey, I Lost The Plot", *The Spectator*, 25 March 2000, p. 16.
43. See Paulo Freire, *Pedagogy of the Oppressed* (New York: Continuum, 1992).
44. William Over, *Human Rights in the International Public Sphere: Civic Discourse for the 21st Century* (Stamford, CT: Ablex, 1999), pp. 79–80.
45. Quoted in Thalif Deen, "Politics: U.N. Hosts Galaxy of Celebrities Promoting Its Ideals", *Inter Press Service*, 23 October 2000.

46. Philip L. Gianos, *Politics and Politicians in American Film* (Westport, CT: Praeger, 1998), pp. xi–xii.

47. See *Slaying The Dragon* (video recording), produced by Pacific Productions; a special project of Asian Women United in association with KQED (New York: Women Make Movies, 1988).

48. *The New York Times*, 15 August 1953, p. 8, column 4.

49. Neil Hickey, "How To Make A Dream Come True", *TV Guide*, 28 December 1964, p. 10.

50. Telephone interview with Ms. Ann Neal, Director, Xerox Archive, 21 March 2001.

51. "What's Good for U.N. is Good for Xerox", *Business Week*, no. 1807, 18 April 1964, pp. 80 and 82.

52. Ibid., p. 80.

53. Robert Lewis Shayon, "They Sang Along With Mitch", *Saturday Review*, 30 May 1964, p. 24.

54. Robert Lewis Shayon, "The Birchbark Curtain", *Saturday Review*, 3 October 1964, p. 29.

55. Quoted in Val Adams, "U.N.-Show Policy Is Set By N.B.C.-TV", *The New York Times*, 11 April 1964, p. 53.

56. Shayon, "The Birchbark Curtain", op. cit.

57. Val Adams, "N.B.C. To Present Rockettes Film", *The New York Times*, Saturday, 13 February 1965, p. 49.

58. See Val Adams, "Susskind Shapes New Play Series", *The New York Times*, 17 September 1964, p. 87; and Irving Spiegel, "Dr. King Examines Rights and Laws", *The New York Times*, 21 May 1965.

59. "UN-precedented", *Newsweek*, 20 April 1964, p. 72.

60. "What's good for U.N. is Good for Xerox", op. cit.

61. Jack Gould, "TV: Weak Premiere of U.N. Series", *The New York Times*, 29 December 1964, p. 55. See also Jack Gould, "TV: Soap Opera Asea", *The New York Times*, 20 February 1965, p. 53; Jack Gould, "TV: 'Once Upon a Tractor' Wanders", *The New York Times*, 10 September 1965, p. 71; and Jack Gould, "TV Review: 'Poppy Also a Flower' Is U.N. Melodrama", *The New York Times*, 23 April 1966, p. 63.

62. Rex Reed, "Director Among the TV Demoniacs", *The New York Times*, 27 December 1964, Section II, p. 15.

63. Quoted in Jay Sharbutt, "The Final Test Of 'Amerika' Is The Ratings", *Los Angeles Times*, 13 February 1987, Section VI, p. 1.

64. Harry F. Waters (with Janet Huck), "ABCs Amerikan Dream", *Newsweek*, 16 February 1987, p. 21.

65. See "'Amerika' Tops Ratings For Sunday", *The New York Times*, 17 February 1987, Section C, p. 21; and "ABC Ranks 3d Week Despite 'Amerika' Series", *The New York Times*, 26 February 1987, Section C, p. 26.

66. Alvin P. Sanoff (with Lisa J. Moore and Elisabeth Blaug), "Will Bad Russians Make Good Ratings?", *US News & World Report*, 16 February 1987, p. 67.

67. Howard Rosenberg, "The 'Amerika' Controversy: Let America Decide", *Los Angeles Times*, 30 January 1987, Part VI, p. 1.

68. Quoted in Jay Sharbutt, "Foreign TV Markets Court 'Amerika'", *Los Angeles Times*, 28 January 1987, Part VI, p. 1.

69. Andrew Feinberg, "Video Deal Brings Amerika to UK", *Campaign* (Copyright Haymarket Publishing Services Ltd.), 13 March 1987. Complete text downloaded from Lexis-Nexis Academic, 5 April 2002.

70. Sanoff *et al.*, op. cit., p. 66.

71. Sharbutt, "The Final Test Of 'Amerika' Is The Ratings", op. cit., p. 22.
72. Andrew Kopkind, "*Amerika*: It Can't Happen Here", *The Nation*, 14 February 1987, p. 195.
73. See "Red Stars and Stripes Forever", *The Economist*, 21 February 1987, p. 43 (US Edition p. 31); " 'Amerika's' Kristofferson To Film Spot On U.N.", *Los Angeles Times*, 11 February 1987, p. 10.
74. Howard Rosenberg, "...And Turner Launches A Counterattack On WTBS", *Los Angeles Times*, 13 February 1987, Part VI, pp. 1 and 22.
75. Quoted in Shirley Hazzard, "Breaking Faith – I", op. cit., p. 76.
76. Lawrence Van Gelder, "John A. Scali, 77, ABC Reporter Who Helped Ease Missile Crisis", (Obituary) *The New York Times*, 10 October 1995, Section A, p. 20.
77. William J. Millard, "International Public Opinion of the United Nations: A Comparative Analysis", *International Journal of Public Opinion Research*, vol. 5, no. 1, spring 1993, pp. 93–96.
78. "Feeling of Renaissance", *World Press Review*, July 1988, p. 45.
79. Shirley Hazzard, "Breaking Faith – I", op. cit., pp. 76–77.

4   Good Propaganda, Bad Propaganda

1. United Nations document A/RES/13(I), ANNEX I, *Recommendations of the Technical Committee on Information Concerning the Policies, Functions and Organization of the Department of Public Information*, 1946.
2. L. John Martin, *International Propaganda: Its Legal and Diplomatic Control* (Gloucester, MA: Peter Smith, 1958, reprinted 1969), pp. 89–90.
3. William Preston Jr., "The History of U.S.-UNESCO Relations", in William Preston Jr., Edward S. Herman and Herbert I. Schiller, *Hope And Folly: The United States and UNESCO 1945–1985* (Minneapolis: University of Minnesota Press, 1989), pp. 26–27.
4. Edward W. Ploman, *International Law Governing Communication and Information: A Collection of Basic Documents* (London: Frances Pinter, 1982).
5. Martin, op. cit., p. 80.
6. Ibid., p. 78.
7. See Garth S. Jowett and Victoria O'Donnell, *Propaganda and Persuasion*, 2nd edn (Newbury Park, CA: Sage, 1992), pp. 185–95.
8. UN document A/RES/37/92, *Principles Governing the Use by States of Artificial Earth Satellites for International Direct Television Broadcasting*, 10 December 1982.
9. UNESCO General Conference, Resolution 4/9.3/2, 1978, *Declaration On Fundamental Principles Concerning The Contribution Of The Mass Media To Strengthening Peace And International Understanding, To Promotion Of Human Rights And to Countering Racialism, Apartheid And Incitement To War*.
10. 32 U.N. GAOR Committee on the Peaceful Uses of Outer Space (173d mtg.) at 42, U.N. Doc. A/AC.105/PV.173 (1977), quoted in Jon T. Powell, "Towards A Negotiable Definition of Propaganda for International Agreements Related to Direct Broadcast Satellites", *Law and Contemporary Problems*, vol. 45, no. 1 (winter 1982), p. 9.
11. United Nations document A/C.5/L.172, *Report of Sub-Committee 8 of the Fifth Committee on Public Information*, 28 January 1952, paragraph 5.
12. United Nations document A/C.5/1320/Rev.1, *Budget Estimates for the Financial Year 1972 – Review and Reappraisal of United Nations Information Policies and Activities: Report of the Secretary-General*, 15 June 1971, pp. 11 and 14.

13. Ibid., pp. 16–17.
14. Alexander Szalai with Margaret Croke and Associates, *The United Nations and the News Media: A Survey of Public Information on the United Nations in the World Press, Radio, and Television* (New York: UNITAR, 1972), p. 98.
15. Ibid., p. 99.
16. See United Nations document A/AC.51/1983/7, *In-Depth Evaluation of the Work of the Department of Public Information: Report of the Secretary-General*, 18 April 1983, paragraph 92, p. 24.
17. Task Force on the Reorientation of United Nations Public Information Activities, *Global Vision, Local Voice* (New York: The United Nations, 1997), p. 10.
18. United Nations document A/AC.198/2001/9, *Activities of the Joint United Nations Information Committee in 2000 – Report of the Secretary-General*, 1 March 2001, p. 2.
19. United Nations document A/55/6/Rev.1, *Medium-Term Plan for the Period 2002–2005*, 23 January 2001, p. 194.
20. United Nations document A/C.5/1320/Rev.1, op. cit., p. 14.
21. United Nations document E/AC.51/84, *Public Information Activities in the United Nations System: Report of the Administrative Committee on Co-ordination*, 29 April 1977, p. 4.
22. See for example Alison Dundes Renteln, *International Human Rights: Universalism Versus Relativism* (Newbury Park, CA: Sage, 1990).
23. See Lone Lindholt, *Questioning the Universality of Human Rights: The African Charter on Human and People's Rights in Botswana, Malawi, and Mozambique* (Brookfield, VT: Ashgate Publishing, 1997); and Pierre de Senarclens, "The Smashed Mirror of Past Illusions", *Society*, vol. 22, no. 6, September/October, 1985, pp. 6–14. See also R. J. Vincent, *Human Rights and International Relations* (Cambridge: Cambridge University Press, 1986), pp. 37–38.
24. de Senarclens, op. cit., p. 7.
25. Ibid., p. 8.
26. Renteln, op. cit., p. 12.
27. Ibid., p. 52.
28. Ibid., pp. 19 and 32.
29. Ibid., pp. 5 and 9.
30. See Sydney D. Bailey, *The United Nations: A Short Political Guide*, 2nd edn (London: Macmillan Press – now Palgrave Macmillan, 1989), pp. 72–74.
31. William H. Meyer, "Toward A Global Culture: Universalism vs. Relativism Regarding International Human Rights". Paper presented at the Annual Meeting of the International Studies Association, Chicago, February 1995, p. 6.
32. William Over, *Human Rights In The International Public Sphere* (Stamford, CT: Ablex Publishing, 1999), p. 13.
33. For more on the educational and advocacy roles of NGOs, see Thomas G. Weiss and Leon Gordenker (eds.), *NGOs, The UN, & Global Governance* (Boulder, CO: Lynne Rienner Publishers, 1996), pp. 38–40.
34. See General Assembly Resolutions 55/94 and 49/184.
35. UN Press Release GA/SM/221 HR/4504, 28 November 2000.
36. UN Press Release HR/4348 PI/1046, 10 December 1997.
37. UN Press Release PI/998, 18 April 1997.
38. Sue Kendall, "OECD Ministers 'Determined' To Launch New Trade Round", *Agence France Presse*, 27 June 2000. Complete text downloaded from Lexis-Nexis Academic, 26 April 2002.

39. See Peter Harmsen, "China's Rights Record Could Worsen After WTO Entry: Analysts", *Agence France Presse*, 11 November 2001. Complete text downloaded from Lexis-Nexis Academic, 25 April 2002.

40. Quoted in John Rice, "Fox Denies Lying About Castro, But Asks Apology; Confirms Radically New Foreign Policy", *Associated Press*, 25 April 2002. Complete text downloaded from Lexis-Nexis Academic, 25 April 2002.

41. UN Department of Public Information (The United Nations Blue Books Series, Vol. 1) *The United Nations and Apartheid: 1948–1994* (New York: The United Nations, 1994), pp. 13 and 29–30.

42. See General Assembly resolutions A/RES/395 (V), *Treatment of People of Indian Origin in the Union of South Africa*, 2 December 1950; and A/RES/616 A (VII), *The Question of Race Conflict in South Africa Resulting from the Policies of Apartheid of the Government of the Union of South Africa*, 5 December 1952; and A/RES/616 B (VII), 5 December 1952. See Security Council Resolution S/RES/134 (1960), *Question Relating to the Situation in the Union of South Africa*, 1 April 1960. See also William Korey, *NGOs and the Universal Declaration of Human Rights* (New York: St. Martin's Press – now Palgrave Macmillan 1998), p. 98.

43. General Assembly resolution A/RES/1761 (XVII), *The Policies of Apartheid of the Government of the Republic of South Africa*, 6 November 1962.

44. UN Department of Public Information (The United Nations Blue Books Series, Vol. 1), op. cit., p. 64.

45. United Nations document UN DPI/S1 1988, *United Nations Yearbook 1988*, Vol. 2, pp. 154–55.

46. UN Department of Public Information (The United Nations Blue Books Series, Vol. 1), op. cit., p. 62.

47. See Danny Schechter, "South Africa now: the challenge of the South African story", in Beverly G. Hawk (ed.), *Africa's Media Image* (Westport, CT: Praeger, 1992). Information on the UN grant of $10 000 was provided by Danny Schecter in an email to Laura Fernandez (Research Assistant to Mark Alleyne), 5 December 2001.

48. "Sanctions Lifted After 31 Years: Interim Constitution Agreed On", *UN Chronicle*, vol. 31, no. 1, March 1994, p. 49.

49. See United Nations Documents A/RES/40/97 (1985); A/RES/41/39 (1986); A/RES/42/14 (1987); and A/RES/43/26 (1988).

50. See United Nations Documents A/RES/39/72 (1984); A/RES/40/64 (1985); A/RES/42/23 (1987); UN/RES/43/50 (1988); and A/RES/44/27 (1989).

51. UN Department of Public Information (The United Nations Blue Books Series, Vol. 1), op. cit., p. 65.

52. See United Nations documents A/RES/40/148 (1985) and A/RES/41/160 (1986).

53. UN Department of Public Information (The United Nations Blue Books Series, Vol. 1), op. cit., p. 44.

54. Korey, op. cit., p. 113.

55. Schechter, op. cit., pp. 245–46.

56. For a chronology of events during South Africa's apartheid era, see UN Department of Public Information (The United Nations Blue Books Series, Vol. 1), op. cit., pp. 149–66.

57. William A. Hachten and C. Anthony Giffard, *The Press and Apartheid: Repression and Propaganda in South Africa* (Madison, WI: University of Wisconsin Press, 1984), pp. 6–7, and also Chapter 10.

58. Michael Kunczik, *Images of Nations and International Public Relations* (Bonn: Friedrich-Ebert-Stiftung, 1990), pp. 155–65.

59. For more on this, see Elaine Windrich, "South Africa's Propaganda War," *Africa Today*, vol. 36, no. 1, 1989, pp. 51–60.
60. See Michele M. Melendez, "Smoke Hasn't Cleared Yet on Anti-Drug Ads; Experts, Teens Unsure Whether Costly Campaign Deters Abuse", *The Times-Picayune* (New Orleans), 15 March 2002, p. 1. Complete text downloaded from Lexis-Nexis Academic, 19 May 2002.
61. See Richard Earle, *The Art of Cause Marketing: How To Use Advertising To Change Personal Behavior and Public Policy* (Lincolnwood, IL: NTC Business Books, 2000).
62. Marlise Simons, "Trial Centers on Role of Press During Rwanda Massacre", *The New York Times*, 3 March 2002. Complete text relayed by Proquest database, 17 April 2002.
63. Daniel Deluce, "Media Wars", *NATO Review*, vol. 48, no. 4, winter 2000/2001. Complete text relayed by Proquest database, 17 April 2002.
64. See Les Back, "White Fortresses in Cyberspace", *The Courier* (UNESCO), January 2001. Complete text downloaded from the magazine's website, *www.unesco.org/courier*, 11 May 2002; and Claire Doole, "Cyber-racists 'Safe in US'", *BBC News Online*, 16 February 2000. Complete text downloaded from the British Broadcasting Corporation website, *news.bbc.co.uk*, 11 May 2002.
65. Yojana Sharma, "Rights: Zero Tolerance For Internet Hate Speech", *Inter Press Service*, 27 June 2000. Complete text downloaded from Lexis-Nexis Academic, 11 May 2002.
66. See Les Back, op. cit.
67. Simons, op. cit.
68. Ian De Freitas, "Worldwide Web of Laws Threatens The Internet", *The Times* (London), 9 January 2001. Complete text downloaded from Lexis-Nexis Academic, 11 May 2002.
69. Ibid.
70. Jamie F. Metzl, "Information Intervention: When Switching Channels Isn't Enough", *Foreign Affairs*, vol. 76, no. 6, Nov/Dec 1997, pp. 15–20.
71. Randall L. Bytwerk, *Julius Streicher* (New York: Stein and Day, 1983).

5   Lubricating the Wheels

1. David Rieff, "Up the Organization," *The New Republic*, 1 February 1999. Complete text relayed by Proquest database, 21 March 2002.
2. Lynette Finch, "Psychological Propaganda: The War of Ideas on Ideas During the First Half of the Twentieth Century", *Armed Forces and Society*, vol. 26, no. 3, pp. 367–86, p. 12 of downloaded database version.
3. Ken Millen-Penn, "Democratic Control, Public Opinion, and League Diplomacy", *World Affairs*, vol. 157, spring 1995, p. 1 of downloaded database version. Full text downloaded from FirstSearch, 16 February 2001.
4. Ibid., p. 4 of downloaded database version.
5. *The Wall Street Journal*, "Technology" (special supplement), 15 November 1993, p. R7.
6. See Debra Johnson, "MTV to Expand International Reach", *Broadcasting & Cable*, March 1996, p. 64; and Phyllis Zagano, "Beavis and Butt-head, Free Your Mind", *America*, 5 March 1994, p. 6.
7. Report of the Committee on Information on the resumed twenty-first session (1–5 November 1999), 9 November 1999, Supplement No. 21A (A/54/21/Add.1),

Annex, "Statement by the Under-Secretary-General for Communications and Public Information at the opening of the resumed twenty-first session of the Committee on Information".

8. Ann M. Florini (ed.), *The Third Force: The Rise of Transnational Civil Society* (Washington DC: Carnegie Endowment for International Peace, 2000), p. 9.

9. United Nations document A/53/170, *Arrangements and Practices for the Interaction of Non-Governmental Organizations in all Activities of the United Nations System: Report of the Secretary General*, 10 July 1998, p.2.

10. Ibid.

11. "Civil society" and the "social movement" that supposedly create it are used with some care here. David Macey, in *The Penguin Dictionary of Critical Theory* (London: Penguin, 2000), says that the term "civil society" "is commonly used to describe a sphere of human activity that is outside or apart from the structures of states and governments and in which free individuals form voluntary associations and establish pluralistic relations based on affinities and common interests rather than coercion". He notes, however, that this is merely the most recent meaning of a term that has represented different concepts for seventeenth- and eighteenth-century theorists of the social contract, Marx, and Gramsci. More recently, Gellner has spoken of civil society as being synonymous with liberal democracy. The UN Secretariat's use of the term in the late 1990s seems to be a conflation of this idea that civil society is a realm of organizations outside the control of governments, and that the existence of these organizations implies the life of liberal-democracy. The UN's developing and maintaining ties with these groups is seen as something positive for international politics, therefore, because it would be a way of gaining the participation of non-state entities in transnational decision-making. As I note below, recent thinkers in international relations, especially Colás, do not share this positive reading of this most recent version of civil society. Although acknowledging the existence of these organizations, Colás focuses attention on the terms under which they participate in global politics. From this perspective, movements for social change (social movements) can reap little if they are prevented from contributing meaningfully to the political process.

12. "The Civil Society," *Canada and the World Backgrounder*, vol. 67, no. 1, September 2001. Complete text downloaded from the Wilson Select Plus database, 18 June 2002, p. 4 of database version.

13. John Keane, *Civil Society: Old Images, New Visions* (Cambridge: Polity Press, 1998), p. 15.

14. Alejandro Colás, *International Civil Society: Social Movements and World Politics* (Cambridge: Polity Press, 2002) p. 138.

15. Craig Warkentin, *Reshaping World Politics: NGOs, the Internet, and Global Civil Society* (Lanham, MD: Rowman & Littlefield, 2001), p. 19.

16. Telephone interview with Gillian Martin Sorensen, Assistant Secretary-General for External Relations, Executive Office of the United Nations Secretary-General, 31 October 2001.

17. United Nations document A/RES/13(I), ANNEX I. See Appendix II.

18. United Nations document E/RES/1297 (XLIV), 4 June 1968.

19. United Nations document A/53/170, op. cit., p. 2.

20. Ibid.

21. Willetts reported that:

> In the euphoria of the Earth Summit, provisions were written into Agenda 21 for a review of the "formal procedures and mechanisms" for involvement of NGOs

in the United Nations system. The pressures for such a review came from NGOs seeking a much greater role in ECOSOC than that provided by existing consultative status, the need to consider whether special procedures were required on sustainable development questions and the desire of some to establish formal relationships in the General Assembly. The Secretariat wanted consideration of the resources allocated to the NGO Unit and the logistics of dealing with much greater numbers of NGOs. Some governments wished to give positive support to NGOs as part of the process of global democratization, while others, which were antagonistic to human rights NGOs and some environmental NGOs, no doubt hoped that the review process would provide opportunities for them to halt, or even reverse, the growth in the activities and the prestige of NGOs.

Peter Willetts (ed.), *"The Conscience of the World": The Influence of Non-Governmental Organisations in the UN System* (Washington DC: The Brookings Institution, 1996), p. 57.
22. DPI/NGO Home page (*http://www.un.org/dpi/ngosection/brochure.htm*). Downloaded 3 July 2002.
23. United Nations document A/53/170, op. cit., p. 15.
24. Keane, op. cit., p. 79.
25. Colás, op. cit., p. 153.
26. Ibid., p. 84.
27. Weiss and Gordenker distinguish between government-organized non-governmental organizations (GONGOs), quasi-non-governmental organizations (QUANGOs), and donor-organized NGOs (DONGO). See Thomas G. Weiss and Leon Gordenker (eds.), *NGOs, The UN, & Global Governance* (Boulder, CO: Lynne Rienner Publishers, 1996), pp. 20–21. Willetts notes that NGOs have links to all the three types of international organizations he says exist in international society: intergovernmental organizations, hybrid international organizations, and international non-governmental organizations. It is only the intergovernmental organizations that do not have NGO members. See Willetts, op. cit., p. 8.
28. Weiss and Gordenker, op. cit., p. 28.
29. Willetts, op. cit., p. 271.
30. See for example Sara Fletcher Luther, *The United States and the Direct Broadcast Satellite* (New York: Oxford University Press, 1988), Chapter 3; and Willard D. Rowland, Jr., "Deconstructing American Communications Policy Literature," *Critical Studies in Mass Communication*, December 1984, pp. 423–35.
31. Paul F. Lazarsfeld, Bernard Berelson and Hazel Gaudet, *The People's Choice* (New York: Columbia University Press, 1948).
32. Elihu Katz, "The Two-Step Flow of Communication: An Up-To-Date Report on an Hypothesis", *Public Opinion Quarterly* 21, 1957, p. 77.
33. Ibid., p. 61.
34. Robert Heine-Geldern, "Cultural diffusion", in David L. Sills (ed.), *An International Encyclopedia of the Social Science* (New York: Crowell-Collier and Macmillan – now Palgrave Macmillan, 1968), pp. 169–73.
35. David Strang and Sarah A. Soule, "Diffusion Organizations and Social Movements: From Hybrid Corn to Poison Pills", *Annual Review of Sociology*, vol. 24, 1998, pp. 265–90, p. 2 of downloaded electronic database version.
36. James A. Muncy and Jacqueline K. Eastman, "The Journal of Advertsing: Twenty-Five Years and Beyond," *Journal of Advertising*, vol. 27, no. 4, winter 1998, pp. 1–8, p. 2 of downloaded electronic database version.
37. Michael S. Sweeney, "Censorship Missionaries of World War II", *Journalism History*, vol. 27, no. 1, spring 2001, pp. 4–13.

38. Lucian W. Pye (ed.), *Communications and Political Development* (Princeton, NJ: Princeton University Press, 1963), pp. 24–26.
39. Writers such as Herbert Schiller, Noam Chomsky and Armand Mattelart built careers in the 1970s, 1980s and 1990s through their prolific writings about how the mass media often serve as handmaidens of the powerful. The American media scholar Michael Parenti said the mass media "invented" reality. See Michael Parenti, *Inventing Reality: The Politics of News Media*, 2nd edn (New York: St. Martin's Press – now Palgrave Macmillan, 1993). The Gulf War sparked a number of critical academic studies of how the media function in relation to power in times of social crisis, for example Susan L. Carruthers, *The Media At War* (New York: St. Martin's Press – now Palgrave Macmillan, 2000). Another area of critical research has been on how the media represent race and perpetuate racism. See for example Christopher P. Campbell, *Race, Myth and the News* (Thousand Oaks, CA: Sage, 1995); and Arthur K. Spears (ed.), *Race and Ideology* (Detroit, MI: Wayne State University Press, 1999). The New World Information and Communication Order (NWICO) debate at UNESCO provoked a number of studies of mass media in transnational context, and this scholarship was refined by globalization theory that became a popular analytical frame from the 1980s on. See for example Anthony D. King (ed.), *Culture, Globalization and the World System: Contemporary Conditions for the Representation of Identity* (Minneapolis: University of Minnesota Press, 1997).
40. Quoted in United Nations document A/3928, *Report of the Expert Committee on United Nations Public Information*, 20 September 1958, p. 88. The Survey Group's report was presented to the tenth session of the UN General Assembly. Responses to it are in various documents by the parties concerned, i.e. the Secretary-General (UN document A/3041), the Advisory Committee on Administrative and Budgetary Questions (A/3031), and the Fifth Committee (A/3103).
41. United Nations document A/AC.51/1983/7, *In-Depth Evaluation of the Work of the Department of Public Information: Report of the Secretary-General*, 18 April 1983, p. 11.
42. Ibid.
43. Ibid., p. 10.
44. James W. Loewen, *Lies My Teacher Told Me: Everything Your American History Textbook Got Wrong* (New York: Touchstone, 1995).
45. "Apartheid Belies Chinese Rhetoric," *Africa Report*, vol. 34, no. 2, March 1989, p. 9; Andrew Giarelli, "Is China Racist?", *World Press Review*, vol. 36, no. 3, March 1989, p. 43; Michael S. Serrill, "The Fallout From Nanjing," *Time*, vol. 133, no. 3, 16 January 1989, p. 38.
46. Gopal Sukhu, "Nanjing Burning", *The Village Voice*, vol. 33, no. 3, 17 January 1989, pp. 21 and 106; "Chinese Chequers," *New Statesman and Society*, vol. 35, no. 2, 3 February 1989, p. 31.
47. Raymond Seidelman, "The Anti-African Protests: More Than Just Chinese Racism", *The Nation*, vol. 248, no. 6, 13 February 1989, pp. 195–96; Melinda Beck, "China: 'Kill The Black Devils' ", *Newsweek*, vol. 113, no. 2, 9 January 1989, p. 35.
48. Both definitions taken from the UN's Peacekeeping Operations website (*http://www.un.org/Depts/dpko/glossary/p.htm*), 5 July 2002.
49. United Nations document A/54/2000, *We The Peoples: The Role of the United Nations in the Twenty-First Century – Report of the Secretary-General*, 27 March 2000, p. 31, paragraph 191.
50. Sir Marrack Goulding (former head of UN peacekeeping), "United Nations Peacekeeping". Public lecture, Chicago, 24 February 2001. See also Marrack Goulding, *Peacemonger* (London: John Murray, 2002).

51. Goulding, op. cit.; United Nations document A/54/2000, op. cit., pp. 34 and 36, paragraph 221.
52. United Nations document S/1999/1257, *Report of the Independent Inquiry Into the Actions of the United Nations During the 1994 Genocide in Rwanda*, 15 December 1999.
53. Paul Jenkins, "Europe: Propaganda Unlimited – Serbs are beaming their view of the war in the former Yugoslavia around the world, on Western television networks. Sanctions, what sanctions? Asks Paul Jenkins", *The Guardian* (Manchester), 3 May 1993. Downloaded from ProQuest database, 3 April 2001.
54. See Carol Matlack, "Serbian-Croatian PR War", *National Journal*, vol. 24, no. 11, 14 March 1992, pp. 644–45; and Rochelle L. Stanfield, "Balkans Wars on K Street", *National Journal*, vol. 24, no. 33, 15 August 1992, pp. 1903–04.
55. Noel Malcolm, " 'The Whole Lot of Them Are Serbs' ", *The Spectator*, vol. 274, no. 8709, 10 June 1995, pp. 14–18.
56. Alexander Cockburn, "Hating Serbs is Fun", *The Nation*, vol. 261, no. 12, 16 October 1995, p. 411.
57. "Poison From Pale: Why Nato should intervene in the Bosnian Serb media battle," (Editorial) *The Times*, 25 August 1997, p. 19A.
58. Jamie F. Metzl, "Information Intervention: When Switching Channels Isn't Enough", *Foreign Affairs*, vol. 76, no. 6, Nov/Dec 1997, pp. 15–20.
59. Keith Spicer, "Propaganda for Peace", *The New York Times*, 10 December 1994, Section 1, p. 23.
60. Aryeh Neier, "Watching Rights", *The Nation*, vol. 258, no. 24, 20 June 1994, p. 862.
61. See Michael Evans, "Nato troops take over 'poisonous' Karadzic TV", *The Times* (London), 2 October 1997, p. 16A.
62. Reported in United Nations document A/54/2000, op. cit., p. 11.
63. Lina Maria Holguin, "The Media in Modern Peacekeeping", *Peace Review*, vol. 10, no. 4, December 1998, pp. 639–45.
64. Ibid.
65. Metzl, op. cit.
66. Holguin, op. cit.
67. United Nations document A/55/305-S/2000/809, *Report of the Panel on United Nations Peace Operations*, 21 August 2000, paragraphs 146–50, 234–38 and 263.
68. "Multidisciplinary Peacekeeping: Lessons Learned From Recent Past," United Nations' *Lessons Learned in Peacekeeping* web page (*http://www.un.org/Depts/dpko/lessons/*). Downloaded 5 July 2002.
69. See United Nations document A/AC.198/2002/5, *Substantive Questions: Role of the Department of Public Information in United Nations Peacekeeping – Report of the Secretary-General*, 2 March 2002.
70. Adapted from United Nations document A/55/977, *Implementation of the Recommendations of the Special Committee on Peacekeeping Operations and the Panel on United Nations Peace Operations: Report of the Secretary-General*, 1 June 2001, Annex M.

6 Using the Tool

1. United Nations document A/RES/13 (I), ANNEX I, *Recommendations of the Technical Advisory Committee on Information Concerning the Policies, Functions and Organization of the Department of Public Information*, 13 February 1946.

2. United Nations document A/C.5/L.172, *Report of Sub-Committee 8 of the Fifth Committee on Public Information*, 28 January 1952, paragraph 6.
3. United Nations document A/7201/ Add.1, paragraph 166, quoted in United Nations document A/C.5/1320/Rev.1, *Budget Estimates for the Financial Year 1972 – Review and Reappraisal of United Nations Information Policies and Activities: Report of the Secretary-General*, 15 June 1971, p. 13.
4. United Nations document A/C.5/1320/Rev.1, op. cit., p. 14.
5. United Nations document E/AC.51/84, *Public Information Activities in the United Nations System: Report of the Administrative Committee on Co-ordination*, 29 April 1977, p. 4.
6. Alexander Szalai with Margaret Croke and Associates, *The United Nations and the News Media: A Survey of Public Information on the United Nations in the World Press, Radio, and Television* (New York: UNITAR, 1972), p. 100.
7. JUNIC was given the following terms of reference:

   The Joint United Nations Information Committee (JUNIC) shall assume, under ACC, principal (sic) responsibility for developing a common United Nations public information system covering all aspects of the activities of the organizations within the system, with special reference to the mobilization of public opinion in support of economic and social development.
   To this end, the Committee shall:

   (a) Advise ACC on general public information policy and co-ordination for the United Nations system as a whole;
   (b) Provide general policy guidance and co-ordination in public information matters throughout the United Nations family at Headquarters and in the field,
   (c) Jointly plan public information operations including the establishment of co-operative arrangements for special projects and events.

   United Nations document JIU/REP/81/2, *Co-ordination in the Field of Public Information Activities Among the Members of the United Nations System* (prepared by Sreten Ilic, Joint Inspection Unit), February 1981, p. 7.
8. Ibid., pp. 1 and 21.
9. United Nations document A/C.5/1320/Rev.1, *Budget Estimates for the Financial Year 1972 – Review and Reappraisal of United Nations Information Policies and Activities: Report of the Secretary-General*, 15 June 1971, p. 15.
10. Ibid.
11. Alexander Szalai with Margaret Croke and Associates, op. cit., p. 103.
12. Ibid., p. 104.
13. Ibid., p. 19.
14. Voluntary Service Overseas (VSO), *The Live Aid Legacy: The Developing World Through British Eyes – A Research Report* (London: VSO, 2002).
15. William J. Millard, "International Public Opinion of the United Nations: A Comparative Analysis", *International Journal of Public Opinion Research*, vol. 5, no. 1, spring 1993, pp. 92–99.
16. Martin Wight, *Power Politics*, 2nd edn (London: Penguin; Royal Institute of International Affairs, 1986).
17. Marcel Merle, *The Sociology of International Relations* (Leamington Spa: Berg, 1987).
18. Graham Evans and Jeffrey Newnham, *The Penguin Dictionary of International Relations* (London: Penguin Books, 1998), p. 340.

19. United Nations Department of Public Information, *Principal Organs of the United Nations* (chart) (New York: DPI, January 2002).
20. Robert W. Cox and Harold K. Jacobson, *et al.*, *The Anatomy of Influence: Decision Making in International Organization* (New Haven, CT: Yale University Press, 1974), pp. 5–6.
21. Warren P. Strobel, *Late-Breaking Foreign Policy* (Washington DC: United States Institute of Peace Press, 1997), pp. 4–6.
22. Susan L. Carruthers, *The Media At War* (New York: St. Martin's Press – now Palgrave Macmillan, 2000), p. 199.
23. Vera Gowlland-Debbas and Hassiba Hadj-Sahraoui (eds), *United Nations Sanctions and International Law* (The Hague, Netherlands: Kluwer Law International, 2001), pp. 1–48.
24. Margaret Doxey, "United Nations Sanctions: Lessons of Experience", *Diplomacy & Statecraft*, vol. 11, no. 1, March 2000, pp. 8–9.
25. See for example Jamie Frederic Metzl, "Popular Diplomacy," *Daedalus*, vol. 128, no. 2, spring 1999, pp. 177–92.
26. United Nations document A/AC.51/1983/7, *In-Depth Evaluation of the Work of the Department of Public Information: Report of the Secretary-General*, 18 April 1983, p. 5.
27. Ibid.
28. See Karl Marx and F. Engels, *The German Ideology* (London: Lawrence & Wishart, 1970), p. 64.
29. John Keane, *Civil Society: Old Images, New Visions* (Cambridge: Polity Press, 1998), p. 169.
30. Jowett and O'Donnell note that Julius Caesar used "massive triumphal processions" as spectacles, and the most blatant examples of the phenomenon in the twentieth century were the Soviets (May Day parades) and the Nazis (the Nuremberg rallies). Garth S. Jowett and Victoria O'Donnell, *Propaganda and Persuasion*, 3rd edn (Thousand Oaks, CA: Sage Publications, 1999).
31. "Lessons from the sporting life," *Chicago Tribune*, 15 July 1998, Section 1, p. 24.
32. Matthew Brace, "Cathy's Triumph Shows How Times are Finally Changing", *The Observer*, 8 October 2000. Downloaded from Lexis-Nexis Academic, 15 August 2002.
33. John Pilger, "Fixed race Australia is gearing up to host the 2000 Olympics, yet its own sporting history is far removed from the spirit of the Games. Some of its greatest sportspeople were denied the chance to make their mark. Why? Because of the colour of their skin. And even today, to be aborigine, is to be a second-class citizen". *The Guardian* (Manchester), 21 August 1999, p. 18.
34. Michael R. Real, "MediaSport: Technology and the Commodification of Postmodern Sport", in Lawrence A. Wenner (ed.), *MediaSport* (London: Routledge, 1998), p. 19.
35. Steve Gorman, "Olympics ratings fall to 32-year low: NBC fails to meet viewership projections given to advertisers". Downloaded from the MSNBC home page, *http://www.msnbc.com*, 3 October 2000.
36. John Sugden and Alan Tomlinson, "Power and Resistance in the Governance of World Football: Theorizing FIFA's Transnational Impact", *Journal of Sport and Social Issues*, vol. 22, no. 3, August 1998, p. 5 of downloaded database version.
37. Real, op. cit., p. 25.
38. Sugden and Tomlinson, op cit., p. 7 of downloaded database version.

7 UN Ideological Work and International Change

1. See for example Cary Nelson, *Shouts From The Wall: Posters and Photographs Brought Home from the Spanish Civil War by American Volunteers* (Waltham, MA: Abraham Lincoln Brigade Archives, 1996).
2. George Orwell, *Homage to Catalonia* (San Diego, CA: Harcourt Brace & Company, 1952), p. 42.
3. United Nations document A/53/170, *Arrangements and Practices for the Interaction of Non-Governmental Organizations in all Activities of the United Nations System: Report of the Secretary-General*, 10 July 1998, p.15.
4. Conor Cruise O'Brien and Feliks Topolski, *The United Nations Sacred Drama* (New York: Simon and Schuster, 1968), p. 281.
5. Bernard D. Nossiter, "The Sins of the U.N.", *The Washington Post Book World*, 8 April, 1990, p. X7.
6. William Over, *Human Rights In The International Public Sphere* (Stamford, CT: Ablex Publishing, 1999), p. 13.
7. François Debrix, *Re-Envisioning Peacekeeping: The United Nations and the Mobilization of Ideology* (Minneapolis: University of Minnesota Press, 1999), p. 18.
8. William H. Baldwin, "As the World Turns: In the face of lackluster American public opinion, financial woes, and, most recently, the controversial mini-series 'America,' will the United Nations shift its public relations focus to aggressive persuasion?" *Public Relations Journal*, vol. 43, no. 3, March 1987, p. 14.
9. "Communicator to the world: An interview with United Nations' Communications Director Shashi Tharoor," *Public Relations Strategist*, vol. 7, no. 2, spring 2001, p. 1 of downloaded electronica database version.
10. Richard Earle, *The Art of Cause Marketing: How to Use Advertising to Change Personal Behavior and Public Policy* (Chicago, IL: McGraw-Hill: 2000), pp. 149–51.
11. "The 1999 IPRA/NEC Golden World Awards for Excellence to 9 Countries," IPRA Press Release. Downloaded from the IPRA web site (*http://www.ipranet.org*), 18 August 2002.
12. Scott M. Cutlip, "Pioneering Public Relations for Foreign Governments", *Public Relations Review*, vol. 18, no. 1, spring 1987, pp. 13–34.
13. Benno H. Signitzer and Timothy Coombs, "Public Relations and Public Diplomacy: Conceptual Convergences," *Public Relations Review*, vol. 18, no. 2, 1992, pp. 137–47.
14. See Mark D. Alleyne, *International Power and International Communication* (London: St. Antony's Press – now Palgrave Macmillan, 1995), chapter 5; also Mark D. Alleyne, *News Revolution: Political and Economic Decisions About Global Information* (New York: St. Martin's Press – now Palgrave Macmillan, 1997), chapter 3.
15. Leah R. Vande Berg, "The Critical Sense: Three Decades of Critical Media Studies in the wake of Samuel L. Becker's 'Rhetorical Studies for the Contemporary World' ", *Communication Studies*, vol. 50. no. 1, spring 1999, pp. 72–81.
16. See Lynette Finch, "Psychological Propaganda: The War of Ideas on Ideas During the First Half of the Twentieth Century", *Armed Forces and Society*, vol. 26, no. 3, spring 2000, pp. 367–86.
17. James E. Grunig and Todd Hunt, *Managing Public Relations* (Fort Worth, TX: Harcourt, Brace, Jovanovich, 1984).
18. See for example Hugh M. Culbertson and Ni Chen, "Communitarianism: A Foundation for Communication Symmetry", *Public Relations Quarterly*, vol. 42, summer 1997, pp. 36–41; and M. Karlberg, "Remembering the Public in Public

Relations Research: From Theoretical to Operational Symmetry", *Journal of Public Relations Research*, 8, 1996, pp. 263–78.

19. James E. Grunig, "Public Relations and International Affairs: Effects, Ethics", *Journal of International Affairs*, vol. 47, no. 1, summer 1993, p. 5 of downloaded database version.

20. Ibid.

21. Ibid., p. 3 of downloaded database version.

22. Ibid., p. 4.

23. See for example Cutlip, op. cit., and Benno and Coombs, op cit.

24. See James E. Grunig and Fred C. Repper, "Strategic Management, Publics, and Issues", in James E. Grunig (ed.), *Excellence in Public Relations and Communication Management* (Fort Worth, TX: Harcourt, Brace, Jovanovich, 1984).

25. United Nations document A/54/2000, *We The Peoples: The Role of the United Nations in the Twenty-First Century – Report of the Secretary-General*, 27 March, 2000, p. 49.

26. Margaret Anstee, "What Price Peace? – and United Nations reform", *Round Table*, Issue 346, April 1998, pp. 227–33.

27. Debrix, op. cit., p. 56.

28. Martin Griffiths, *Fifty Key Thinkers in International Relations* (London: Routledge, 1999).

29. Paul R. Viotti and Mark V. Kauppi, *International Relations Theory: Realism, Pluralism, Globalism* (New York: Macmillan Press – now Palgrave Macmillan, 1993).

30. V. I. Lenin, *Imperialism, The Highest Stage of Capitalism* (Peking: Foreign Languages Press, 1975).

31. Immanuel Wallerstein, *The Capitalist World Economy* (Cambridge: Cambridge University Press, 1979).

32. Argentine economist Raul Prebisch is considered a founder of this school. See his "Five stages in my thinking on development", in Gerald M. Meier and Dudley Seers (eds.), *Pioneers In Development* (New York: Oxford University Press for the World Bank, 1984).

33. See for example Elizabeth C. Hanson, "The global media system and international relations", in Kanti P. Bajpai and Harish C. Shukul (eds.), *Interpreting World Politics* (New Delhi: Sage, 1995), p. 274, where globalization is defined as a term that "implies increasing volume and expanding scope of interactions among a broad range of actors in the international system, as well as a greater degree of interdependence resulting from this interconnectivity".

34. See Mark D. Alleyne, "Exaggerated Rumors of the Death of the State: The Alliance Between Media Firms and States in Globalization", *Jornadas Internacionales XII*, Facultad de Comunicación, Universidad de Navarra, Spain, July 1998, pp. 26–62.

35. Malcolm Waters, *Globalization* (London: Routledge, 1995), p. 42.

36. Arjun Appadurai, *Modernity at Large* (Minneapolis: University of Minnesota Press, 1996), p. 41.

37. Ibid., pp. 33–43.

38. Karl W. Deutsch, *The Nerves of Government: Models of Political Communication and Control* (New York: Free Press, 1966).

39. Immanuel Wallerstein, *The Modern World-System: Capitalist Agriculture and the Origins of the European World-Economy in the Sixteenth Century* (New York: Academic Press, 1974).

40. Vendulka Kubálková, Nicholas Onuf and Paul Kowert (eds.), *International Relations in a Constructed World* (Armonk, New York: M. E. Sharpe, 1998), pp. 6–7.
41. See Sarah Franklin, Celia Lury and Jackie Stacey, "Feminism and cultural studies", in Paddy Scannell, Philip Schlesinger and Colin Sparks (eds.) *Culture and Power: a Media, Culture & Society Reader* (London: Sage, 1992), pp. 90–111.
42. See Anthony Giddens, *The Constitution of Society: Outline of a Theory of Structuration* (Berkeley, CA: University of California Press, 1984).
43. See Scott Burchill, Richard Devetak, Andrew Linklater, Matthew Paterson, Christian Reus-Smit and Jacqui True, *Theories of International Relations*, 2nd edn (Basingstoke: Palgrave Press – now Palgrave Macmillan, 2001).

Select Bibliography

A note on page numbers

Every effort has been taken to provide here the exact page numbers of articles published in periodicals. Where page numbers are not provided the article was published electronically in its original form, or also published in an electronic database, and that is the version consulted for this book. In the endnotes, sources acquired from electronic databases are identified as such and the page numbers of database documents are given to distinguish them from page numbers in the printed documents that may be different from the electronic versions.

Primary sources

Books

Central Office of Information (1954) *Summary of the Report of the Independent Committee of Enquiry into the Overseas Information Services (the Drogheda Committee)*. London: Her Majesty's Stationery Office.

—— (1988) *Britain 1988: An Official Handbook*. London: Her Majesty's Stationery Office.

Commission on Global Governance (1994) *Our Global Neighborhood*. New York: Oxford University Press.

Cruise O'Brien, Conor (1968) *The United Nations Sacred Drama*. New York: Simon and Schuster.

Goulding, Marrack (2002) *Peacemonger*. London: John Murray.

International Commission on the Balkans (1996) *Unfinished Peace*. Washington DC: Carnegie Endowment for International Peace.

Landskron, William A. (ed.) (1983) *Annual Review of United Nations Affairs 1982*. Dobbs Ferry, New York: Oceana Publications.

Lehmann, Ingrid A. (1999) *Peacekeeping and Public Information: Caught in the Crossfire*. London: Frank Cass.

Lie, Trygve, with Brock Chisholm, Herbert V. Evatt, John Boyd-Orr, Charles Malik, Ralph Bunche, Eleanor Roosevelt, Benjamin Cohen, Jaime Torres Bodet, Ludwik Rajchman and Carlos Romulo (1949) *Peace on Earth*. New York: Hermitage House.

New Zealand Ministry of Foreign Affairs and Trade (1999) *United Nations Handbook 1999*. Wellington, New Zealand: New Zealand Ministry of Foreign Affairs and Trade.

Orwell, George (1952) *Homage to Catalonia*. San Diego, CA: Harcourt Brace & Company.

Ploman, Edward W. (1982) *International Law Governing Communication and Information: A Collection of Basic Documents*. London: Frances Pinter.

Sher, Neil M. (1994) *Kurt Waldheim and Nazi Wartime Atrocities: The Uncensored Justice Department Report*. Collingdale, PA: DIANE Publishing Company.

Szalai, Alexander, with Margaret Croke and Associates (1972) *The United Nations and the News Media*. New York: United Nations Institute for Training and Research (UNITAR).

Task Force on the Reorientation of United Nations Public Information Activities (1997) *Global Vision, Local Voice*. New York: The United Nations.

Tavares De Sá, Hernane (1966) *The Play Within The Play*. New York: Alfred A. Knopf.

Templer, William (1993) *Waldheim Report: International Commission of Historians*. Copenhagen: Museum Tusculanum.
UN Department of Public Information (The United Nations Blue Books Series, Vol. 1) (1994) *The United Nations and Apartheid: 1948–1994*. New York: The United Nations.
UNESCO (1999) *World Communication and Information Report 1999–2000*. Paris: UNESCO.
——(2000) *Culture, Trade and Globalization: Questions and Answers*. Paris: UNESCO.
——(2000) *World Culture Report 2000: Cultural Diversity, Conflict and Pluralism*. Paris: UNESCO.
United Nations Department of Public Information (1995) *A Guide to Information at the United Nations*. New York: DPI.
World Commission on Environment and Development (1987) *Our Common Future*. Oxford: Oxford University Press.

Articles, pamphlets, speeches and documents

"8 Assistant Secretaries General Of UN Have Varied Backgrounds", *The New York Times*, 11 April 1946.
"Canadian Woman to Get Top U.N. Job", *The Toronto Star*, 26 November 1986, p. A4.
"Communicator to the world: An interview with United Nations' Communications Director Shashi Tharoor", *Public Relations Strategist*, vol. 7, no. 2, spring 2001.
"Diplomacy: The UN at 50", *Los Angeles Times*, 20 October 1995.
"Dubious Economies: Uniprop" (Editorial), *The New York Times*, 5 June 1981, Section A, p. 26.
"Europe freed, radio signs off?", *The Economist*, 27 February 1993.
"Feeling of Resistance", *World Press Review*, vol. 35, no. 7, July 1988, p. 45.
"Kobayashi Named Chief of Protocol", *Jiji Press Ticker Service*, 20 April 2001.
"Multidisciplinary Peacekeeping: Lessons Learned from Recent Past", United Nations' *Lessons Learned in Peacekeeping* website, *http://www.un.org/Depts/dpko/lessons/*, complete text downloaded 5 July 2002.
"Poison From Pale: Why Nato should intervene in the Bosnian Serb media battle" (Editorial), *The Times*, 25 August 1997, p. 19A.
"Sanctions Lifted After 31 Years: Interim Constitution Agreed On", *UN Chronicle*, vol. 31, no. 1, March 1994.
"Sec-Gen Announces Membership of Task Force on Reorientation of UN Public Information Activities", *M2 Presswire*, 24 April 1997.
"Secretariat – Public Information", *United Nations Weekly Bulletin*, vol. 1, 23 September 1946, p. 19.
"United Nations Operation in Somalia II", United Nations website, *http://www.un.org/Depts/dpko/dpko/co_mission/unosom2.htm*. Complete text downloaded 21 March 2002.
"United Nations: Paying for Puffs, and Then Puffing", *The Economist*, 6 June 1981, p. 56 (US edition p. 46).
"UNO Aides Appointed", *The New York Times*, 5 March 1946, p. 5.
"Waldheim apologises for misleading Israelis about past", UPI report, 11 May 1990.
"What's good for U.N. is Good for Xerox", *Business Week*, no. 1807, 18 April 1964.
Amdur, Meredith (1993) "BBC World Service TV looks west", *Broadcasting & Cable*, 19 April.
Anstee, Margaret (1998) "What Price Peace? – and United Nations reform", *Round Table*, Issue 346, April, pp. 227–33.
Back, Les (2001) "White Fortresses in Cyberspace", *The Courier* (UNESCO), January.

Cohen, Benjamin (1947) "Voice of UN – The Department of Public Information", *United Nations World*, March, pp. 54–57.

Commonwealth Secretariat (1987) *Racism in Southern Africa: The Commonwealth Stand*. London: Commonwealth Secretariat.

De Freitas, Ian (2001) "Worldwide Web of Laws Threatens The Internet", *The Times* (London), 9 January.

Deluce, Daniel (2000) "Media Wars", *NATO Review*, vol. 48, no. 4, winter.

Dhanapala, Jayantha (2001) "Communicating the Disarmament Message". Speech at the Centre for International Communication, Macquarie University, Sydney, Australia, 30 August.

Doole, Claire (2000) "Cyber-racists 'Safe in US'", *BBC News Online*, the British Broadcasting Corporation website, *news.bbc.co.uk*, 16 February.

Erlanger, Steven (1999) "NATO Peacekeepers Plan a System of Controls for the News Media in Kosovo", *The New York Times*, 16 August, p. A8 (Late Edition, East Coast).

Gould, Jack "TV: Weak Premiere of U.N. Series", *The New York Times*, 29 December 1964, p. 55.

Hickey, Neil (1964) "How To Make A Dream Come True", *TV Guide*, 28 December.

Jenkins, Paul (1993) "Europe: Propaganda Unlimited – Serbs are beaming their view of the war in the former Yugoslavia around the world, on Western television networks. Sanctions, what sanctions? Asks Paul Jenkins", *The Guardian* (Manchester), 3 May.

Kopkind, Andrew (1987) "*Amerika*: It Can't Happen Here", *The Nation*, 14 February.

Malcolm, Noel (1995) "'The Whole Lot of Them Are Serbs'", *The Spectator*, vol. 274, no. 8709, 10 June.

Mann, Jim (1997) "National Perspective: UN Hate-Radio Jamming Would Send Wrong Signal", *Los Angeles Times*, 3 December, p. 5 (Record edition).

Marshall, Pearl (1988) "Waldheim 'Inquiry' Will Make TV History", *Los Angeles Times*, 28 May.

Matlack, Carol (1992) "Serbian-Croatian PR War", *National Journal*, vol. 24, no. 11, 14 March.

Melendez, Michele M. (2002) "Smoke Hasn't Cleared Yet on Anti-Drug Ads: Experts, Teens Unsure Whether Costly Campaign Deters Abuse", *The Times-Picayune* (New Orleans), 15 March, p. 1.

The Norwegian Nobel Committee (2001) "The Nobel Peace Prize 2001", Press Release, Oslo, 12 October.

Nossiter, Bernard D. (1981) "U.N. Gave $432,000 to the Foreign Press to Publish Its Views", *The New York Times*, 28 May, Section A, p. 1.

Rice, John (2002) "Fox Denies Lying About Castro, But Asks Apology; Confirms Radically New Foreign Policy", *Associated Press*, 25 April.

Rosenberg, Howard (1987) "The 'Amerika' Controversy: Let America Decide", *Los Angeles Times*, 30 January, Part VI, p. 1.

Rowe, Trevor (1987) "Canadian UN Official Defends Her Role in Row Over Contracts", *The Toronto Star*, 5 November, p. A3.

Serrill, Michael S. (1989) "The Fallout From Nanjing", *Time*, vol. 133, no. 3, 16 January.

Sharma, Yojana (2000) "Rights: Zero Tolerance For Internet Hate Speech", *Inter Press Service*, 27 June.

Simons, Marlise (2002) "Trial Centers on Role of Press During Rwanda Massacre", *The New York Times*, 3 March.

Stanfield, Rochelle L. (1992) "Balkans Wars on K Street", *National Journal*, vol. 24, no. 33, 15 August.

Sukhu, Gopal (1989) "Nanjing Burning", *The Village Voice*, vol. 33, no. 3, 17 January.

Tharoor, Shashi (1999/2000) "Are Human Rights Universal?", *World Policy Journal*, vol. 16, no. 4.

UNESCO General Conference, Resolution 4/9.3/2, 1978, *Declaration On Fundamental Principles Concerning The Contribution Of The Mass Media To Strengthening Peace And International Understanding, To Promotion Of Human Rights And To Countering Racialism, Apartheid And Incitement To War.*

United Nations Press Release GA/SM/221 HR/4504 (2000) "General Assembly President, in Human Rights Day Message, Stresses Importance of Education for Exercise of Rights", 28 November.

United Nations Press Release HR/4348 PI/1046 (1997) "Human Rights Day Events at United Nations Mark Beginning of Year-Long Observance of Fiftieth Anniversary of Universal Declaration", 10 December.

United Nations Press Release ORG/982; PI/384 (1982) "DPI Launches Oral History of United Nations", 17 September.

United Nations Press Release PI/998 (1997) "Department of Public Information, Columbia University Roundtable to Address Impact of Communications on Global Issues", 18 April.

United Nations Press Release SG/A/366; BIC/2219; PI/558 (1986) "Secretary-General Appoints Therese Paquet-Sevigny Under-Secretary-General for Public Information", 26 November.

United Nations Press Release, No. PI/1245 (2000) "World Freedom Day Observed at Headquarters With Panel discussion on 'Reporting the News in a Dangerous World'", 3 May.

Voluntary Service Overseas (VSO) (2002) *The Live Aid Legacy: The Developing World Through British Eyes – A Research Report*. London: VSO.

Wada, Tsutomu (1998) "Japanese Lament How Few of Them Hold Top U.N. Jobs; Latest Appointee Tapped To Head Public Relations Team", *The Nikkei Weekly*, 16 February, p. 1.

Waters, Harry F. with Janet Huck (1987) "ABCs Amerikan Dream", *Newsweek*, 16 February, p. 21.

Wren, Christopher S. (2001) "Era Waning, Holbroke Takes Stock", *The New York Times*, 14 January (Late Edition, East Coast), section 1, p. 10.

United Nations Official Documents

Because the United Nations generates thousands of documents every year it maintains a numbering system that gives each document a separate identity. In the entries below, the numbers for these documents (called "symbols" by the UN) are listed first. The online Official Document System of the United Nations (ODS) (*http:// www.ods.unog.ch/ods/*), or the free online UN Documentation Centre (*http://www. un.org/documents/*), can be used to quickly locate most of these documents via their document numbers. The document number does not include the year when the item was passed or written; this is provided in brackets after the number. According to the UN (*http://www.ods.unog.ch/ods/Help_E.htm*): "Searching by document symbol is the most precise search option as it allows searching for one specific document, including any revisions, addenda and corrigenda.

Examples
A/52/100 – General Assembly document from the fifty-second session
S/1997/100 – Security Council document issued in 1997

E/1997/100 – Economic and Social Council document from the 1997 sessions
ST/AI/405 – Administrative instruction issued by the Secretariat
E/CN.4/1997/1 – Document of the Commission on Human Rights, a subsidiary
body of the Economic and Social Council
E/CN.4/Sub.2/1997/1 – Document of the Sub Commission on Prevention of
Discrimination and Protection of Minorities of the Commission on Human
Rights."

A/3928 (1958) *Report of the Expert Committee on United Nations Public Information.*
A/42/21 (1987) *Report of the Committee on Information.*
A/51/829 (1997) *Strengthening of the United Nations System, letter of the Secretary-General to the President of the General Assembly,* 17 March.
A/53/170 (1998) *Arrangements and Practices for the Interaction of Non-Governmental Organizations in all Activities of the United Nations System: Report of the Secretary-General.*
A/54/2000 (2000) *We The Peoples: The Role of the United Nations in the Twenty-First Century: Report of the Secretary-General.*
A/54/21 (1999) *Committee on Information, Report on the Twenty-First Session (3–14 May 1999), Supplement No. 21, Annex, "Statement by the Under-Secretary-General for Communications and Public Information at the Opening of the Twenty-First Session of the Committee on Information".*
A/54/21/Add.1 (1999) *Report of the Committee on Information on the Resumed Twenty-First Session (1–5 November 1999), Supplement No. 21A, Annex, "Statement by the Under-Secretary-General for Communications and Public Information at the Opening of the Resumed Twenty-First Session of the Committee on Information".*
A/54/549 (1999) *Report of the Secretary-General Pursuant to General Assembly Resolution 53/35: The Fall of Srebrenica.*
A/54/6/Rev.1 (1999) *Proposed Programme Budget for the Biennium 2000–2001, Vol. 1 (Foreword and Introduction), GA: Official Records, 54th Session, Supplement No. 6.*
A/54/6/Rev.1 (1999) *Proposed Programme Budget for the Biennium 2000–2001, Vol. III, Expenditure Sections 16 to 33 and Income Sections 1 to 3.*
A/55/21 (2000) *Committee on Information, Report on the Twenty-Second Session (1–2 May).*
A/55/305-S/2000/809 (2000) *Report of the Panel on United Nations Peace Operations.*
A/55/6/Rev.1 (2001) *Medium-Term Plan for the Period 2002–2005.*
A/55/977 (2001) *Implementation of the Recommendations of the Special Committee on Peacekeeping Operations and the Panel on United Nations Peace Operations: Report of the Secretary-General.*
A/56/21 (2001) *Committee on Information: Report on the Twenty-Third Session (30 April–11 May).*
A/AC.198/2000/5 (2000) *United Nations Information Centres in 1999: Allocation of Resources from the Regular Budget of the United Nations.*
A/AC.198/2001/9 (2001) *Activities of the Joint United Nations Information Committee in 2000: Report of the Secretary-General.*
A/AC.198/2002/5 (2002) *Substantive Questions: Role of the Department of Public Information in United Nations Peacekeeping: Report of the Secretary General.*
A/AC.198/53 (1982) *Proposals for Developing Systematic Evaluation Procedures for Activities of the Department of Public Information.*
A/AC.51/1983/7 (1983) *In-Depth Evaluation of the Work of the Department of Public Information: Report of the Secretary-General.*

A/C.5/1320/Rev.1 (1971) *Budget Estimates for the Financial Year 1972 – Review and Reappraisal of United Nations Information Policies and Activities: Report of the Secretary-General.*

A/C.5/L.172 (1952) *Report of Sub-Committee 8 of the Fifth Committee on Public Information.*

A/RES/13(I), ANNEX I (1946) *Recommendations of the Technical Advisory Committee on Information Concerning the Policies, Functions and Organization of the Department of Public Information.*

A/RES/1761(XVII) (1962) *The Policies of Apartheid of the Government of the Republic of South Africa.*

A/RES/3201(S-VI) (1974) *Declaration on the Establishment of a New International Economic Order.* [This Declaration was adopted by the General Assembly at its 6th special session, 2229th plenary meeting, 1 May, 1974.]

A/RES/34/182 (1979) *Questions Relating to Information.*

A/RES/37/92 (1982) *Principles Governing the Use by States of Artificial Earth Satellites for International Direct Television Broadcasting.*

A/RES/39/72 (1984) *Policies of Apartheid of the Government of South Africa.*

A/RES/395 (V) (1950) *Treatment of People of Indian Origin in the Union of South Africa.*

A/RES/40/148 (1985) *Measures to be taken against Nazi, Fascist and neo-Fascist activities and all other forms of totalitarian ideologies and practices based on racial intolerance, hatred and terror.*

A/RES/40/64 (1985) *Policies of Apartheid of the Government of South Africa.*

A/RES/40/97 (1985) *Question of Namibia.*

A/RES/41/160 (1986) *Measures to be taken against Nazi, Fascist and neo-Fascist activities and all other forms of totalitarian ideologies and practices based on racial intolerance, hatred and terror.*

A/RES/41/39 (1986) *Question of Namibia.*

A/RES/42/14 (1987) *Question of Namibia.*

A/RES/42/23 (1987) *Policies of Apartheid of the Government of South Africa.*

A/RES/43/26 (1988) *Question of Namibia.*

A/RES/43/50 (1988) *Policies of Apartheid of the Government of South Africa.*

A/RES/44/27 (1989) *Policies of Apartheid of the Government of South Africa.*

A/RES/49/184 (1995) *United Nations Decade for Human Rights Education.*

A/RES/55/94 (2001) *United Nations Decade for Human Rights Education, 1995–2004, and Public Information Activities in the Field of Human Rights.*

A/RES/616 A(VII) (1952) *The Question of Race Conflict in South Africa Resulting from the Policies of Apartheid of the Government of the Union of South Africa.*

E/AC.5/1999/4 (1999) *Report of the Office of Internal Oversight Services on the Triennial Review of the Implementation of the Recommendations made by the Committee for Programme and Coordination at its Thirty-Sixth Session on the Evaluation of the Department of Public Information. Note by the Secretary-General.*

E/AC.51/1986/10 (1986) *Triennial Review of the Implementation of the Recommendations made by the Committee for Programme and Co-ordination at its Twenty-Third Session on the Work of the Department of Public Information: Report of the Secretary-General.*

E/AC.51/1986/10 (1986) *Triennial Review of the Implementation of the Recommendations made by the Committee for Programme and Coordination at its Twenty-Third Session on the Work of the Department of Public Information: Report of the Secretary-General.*

E/AC.51/1999/L.6/Add.40 (1999) *Draft Report. Addendum. Programme Questions: Evaluation (4(c)). Triennial Review of the Implementation of the Recommendations Made by the Committee For Programme Coordination at its Thirty-Sixth Session on the Evaluation of the Department of Public Information.*

E/AC.51/80Add.2 (1977) *Programme Evaluation for the Biennium 1974–1975, Public Information: Report of the Secretary-General.*
E/AC.51/84 (1977) *Public Information Activities in the United Nations System: Report of the Administrative Committee on Co-ordination.*
E/RES/1297(XLIV) (1968) *Non-Governmental Organizations.*
JIU/REP/81/2 (1981) *Co-ordination in the Field of Public Information Activities Among the Members of the United Nations System* (Prepared by Sreten Ilic, Joint Inspection Unit).
S/1994/653 (1994) *Report of the Commission of Inquiry Established Pursuant to Security Council Resolution 885 (1993) To Investigate Armed Attacks on UNOSOM II Personnel Which Led to Casualties Among Them.*
S/1999/1257 (1999) *Report of the Independent Inquiry Into the Actions of the United Nations During the 1994 Genocide in Rwanda.*
S/RES/134 (1960) *Questions Relating to the Situation in the Union of South Africa.*
ST/SGB/1999/10 (1999) *Organization of the Department of Public Information,* 30 June.
ST/SGB/Organization, Section DPI/Rev.2 (1996) *Functions and Organization of the Department of Public Information.*
UN DPI/S1 1988 (1988) *United Nations Yearbook 1988,* Vol. 2.

Secondary sources

Books

Alleyne, Mark D. (1995) *International Power and International Communication.* London: St. Antony's/Macmillan Series – now Palgrave Macmillan.
——(1997) *News Revolution: Political and Economic Decisions About Global Information.* New York: St. Martin's Press – now Palgrave Macmillan.
Anderson, Benedict (1983) *Imagined Communities: Reflections on the Origin and Spread of Nationalism.* London: Verso.
Appadurai, Arjun (1996) *Modernity at Large.* Minneapolis: University of Minnesota Press.
Bailey, Sydney D. (1989) *The United Nations: A Short Political Guide,* 2nd edn. London: Macmillan Press – now Palgrave Macmillan.
Bajpai, Kanti P. and Shukul, Harish C. (eds) (1995) *Interpreting World Politics.* New Delhi: Sage.
Best, Steven and Kellner, Douglas (1991) *Postmodern Theory: Critical Interrogations.* New York: Guilford Press.
Black, Allida M. (1996) *Casting Her Own Shadow: Eleanor Roosevelt and the Shaping of Postwar Liberalism.* New York: Columbia University Press.
Burchill, Scott, Devetak, Richard, Linklater, Andrew, Paterson, Matthew, Reus-Smit, Christian and True, Jacqui (2001) *Theories of International Relations,* 2nd edn. Basingstoke: Palgrave Press – now Palgrave Macmillan.
Bytwerk, Randall L. (1983) *Julius Streicher.* New York: Stein and Day.
Campbell, Christopher P. (1995) *Race, Myth and the News.* Thousand Oaks, CA: Sage.
Carr, E. H. (1939) *The Twenty Years' Crisis.* London: Macmillan Press – now Palgrave Macmillan.
Carruthers, Susan L. (2000) *The Media At War.* New York: St. Martin's Press – now Palgrave Macmillan.
Colás, Alejandro (2002) *International Civil Society.* Cambridge: Polity Press.
Cox, Robert W., Jacobson, Harold K. with Gerard Curzon, Victoria Curzon, Joseph S. Nye, Lawrence Scheinman, James P. Sewell and Susan Strange (1974) *The Anatomy*

of Influence: Decision Making in International Organization. New Haven, CT: Yale University Press.

Debrix, François (1999) *Re-Envisioning Peacekeeping: The United Nations and the Mobilization of Ideology*. Minneapolis: University of Minnesota Press.

Deutsch, Karl W. (1954) *Political Community at the International Level: Problems of Definition and Measurement*. Garden City, New York: Doubleday.

—— (1966) *The Nerves of Government: Models of Political Communication and Control*. New York: Free Press.

Dovring, Karin (1997) *English as Lingua Franca: Double Talk in Global Persuasion*. Westport, CT: Praeger.

Dundes Renteln, Alison (1990) *International Human Rights: Universalism Versus Relativism*. Newbury Park, CA: Sage.

Earle, Richard (2000) *The Art of Cause Marketing: How to Use Advertising to Change Personal Behavior*. Lincolnwood, IL: NTC Business Books.

Evans, Graham and Newnham, Jeffrey (1998) *The Penguin Dictionary of International Relations*. London: Penguin Books.

Fletcher Luther, Sara (1988) *The United States and the Direct Broadcast Satellite*. New York: Oxford University Press.

Florini, Ann M. (ed.) (2000) *The Third Force: The Rise of Transnational Civil Society*. Washington DC: Carnegie Endowment for International Peace.

Freire, Paulo (1992) *Pedagogy of the Oppressed*. New York: Continuum.

George, Susan and Sabelli, Fabrizio (1994) *Faith and Credit: The World Bank's Secular Empire*. New York: Penguin Books.

Gianos, Phillip L. (1998) *Politics and Politicians in American Film*. Westport, CT: Praeger.

Giddens, Anthony (1984) *The Constitution of Society: Outline of a Theory of Structuration*. Berkeley, CA: University of California Press.

Gill, Stephen (1994) *American Hegemony and the Trilateral Commission*. Cambridge: Cambridge University Press.

Gordenker, Leon and Weiss, Thomas G. (eds) (1996) *NGOs, the UN, and Global Governance*. Boulder, CO: Lynne Rienner.

Gowlland-Debbas, Vera and Hadj-Sahraoui, Hassiba (eds) (2001) *United Nations Sanctions and International Law*. The Hague, Netherlands: Kluwer Law International.

Griffiths, Martin (1999) *Fifty Key Thinkers in International Relations*. London: Routledge.

Grunig, James E. (1992) *Excellence in Public Relations*. Hillsdale, NJ: Lawrence Earlbaum Associates.

—— and Hunt, Todd (1984) *Managing Public Relations*. Fort Worth, TX: Harcourt, Brace, Jovanovich.

Hables Gray, Chris (1997) *Postmodern War: The Politics of Conflict*. London: The Guilford Press.

Hachten, William A. (1987) *The World News Prism*. Ames, Iowa: Iowa State University Press.

—— and Giffard, Anthony C. (1984) *The Press and Apartheid: Repression and Propaganda in South Africa*. Madison, WI: University of Wisconsin Press.

Hawk, Beverly G. (ed.) (1992) *Africa's Media Image*. Westport, CT: Praeger.

Hazzard, Shirley (1990) *Countenance of Truth: The United Nations and the Waldheim Case*. New York: Viking.

Hein, Laura and Seldon, Mark (eds) (2000) *Censoring History: Citizenship and Memory in Japan, Germany, and the United States*. Armonk, New York: M. E. Sharpe.

Hilliard, Robert L. and Keith, Michael C. (1996) *Global Broadcasting Systems*. Boston, MA: Focal Press.

Iriye, Akira (1997) *Cultural Internationalism and World Order*. Baltimore, MD: Johns Hopkins University Press.

Jowett, Garth S. and O'Donnell, Victoria (1999) *Propaganda and Persuasion*, 3rd edn. Thousand Oaks, CA: Sage.

Keane, John (1998) *Civil Society: Old Images, New Visions*. Cambridge: Polity Press.

Kellner, Douglas (1992) *The Persian Gulf TV War*. Boulder, CO: Westview.

Kihl, Young Whan (1963) *A Study of Functionalism In International Organization*. PhD dissertation, New York University.

King, Anthony D. (ed.) (1997) *Culture, Globalization and the World System: Contemporary Conditions for the Representation of Identity*. Minneapolis: University of Minnesota Press.

Korey, William (1998) *NGOs and the Universal Declaration of Human Rights*. New York: St. Martin's Press – now Palgrave Macmillan.

Kubálková, Vendulka, Onuf, Nicholas and Kowert, Paul (eds.) (1998) *International Relations in a Constructed World*. Armonk, New York: M. E. Sharpe.

Kunczik, Michael (1990) *Images of Nations and International Public Relations*. Bonn: Friedrich-Ebert-Stiftung.

Lasswell, Harold D. (1927) *Propaganda Technique in World War I*. Cambridge, MA: MIT Press, 1971.

——Lerner, Daniel and Speier, Hans (eds.) (1980). *Propaganda and Communication in World History – Vol. II: Emergence of Public Opinion in the West*. Honolulu: The University Press of Hawaii.

Lazarsfeld, Paul F., Berelson, Bernard and Gaudet, Hazel (1948) *The People's Choice*. New York: Columbia University Press.

Lindholt, Lone (1997) *Questioning the Universality of Human Rights: The African Charter on Human and Peoples' Rights in Botswana, Malawi and Mozambique*. Aldershot: Ashgate Publishing.

Lippmann, Walter (1922) *Public Opinion*. New York: Free Press.

Loewen, James W. (1995) *Lies My Teacher Told Me: Everything Your American History Textbook Got Wrong*. New York: Touchstone.

Maas, Peter (1996) *Love Thy Neighbor: A Story of War*. New York: Alfred A. Knopf.

Martin, L. John (1958) *International Propaganda: Its Legal and Diplomatic Control*. Gloucester, MA: Peter Smith.

Marx, Karl and Engels, F. (1970) *The German Ideology*. London: Lawrence & Wishart.

Meier, Gerald M. and Dudley Seers, Dudley (eds.) (1984) *Pioneers in Development*. New York: Oxford University Press for the World Bank.

Merle, Marcel (1987) *The Sociology of International Relations*. Leamington Spa: Berg.

Mitchell, J. M. (1986) *International Cultural Relations*. London: Allen & Unwin.

Mitrany, David (1943) *A Working Peace System: An Argument for the Functional Development of International Organization*. London: Royal Institute of International Affairs.

Morganthau, Hans (1973) *Politics Among Nations*, 5th edn. New York: Alfred A. Knopf.

Mosco, Vincent (1996) *The Political Economy of Communication*. London: Sage.

Nelson, Cary (1996) *Shouts from the Wall: Posters and Photographs Brought Home from the Spanish Civil War by American Volunteers*. Waltham, MA: Abraham Lincoln Brigade Archives.

Onuf, Nicholas Greenwood (1989) *World of Our Making: Rules and Rule in Social Theory and International Relations*. Columbia, SC: University of South Carolina Press.

Over, William (1999) *Human Rights in the International Public Sphere*. Stamford, CT: Ablex.

Parenti, Michael (1993) *Inventing Reality: The Politics of News Media*, 2nd edn. New York: St. Martin's Press – now Palgrave Macmillan.

Pitt, David and Weiss, Tom (eds.) (1986) *The Nature of United Nations Bureaucracies*. London: Croom Helm.

Preston, William Jr., Herman, Edward S. and Schiller, Herbert I. (1989) *Hope and Folly: The United States and UNESCO 1945–1985*. Minneapolis: University of Minnesota Press.

Pye, Lucian W. (ed.) (1963) *Communications and Political Development*. Princeton, NJ: Princeton University Press.

Righter, Rosemary (1995) *Utopia Lost: The United Nations and World Order*. New York: Twentieth Century Fund Press.

Sarup, Madan (1993) *An Introductory Guide to Post-Structuralism and Postmodernism*, 2nd edn. Athens: The University of Georgia Press.

Scannell, Paddy, Schlesinger, Philip and Sparks, Colin (eds.) (1992) *Culture and Power: A Media, Culture & Society Reader*. London: Sage.

Sills, David L. (ed.) (1968) *An International Encyclopedia of the Social Science*. New York: Crowell-Collier and Macmillan.

Sim, Stuart (ed.) (1999) *The Routledge Critical Dictionary of Postmodern Thought*. New York: Routledge.

Spears, Arthur K. (ed.) (1999) *Race and Ideology*. Detroit MI: Wayne State University Press.

Strobel, Warren P. (1997) *Late-Breaking Foreign Policy*. Washington DC: United States Institute of Peace Press.

Task Force on the Reorientation of United Nations Public Information Activities (1997) *Global Vision, Local Voice*. New York: The United Nations.

Taylor, Philip M. (1997) *Global Communications, International Affairs and the Media Since 1945*. New York: Routledge.

UNESCO (2000) *World Culture Report 2000: Cultural Diversity, Conflict and Pluralism*. Paris: UNESCO.

Vincent, R. J. (1986) *Human Rights and International Relations*. Cambridge: Cambridge University Press.

Viotti, Paul R. and Kauppi, Mark V. (1993) *International Relations Theory: Realism, Pluralism, Globalism*. New York: Macmillan Press – now Palgrave Macmillan.

Wallerstein, Immanuel (1974) *The Modern World-System: Capitalist Agriculture and the Origins of the European World-Economy in the Sixteenth Century*. New York: Academic Press.

—— (1979) *The Capitalist World Economy*. Cambridge: Cambridge University Press.

Warkentin, Craig (2001) *Reshaping World Politics: NGOs, the Internet, and Global Civil Society*. Lanham, MD: Rowman & Littlefield.

Warner, Daniel (1997) *Human Rights and Humanitarian Law: The Quest for Universality*. New York: Kluwer Law.

Waters, Malcolm (1995) *Globalization*. London: Routledge.

Wenner, Lawrence A. (ed.) (1998) *MediaSport*. London: Routledge.

Wight, Martin (1986) *Power Politics*, 2nd edn. London: Penguin, Royal Institute of International Affairs.

Willetts, Peter (ed.) (1996) *'The Conscience of the World': The Influence of Non-Governmental Organisations in the UN System*. Washington DC: The Brookings Institution.

Articles

"Apartheid Belies Chinese Rhetoric", *Africa Report*, vol. 34, no. 2, March 1989.

"Chinese Chequers", *New Statesman and Society*, vol. 35, no. 2, 3 February 1989.

"The Civil Society", *Canada and the World Backgrounder*, vol. 67, no. 1, September 2001.

Alleyne, Mark D. (1998) "Exaggerated Rumors of the Death of the State: The Alliance Between Media Firms and States in Globalization", *Jornadas Internacionales XII*, Facultad de Comunicación, Universidad de Navarra, Spain, July, pp. 26–62.

——(2000) "Education for Peace: The UN and New Ideas for the 'Information Age'", *Media Development*, no. 4, pp. 12–14.

Baldwin, William H. (1987) "As the World Turns: In the face of lackluster American public opinion, financial woes, and, most recently, the controversial mini-series 'America', will the United Nations shift its public relations focus to aggressive persuasion?", *Public Relations Journal*, vol. 43, no. 3, March.

Cockburn, Alexander (1995) "Hating Serbs is Fun", *The Nation*, vol. 261, no. 12, 16 October.

Corry, John (1998) "A formula for genocide", *American Spectator*, vol. 31, no. 9, September, pp. 22–27.

Culbertson, Hugh M. and Chen, Ni (1997) "Communitarianism: A Foundation For Communication Symmetry", *Public Relations Quarterly*, vol. 42, summer, pp. 36–41.

Cutlip, Scott M. (1987) "Pioneering Public Relations for Foreign Governments", *Public Relations Review*, vol. 18, no. 1, spring, pp. 13–34.

de Senaclens, Pierre (1985) "The Smashed Mirror of Past Illusions", *Society*, vol. 22, no. 6, September/October.

Doxey, Margaret (2000) "United Nations Sanctions: Lessons of Experience", *Diplomacy & Statecraft*, vol. 11, no. 1, March.

Evans, Michael (1997) "Nato troops take over 'poisonous' Karadzic TV", *The Times* (London), 2 October.

Finch, Lynette (2000) "Psychological Propaganda: The War of Ideas on Ideas During the First Half of the Twentieth Century", *Armed Forces and Society*, vol. 26, no. 3, pp. 367–86.

Giarelli, Andrew (1989) "Is China Racist?", *World Press Review*, vol. 36, no. 3, March.

Gordenker, Leon. (1954) "United Nations Use of Mass Communications in Korea, 1950–1951." *International Organization*, vol. 8, no. 3, August, pp. 331–45.

——(1960) "Policy-making and Secretariat Influence in the U.N. General Assembly: The Case of Public Information", *American Political Science Review*, 54, June, pp. 359–73.

Gordon, Hoxie R. (1995) "The United Nations at 50 Years", *Presidential Studies Quarterly*, vol. 25, no. 4, fall.

Grunig, James E. (1993) "Public Relations and International Affairs: Effects, Ethics", *Journal of International Affairs*, vol. 47, no. 1.

Hazzard, Shirley (1989) "Breaking Faith – I", *The New Yorker*, 25 September.

——(1989) "Breaking Faith – II", *The New Yorker*, 2 October.

Heine-Geldern, Robert (1968) "Cultural Diffusion", in David L. Sills (ed.) *International Encyclopedia of the Social Sciences*. New York: Macmillan Press – now Palgrave Macmillan.

Herberichs, Gerard (1966) "On Theories of Public Opinion and International Organization", *Public Opinion Quarterly*, vol. 30, no. 4, winter, pp. 624–36.

Holguin, Lina Maria (1998) "The Media in Modern Peacekeeping", *Peace Review*, vol. 10, no. 4.

Karlberg, M. (1996) "Remembering the Public in Public Relations Research: From Theoretical to Operational Symmetry", *Journal of Public Relations Research*, 8, pp. 263–78.

Katz, Elihu (1957) "The Two-Step Flow of Communication: An Up-To-Date Report on an Hypothesis", *Public Opinion Quarterly*, vol. 21, pp. 61–78.

Katzenstein, Peter J. and Keohane, Robert O. (1998) "International Organization and the Study of World Politics", *International Organization*, vol. 52, no. 4, autumn.

L'Etang, Jacquie (1998) "State Propaganda and Bureaucratic Intelligence: The Creation of Public Relations in 20th Century Britain", *Public Relations Review*, vol. 24, no. 4, winter.

Meisler, Stanley (1997) "A Dream Deferred", *The Washington Monthly*, vol. 29, no. 7, July/August.

Metzl, Jamie F. (1997) "Information Intervention – When Switching Channels Isn't Enough", *Foreign Affairs*, vol. 76, no. 6, pp. 15–20.

—— (1999) "Popular Diplomacy", *Daedalus*, vol. 128, no. 2, spring.

Meyer, William H. (1995) "Toward A Global Culture: Universalism vs. Relativism Regarding International Human Rights". Paper presented at the Annual Meeting of the International Studies Association, Chicago, February.

Millard, William J. (1993) "International Public Opinion of the United Nations: A Comparative Analysis", *International Journal of Public Opinion Research*, vol. 5, no. 1, spring.

Millen-Penn, Ken (1995) "Democratic Control, Public Opinion, and League Diplomacy", *World Affairs*, vol. 157, spring.

Muncy, James A. and Eastman, Jacqueline K. (1998) "The Journal of Advertising: Twenty-Five Years and Beyond", *Journal of Advertising*, vol. 27, no. 4, winter.

Murphy, Laura K. (1999) "China's Psychological Warfare", *Military Review*, vol. 79, no. 56, pp. 13–23.

Neier, Aryeh (1994) "Watching Rights", *The Nation*, vol. 258, no. 24, 20 June.

Nelson, Michael (1992) "Why The 'Big Three' Must Still Broadcast Across The Old Iron Curtin", *Intermedia*, vol. 20, no. 6, November–December.

Pilger, John (1999) "Fixed race Australia is gearing up to host the 2000 Olympics, yet its own sporting history is far removed from the spirit of the Games. Some of its greatest sportspeople were denied the chance to make their mark. Why? Because of the colour of their skin. And even today, to be aborigine, is to be a second-class citizen", *The Guardian* (Manchester), 21 August.

Powell, Jon T. (1982) "Towards a Negotiable Definition of Propaganda for International Agreements Related to Direct Broadcast Satellites", *Law and Contemporary Problems*, vol. 45, no. 1, winter.

Rampal, Kuldip R. and Adams, W. Clifton (1990) "Credibility of the Asian News Broadcasts of the Voice of America and the British Broadcasting Corporation", *Gazette*, vol. 46, no. 2, September, pp. 93–111.

Rieff, David (1999) "Up the Organization", *The New Republic*, 1 February.

Rowland, Jr., Willard D. (1984) "Deconstructing American Communications Policy Literature", *Critical Studies in Mass Communication*, December, pp. 423–35.

Schechter, Danny (2000) "The UN Is Dead: Long Live the UN", *www.mediachannel.org*, 13 September.

Seidelman, Raymond (1989) "The Anti-African Protests: More Than Just Chinese Racism", *The Nation*, vol. 248, no. 6, 13 February.

Shaw, Tony (1999) "The Information Research Department of the British Foreign Office and the Korean War 1950–53", *Journal of Contemporary History*, vol. 34, no. 2.

Signitzer, Benno H. and Coombs, Timothy (1992) "Public Relations and Public Diplomacy: Conceptual Convergences", *Public Relations Review*, vol. 18, no. 2, pp. 137–47.

Snow, Nancy (1998) "The Smith-Mundt Act of 1948", *Peace Review*, vol. 10, no. 4, pp. 619–24.

Speier, Hans (1948) "The Future of Psychological Warfare", *Public Opinion Quarterly*, vol. 12, pp. 5–18.

Spicer, Keith (1994) "Propaganda for Peace", *The New York Times*, 10 December.
Strang, David and Soule, Sarah A. (1998) "Diffusion Organizations and Social Movements: From Hybrid Corn to Poison Pills", *Annual Review of Sociology*, vol. 24.
Sugden, John and Tomlinson, Alan (1998) "Power and Resistance in the Governance of World Football: Theorizing FIFA's Transnational Impact", *Journal of Sport and Social Issues*, vol. 22, no. 3, August.
Sweeney, Michael S. (2001) "Censorship Missionaries of World War II", *Journalism History*, vol. 27, no. 1, spring.
Swift, Richard N. (1960) "The United Nations and Its Public", *International Organization*, vol. 14, no. 1, winter, pp. 60–91.
Vande Berg, Leah R. (1999) "The Critical Sense: Three Decades of Critical Media Studies in the Wake of Samuel L. Becker's 'Rhetorical Studies for the Contemporary World'", *Communication Studies*, vol. 50. no. 1, spring, pp. 72–81.
Windrich, Elaine (1989) "South Africa's Propaganda War", *Africa Today*, vol. 36, no. 1, pp. 51–60.

Website resources

Agence France-Presse (AFP): *www.afp.com*
Alliance Française: *www.afusa.org*
Associated Press (AP): *www.ap.org*
DirecTV: *www.directv.com*
Gallup International: *www.gallup-international.com*
Globalvision New Media: *www.mediachannel.org*
Goethe Institut: *www.goethe.de/eindex.htm*
Instituto Cervantes: *www.cervantes.es*
International Telecommunication Union: *www.itu.int*
ITAR-TASS (The Information Telegraph Agency of Russia): *www.itar-tass.com*
Reuters: *www.reuters.com*
The British Council: *www.britcoun.org*
The Japan Foundation: *www.jpf.go.jp*
The United Nations System: *www.unsystem.org*
UNESCO (United Nations Educational, Scientific and Cultural Organization): *www.unesco.org*
United Press International (UPI): *www.upi.com*
Universal Postal Union (UPU): *www.upu.int*
US State Department Bureau of Educational and Cultural Affairs: *//exchanges.state.gov*
US State Department International Information Programs: *//usinfo.state.gov*
US State Department Press and Public Affairs: *www.state.gov/press*
World Federation of United Nations Associations: *www.wfuna.org*
World Intellectual Property Organization (WIPO): *www.wipo.int*
World Radio Network: *www.wrn.org*
World Trade Organization (WTO): *www.wto.org*

Index